PARENTS' INVOLVEMENT in EDUCATION

The Experience of an African Immigrant Community in Chicago

OBIEFUNA J. ONWUGHALU

iUniverse, Inc.
Bloomington

Parents' Involvement in Education
The Experience of an African Immigrant Community in Chicago

iUniverse books may be ordered through booksellers or by contacting:

iUniverse
1663 Liberty Drive
Bloomington, IN 47403
www.iuniverse.com
1-800-Authors (1-800-288-4677)

Because of the dynamic nature of the Internet, any Web addresses or links contained in this book may have changed since publication and may no longer be valid. The views expressed in this work are solely those of the author and do not necessarily reflect the views of the publisher, and the publisher hereby disclaims any responsibility for them.

Any people depicted in stock imagery provided by Thinkstock are models, and such images are being used for illustrative purposes only.

Certain stock imagery © Thinkstock.

ISBN: 978-1-4502-9612-0 (sc)
ISBN: 978-1-4502-9611-3 (hc)
ISBN: 978-1-4502-9610-6 (e)

Library of Congress Control Number: 2011909087

Printed in the United States of America

iUniverse rev. date: 07/12/2011

To all Igbo parents making sacrifices for
the education of their children

These education policies will open the doors of opportunity for our children. But it is up to us to ensure they walk through them. In the end, there is no program or policy that can substitute for a mother or father, who will attend those parent-teacher conferences or help with homework after dinner or turn off the TV, put away the video games, and read to their child. I speak to you not just as a president but as a father, when I say that responsibility for our children's education must begin at home.

—President Barack Obama's address to the joint
session of Congress on February 24, 2009

Contents

List of Figures

List of Tables

Foreword

"But let us be honest. For teachers to succeed,
they must have parents as partners.
To give our children the education they deserve,
parents must get off the sidelines and get involved.
The most important door to a child's education is
the front door of the home.
And nothing I do at the schools can ever replace that.
Working together, we will create a seamless partnership,
from the classroom to the family room,
to help our children learn and succeed."
"We will do our part. And parents, we need you to do yours."
—Mayor Rahm Emanuel, Inaugural Address, May 16, 2011

In his May 16, 2011 inaugural address Rahm Emanuel, the new mayor of Chicago, candidly enunciated one of the top priorities of his education reform agenda—the responsibility of parents to be actively involved in their childrens' education. In this, he echoes the remarks of his former boss President Barack Obama in the latter's February 2009 address to Congress (see the front of this book).

The necessity of parental involvement, especially in the early years of their childrens' education, is one thing everyone in America agrees with. Parents must take this responsibility to heart and make it a top priority in their parenting and family life. This reflects an ancient but still an essential wisdom that, "Parents are the primary educators of their children."

First-rate education of our children is essential if the United States is to remain a leader in a global economy that is increasingly complex, high tech, competitive and fast moving. Effective and interested involvement by parents in the education of their children is essential for a quality education.

All efforts at the renewal of education, whether directed at curriculum, teacher training and evaluation, teaching methods or funding will fail to renew education if not complemented by consistent and effective parental involvement. Such involvement provides not only immediate educational benefits to their children but implants an essential value deep in their psyches—education as one of their high priority values in life.

Dr. Jerome Onwughalu recounts the fascinating experience of parents from Igboland in southern Nigeria who have made America their new home. Knowing their children won't achieve the American dream without a good education, they devote themselves to active involvement in their childrens' learning.

This book is a must read for parents, educators and all interested in the renewal of education in America and around the world.

Rev. William E. Zimmer, C.P.A., M.B.A., S.T.L., D.Min.

Chicago, IL

Preface

As an educator in rural Ethiopia, I worked with parents, families and the community in educating the children of the nomadic Borana community. There were challenges but my collaboration with the education stakeholders of this rural community positively impacted the education of the children and was also fulfilling for me. In addition, my educational leadership internship at an urban Catholic School in Chicago afforded me the opportunity to witness other ways that parents, families and communities are involved in the education of their children in an industrialized metropolitan setting. As I reflect on both experiences, it dawns on me that in both school communities—parents, families and communities—involved themselves in the education of children, yet in different ways. Moreover, since then I have developed an interest in understanding the dynamics of parents and families working with schools in the education of children. This study is an expression of that interest.

The study was conducted using a narrative inquiry methodology, which provides a good platform to hear these important stories about education and schooling and to better understand the particular experience of Igbo parents in Chicago regarding to their involvement in the education of their children. Epstein's theory of overlapping spheres of influence and Bronfenbrenner's ecological systems theory frame the study.

Ten parents were interviewed in this study—six women and four men.

Ka umu anyi wee karia anyi (So that our children will be better than us) is one of the many reasons Igbo families in Chicago--an African immigrant community--are involved in the education of their children.

Other themes that emerged include: Educating children (what it takes to educate children), the Igbo parents' perception and practice of parental involvement, Igbo parents' relationship with the schools, the parents' environment, the challenges encountered and support systems for parents.

It is immaterial whether their kind of involvement fits the prescribed or standardized form of parental involvement in the literature or in practice elsewhere. But the crucial question is, given their circumstances, are Igbo parents' perceptions and practices of parental involvement promoting the education of their children in Chicago?

About this Book

Parents' Involvement in Education—The Experience of an African Immigrant Community in Chicago is the fruit of my doctoral dissertation that used narrative inquiry, to study how Igbo families in Chicago are involved in the education of their children—their perceptions and practices of parental involvement, the challenges they face and supports they have.

The book has four parts. Part one has three main chapters. The first chapter, the introduction, gives the inspiration and rationale for the study. It also explains the basic concepts of the study. The next chapter gives background information on the Igbo people of Nigeria and their life in Chicago as an immigrant community. This chapter will help the reader better appreciate the parental involvement stories of Igbo families in Chicago in the later chapters. Chapter three presents the theoretical framework of the study and reviews the literature. This last chapter of part one has four main sections: Theories of the overlapping spheres of influence and ecological systems, theory and practice of parental involvement, parental involvement and communication and finally the challenges to parental involvement.

Part two is chapter four. I imagine that readers will like to know how the study was carried out and what informed the decisions regarding methodology. While laying out the blueprint of the study, I articulate the problem, research questions and explain why the study is important and how it contributes to scholarship. I also present the step-by-step process of how I gathered, analyzed and reported the data. I end the chapter by examining both the quality and ethical research issues relevant to this study.

Part three, though longest with seven chapters, gets to the heart of the book. In chapter five, the reader will not only learn something of the stories of the ten parents who participated in the study, but will hear and even feel their voices. In the remaining chapters (6-11), I present parents' voices on: Education and schooling; perceptions and practices of parental involvement; their relationship with the schools their children attend; parents' environment and challenges (and support) in parent involvement.

Part four has two chapters. Chapter twelve muses on what the Igbo parents said about their experience of parental involvement in light of the conceptual framework of the study. The concluding chapter summarizes the study noting its implication for practice, stating its limitations and offering suggestions for future research.

Acknowledgments

This book has deep roots in my educational leadership doctoral program at DePaul University. I characterize its publication as a journey that started with my experience as a teacher and administrator at an elementary school in Borana Ethiopia, and all the way through my doctoral dissertation, which relates and analyzes the findings of interviews with ten Igbo parents in Chicago regarding their perceptions and practices of parental involvement. It also presents the challenges they face and the sources of support they find as they interact with the local schools in the education of their children.

Many people accompanied me in this journey. First, I would like to thank the members of my committee: Dr. Karen Monkman, Dr. Andrea Kayne Kaufman and Dr. Darrick Tovar-Murray. I thank you all for your invaluable advice. Special thanks to Dr. Monkman, my chair, for her wonderful accompaniment on this journey and her kind patience in reviewing various drafts of the paper. Dr. Kaufman, you helped to plant the seed of this research and, in many gracious ways, you watered and nurtured it; I sincerely thank you. Dr. Tovar-Murray, thanks for your special interest in my study and for the many ways you helped to sustain my interest.

For the several wonderful professors at the DePaul Graduate School of Education, thanks to all for your inspiration and the many productive educational insights you provided. I also appreciate the attention given by my colleagues, who not only read my work in its early stages and offered suggestions, but also sent helpful materials and suggested relevant articles and websites. They also provided support and assistance whenever there was a need such as the time I needed someone for a mock interview. I thank in particular Donna Smith, Felicia Richardson, Troy Harden and Stephanie Konkol and many others as well.

I am grateful to the Archdiocese of Chicago for providing accommodation throughout these years of my studies. To the Resurrection Medical Center, I thank you for providing different kinds of assistance, such as the opportunity to work and go to school, thereby earning my graduate school tuition. The chaplaincy, which you provided as a learning platform, added to my graduate school experience.

To my Spiritan (Congregation of the Holy Spirit) confreres here in Chicago, regardless of the fact that your numbers have changed over time, your support remained constant during the whole process. I want to mention Frs. James Okoye, Casmir Eke, Freddy Washington, Eze Umunnakwe and Clement Uchendu. You are all wonderful brothers to me in the Spiritan family. My study spans the tenure of several Provincial Superiors of the Nigerian Province of the Congregation of the Holy Spirit. I am grateful to Fr. Mike Onwuemelie and his council for approving my further studies. Fr. Luke Mbefo and his council implemented it and I thank them for their support. Frs. Gabriel Ezewudo and Augustine Onyeneke continued to support me throughout the study and even provided a listening ear to my many woes. I am equally indebted to Fr. Peter Agbonome, Provincial of the South-East Nigeria province and Fr. John Fogarty, Provincial of the U.S. province. Frs. Donatus Chukwu (Oluwa), Oby Zunmas and Benedict Ezeoke (Benzello): You are truly brothers. Thank you.

My special thanks to Bryan Thalhammer. I thank you for your special role not only in showing me how to do certain things I never thought could be done with Microsoft Word but also reviewing the drafts and offering valuable suggestions. Sharing the experience of your dissertation journey was very helpful too. I will remain ever grateful and remember with nostalgia our discussions about British, American and Nigerian English. I thank Fr. Bill Zimmer, a priest of the Archdiocese of Chicago and resides at St. Angela rectory. He was instrumental in encouraging me to give this study a wider exposure by publishing it as a book. Bill not only read several drafts and provided some very valuable feedback and corrections, but also wrote the foreword to this book.

I am also grateful to the Igbo community in Chicago and especially the parents who graciously agreed to be interviewed. I will not mention your names here to preserve confidentiality, but you all know that I cannot thank you enough. You simply made me proud as one of your own. *Jide nuu ka unu ji!* (Keep on going with what is good! Keep the flag flying!)

Finally, I thank Almighty God Who surprised me in many ways and Who continues to do so everyday, providing me with energy, good health and courage as well as blessings that keep me going strong, against all odds.

CHAPTER 1

Parental Involvement in Education — Who Educates Children?

U nlike the Igbo parents in this study, I have no children of my own and therefore do not have any practical experience in being involved with the education of my own children. However, as a teacher, as well as an administrator in Nigeria and Ethiopia, I have worked with parents and communities in the education of children. Based on that experience, I see myself as having the role of a partner but "on the other side" of the educational process, the school side. Some parents in this study are actually on both sides of the process because they are also professional teachers. So they are involved as parents in some cases, and as teachers in others, which gives them both an interesting and a valuable perspective on parental involvement as a teacher, parent, family member and school employee.

One of the lessons I learned during my years as a teacher and an administrator is how important parent involvement is in the education of children. I had many experiences in my previous profession, where it was quite evident that the school alone could not completely educate a child, just as in the case of parents or families trying to provide schooling in isolation from others. Igbo parents in Chicago say as much: "It [education of children] takes the involvement of parents and teachers working together. It cannot be just the teachers. It cannot be just parents. The involvement of both [is required]" (Nwakaego). Nsobundu warns that there will be a price to pay if either the parents or the school/teachers are not truly involved in a child's education. I doubt whether anyone can dispute Nsobundu's proposition because family and school are the most important institutions in the education and development of children (Lightfoot, 1978; 2003; Bronfenbrenner, 1989; Epstein, 2001). Home and school are two complementary contexts of childrens' teaching and learning.

My work as a teacher and an administrator got me interested in the issues related to parental involvement in the education of children and consequently inspired me to want to know more about the dynamics of the phenomenon. So I placed it on my list of things to do. Therefore, when I started my doctoral program at the DePaul University College of Education, I began to think seriously again about parental involvement. During one of the classes, I came across Epstein's theory of overlapping spheres of influence, and it was like "Eureka, I have an important tool to start my digging." In a nutshell, the theory explains why the family, school and community should work together to achieve a common educational mission for children and society. The education of children takes place in the home, school and community. These environments are not self-contained or isolated from one another because the child lives and grows within the influence of all three virtually simultaneously. It was a big insight for me into the world of parental involvement. However, like all theories it was generic. There is still the need to see how it plays out in the life of ordinary parents. From then on, I paid particular attention to articles, books, newspaper stories and radio or television documentaries that dealt with parental involvement and related issues. In addition, autobiographies and biographies usually attracted my attention, especially the chapters on child-rearing and early education strategies that related to parental involvement. Also, I have to confess to intentionally buying books about some individuals, simply to read about their early upbringing and education vis-à-vis parental involvement.

In reading the literature, listening to radio interviews or watching videos about parents who involve themselves more actively in their childrens' education, I learned how important the educational environment is to a child's learning process. So when I came across Bronfenbrenner's ecological systems theory, it became yet another important tool that could be used to probe the phenomenon of parental involvement in education. As we shall see later, Bronfenbrenner posits that child development, teaching, and learning activities do not occur in a vacuum. They occur in a context, which influences the way individuals grow and function. In relation to parental involvement, the context of parents influences their decisions and actions about the education of their children.

In this study, I integrated the two theories as my theoretical framework. The two theories together read as follows: the context of Igbo parents in Chicago shapes their perceptions, their practices and the challenges (Bronfenbrenner, 1977) of their involvement in the education of their children, which is their overlapping spheres of influence (Epstein, 2001). The next step was to identify the specific area my inquiry should focus on, that is, what should be the object of my study.

I am a firm believer that for any nation to become developed, the quality of education from early childhood through elementary school should be first-rate and solid. And then not only must this foundational level of education be right, but all other subsequent education should also be built on this solid base and continue on seamlessly in the same way. Therefore, I was very pleased to read that the new democratic government of Nigeria launched a Universal Basic Education program in 1999 as one of many steps towards meeting the Millennium Development Goals of 2015. So I thought then that it would be interesting to explore Nigerian parents' involvement in this foundational educational program—Nigerian Universal Basic Education—which is so important for the development of the country. My intention was to select a section of the country or a group of parents and then carry out the study. Fortunately or unfortunately, because of logistics and finances I was unable to carry out that study for my doctoral program. On the advice of my supervisor and committee, I decided to change the focus. I chose to study how Igbo parents in Chicago are involved in the education of their children. It turned out to be one the best decisions I made with regard to my doctoral program.

This study seeks to understand how Igbo parents in Chicago are involved in the education of their children. I chose a qualitative, narrative methodology because I wanted primarily to understand the experience of Igbo parents in relation to their involvement in their childrens' education. Their experiences are embedded in stories. After all, it is hard to separate experience and narrative (Clandinin and Connelly, 2000).

This book is the report of the research on how Igbo parents in Chicago are involved in the education of their children. Through interviews, the parents of ten families of the Igbo community in Chicago share their experiences as they engage with local schools in the education of their children. Before giving the rationale for this study, I will say something about the key concepts and terminologies of this research.

Concepts and Terminology

The key concepts and terminologies used in this study are as follows: parental involvement, education, schooling and context.

Parental Involvement

Parents, family, school and community constitute the overall environment in which the education and development of children take place (Epstein, 2001). Children spend all or most of their childhood years in family, school and community. It is against this background that Riley (1999) notes that the best hope for getting all American children on the right educational path is to increase parental and community involvement, which is the strongest common link among good schools all across America. Similarly, Brandt and Robelen (1998) are of the opinion that it will be very difficult for schools to meet the challenges of true reform, that is, better educational outcomes and benefits without first doing a better job of connecting with parents and the public.

Words like "collaboration," "partnership," "involvement," "engagement" and "participation" are used to characterize the relationship between these institutions—family, school and community—as they work together to educate the children of their community. These words, though not synonyms, primarily describe a broad array of the beliefs, behaviors and practices of parents, family, community and school as they work together to provide a good education for the children of the community (Patrikakou, Weissberg, Redding and Walberg, 2005).

Furthermore, as Bronfenbrenner (1979) points out, schooling that is isolated from the home will have significant consequences on the behavior and development of children. Yet there is a need to find out the nature of this link between school and home in the education of children.

Family, school and community—environments for the education and development of children—engage in mutual interactions that ultimately influence the child's education and development (Bronfenbrenner, 1977, 1979, 1986, 1989). In this way these environments strive for the ideal of becoming allies that work together to accomplish the educational mission, that is, the social, intellectual, psychological and physical development of children that also benefits society. In sum, "Children learn and grow at home, at school, and in the community. Their experiences may be positive or negative, but it is clear that the people in these three contexts influence student learning and development from infancy on" (Epstein, 2005, p. vii).

Context and Parental Involvement

"Context", an important concept in this study, will be used interchangeably with the terms "ecological systems" and "environment." "Context" transcends geographical settings to include socio-cultural, political, economic and psychosocial forces outside the home (Delgado-Gaitan, 1992). In this study, it is construed as the totality of all the elements that influence the day-to-day life of parents, family, school and community.

A fact of life is that people's socio-political, cultural and historical life situation, simply their context or environment or what Bronfenbrenner (1977, 1979, 1986, 1989) refers to as an ecological system, certainly affects their way of thinking and doing things. Similarly, the ecological systems of parents, family, school and community affect and define the way each lives and functions including the influence each wields over the education of the children.

Education and Schooling

In this study, education is understood to mean more than schooling. It includes "learning" which occurs both within and outside school settings and focuses on the development of the individual, who in turn contributes towards meeting the needs and the development of society. Furthermore, education is a broad term used to capture teaching and learning processes inspired by the prevailing needs of the individual and society. These needs could be cultural, political, social, spiritual, psychological, economic, cognitive or health related. Obanya (2004) names the individual as the direct beneficiary while the society is the ultimate beneficiary of education (p. 22).

Schooling, in contrast to education, is a more limited concept (Dodd and Konzal, 2002, p.101). While schooling includes only the responsibilities given to teachers and administrators, education includes the responsibilities of everyone and by extension, everything that influences what children learn (Dodd and Konzal, 2002, pp. 100ff). In addition, "schooling" refers to what happens in school settings and is related primarily to the explicit curriculum and educational policy.

In the same vein, this study prefers to use the phrase "parental involvement in the education of children" rather than "parental involvement in school." The term "parental involvement in school" tends to restrict the participation of family to schooling activities. On the other hand, parental involvement in the education of children encompasses education-related activities both at home and school. This involves some activities related to school (e.g., homework) and some that are not (e.g., emergent literary activities like reading to young children at home). For Igbo parents in Chicago, it can also include choosing the schools their children attend and creating a learning friendly home environment. As such, the distinction between education and schooling is somewhat blurred.

Rationale for the Study

The Igbo community in Chicago is a newer immigrant community compared to the German, Polish or Irish. Just as for these older immigrant groups, education is essential for Igbo immigrants who have come to start a new life in the United States. Adapting well and thriving in the new environment requires immigrants to tread the path of education. The number of Igbo children and other such immigrants are increasing. The way they are educated is important not only to the individual child but also to society. Igbo children are enrolled in both public and private schools in the Chicago metropolitan area (Chicagoland).

Little has been written about Igbo parents in Chicago with respect to their involvement in their children's education. In other words, there is a lack of knowledge about their perception of their own involvement, of what actually constitutes parental involvement activities and of the challenges they face in their day-to-day engagement in the education of their children in Chicago. Since the education of children takes place both at home and school, it is important to explore and characterize the nature of the role parents play as well as the challenges they face. We must first seek out the nature of Igbo parents' involvement in the education of their children in Chicago. Besides, not all immigrants are the same. Knowing about Igbo experiences will enable scholars and educators to recognize commonalities and differences between the Igbo community and other immigrant communities from Europe, Asia, the Caribbean, the Middle East, Latin America or Africa.

CHAPTER 2

Nigeria: The Homeland of the Igbo in Chicago

> The United States has always been a nation
> of nations where people from every region
> of the world come to begin a new life.
>
> —Ronald Bayor in *The Nigerian Americans*

Since the Igbo community in Chicago is the subject of this study, it is important to get a sense of who they are, where they come from, why they emigrated to Chicago, and how their lives are constantly challenged as immigrants.

This section of the chapter will present some introductory background information about the Igbo people in Chicago vis-à-vis Nigeria, their native country. The goal is to situate them in the context of their homeland, Nigeria. The Igbo form a significant percentage of the Nigerian population. It is also important to examine the traditional Nigerian family structure in relation to its role in both informal and formal education. The essence of the section on the history and waves of Nigerian immigration to the United States (whether deliberate or forced by circumstances to emigrate) is to show how some Igbo came to Chicago. Finally, I will look at the Igbo community in Chicago in terms of demography, education of the children, the challenges they face in their new environment, especially as immigrants.

Nigeria

Nigeria is a West African country that shares boundaries with Cameroon on the east, Benin Republic to the west, and Chad and the Niger Republic to the northeast and north respectively. It is bound by the Atlantic Ocean on the south (see figure 1).

Nigeria was a colony of Britain until October 1, 1960. Despite the so-called political independence won over fifty years ago, British influence is still very much obvious in the Nigerian landscape and life. The most prominent example is the adoption of English as the national language. This is not surprising, however, considering that for over seventy years (including the years before the 1914 British amalgamation of the northern and southern protectorates) Britain had a firm grip on Nigeria and its people.

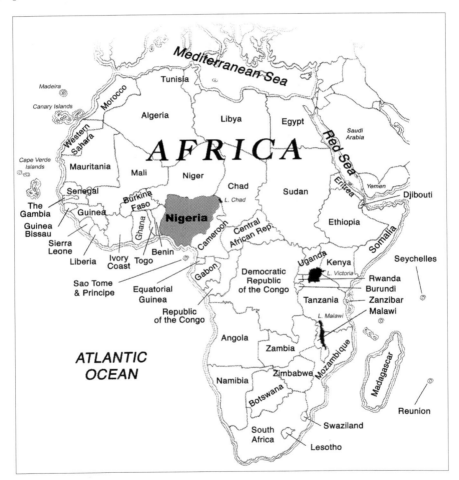

Figure 1. Map of Africa, showing Nigeria and neighboring countries.

The British parliamentary system of government, a carryover from the colonial period, was jettisoned in 1979 for an American-style presidential system of government. Since independence, Nigeria has experienced several spates of intrusions and rule by the military. In her over fifty years as a sovereign nation, the military has ruled for thirty-three years. The present democratic government is the fourth experiment with democracy. However, this burgeoning democracy is still on a very shaky foothold. Free and fair elections are still on the far horizon. The present lack of free and fair elections in Nigeria has had negative consequences on the development of Nigeria. The hope is that as literacy increases and more Nigerians become genuinely educated, democracy will mature, and governance will be more accountable and purposeful.

The 923,768 sq. km. of Nigerian landmass makes it a little larger in area than the state of Texas (see figure 2).

Politically, it is made of 36 states, 774 local government councils, and a federal capital territory. On the regional level, Nigeria is sub-grouped into six geopolitical sections, namely, north central, northeast, northwest, southeast, southwest, and south-south regions. According to the 2006 national census, Nigeria is the most populous black nation on earth, having an estimated population of 140 million people belonging to about 250 different ethnic groups. The population of these ethnic groups ranges between thirty million to less than a million people.

Seventy percent of Nigerians live in rural areas, where the basic infrastructure is either grossly inadequate or simply nonexistent. Like most developing countries, urbanization is increasing at an alarming rate and causing social dislocation in most urban cities. Most of these cities are ill-equipped for the influx of people relocating on a daily or monthly basis. Nigeria is among the twenty least developed and poorest countries of the world. It ranks 159th out of 177 countries analyzed (UNDP, 2006). This ranking is surprising, if not embarrassing, considering that Nigeria is the eighth largest producer of oil in the world.

The educational system followed the British system until the 1977 national policy on education introduced a new system of education, tagged the 6-3-3-4 system: six years of primary education, three years of junior secondary education, three years of senior secondary education, and four years of tertiary education. Nigerian educational policy and management is centralized. The federal government, through the Federal Ministry of Education, formulates policies, manages the system, and carries the bulk of the financial burdens of education. The state and local governments have limited authority to make policy and, thus, are mainly organs for carrying out the federal government educational policies.

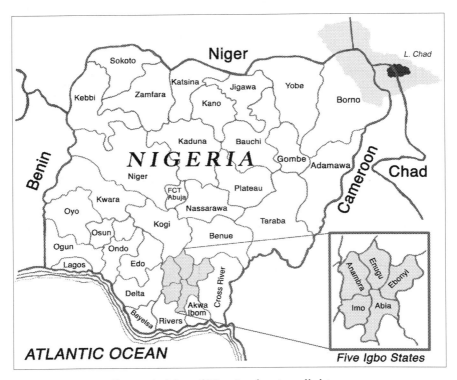

Figure 2. Map of Nigeria, showing all thirty-
six states and the federal capital Abuja.

The 2006 Human Development Index (HDI)[1] puts Nigeria's adult literacy at 55 percent (UNDP, 2006). Forty-five percent of the population consists of children between zero to fifteen years of age. This is the target group of the Nigerian Universal Basic Education (UBE) program, and about 42 percent of this age group is eligible for primary education (Nnaike, 2007).

Having presented some brief information about Nigeria, I will say more regarding the Igbo, thus distinguishing them from the rest of Nigerians.

---

1   Human Development Index (HDI) is an instrument that the United Nations Development Program (UNDP) uses to measure human development of countries worldwide. HDI measures life expectancy, educational attainment, and GDP per capita and ranks them accordingly. Retrieved August 21, 2009, from http://hdr.undp.org/hdr2006/statistics/countries/country_fact_sheets/cty_fs_NGA.html

The Igbo of Southeast Nigeria

The Igbo[2], the third largest ethnic group in Nigeria (after the Hausa in the north and the Yoruba in the southwest) inhabit the five southeastern states of the country, namely, Abia, Anambra, Ebonyi, Enugu and Imo (see figure 2). Also, significant land areas and populations of neighboring states, such as the Rivers and Delta, form part of Igboland (see figures 2 and 3).

Apart from the states that form the Igbo homeland, significant numbers of Igbo are scattered in other parts of Nigeria and around the world. The Igala, Idoma, and Tiv people are neighbors of the Igbo to the north. While the Ijaw and Ogoni are their neighbors to the south, the Ibibio, the Yako, and Anang are their eastern neighbors. To the west, the Bini, Urhobo, and Itserkri people border the Igbo (figure 3).

Figure 3. Map of Igboland showing the principal towns

---

2   *Igbo* is a term used to describe both the people and their language (Reynolds, 2004; Ebelebe, 2007).

The issue of the population of the Igbo has been greatly politicized, making it somewhat difficult to determine the exact population of Ndigbo[3]. For example, using only the data from the five south eastern states (Abia, Anambra, Ebonyi, Enugu, and Imo), the 2006 national census put the population of the Igbo at 16.36 million without taking into consideration the Igbo people living in the Delta and Rivers states and the other parts of the nation and the world. Nevertheless, a conservative estimate of the worldwide Igbo population is 20–25 million (Ebelebe, 2007, p.1).

As for political organization and structure, the largest traditional Igbo political unit is the village group or town. The political system has no kingdoms or city states under the effective control of a monarch, such as the Bini, Yoruba, Igala, Hausa-Fulani, or other ethnic groups in Nigeria (Ebelebe, 2007, p. 38). *Igbo enwe eze* or *Igbo ama eze,* which literally means "Igbo people have no king" or "Igbo people do not recognize a king" is both a well-known saying and a political philosophy. Behind this political philosophy is the Igbo belief in egalitarianism. For the Igbo, the highest form of political power is the community. Family and education are also important not only for Ndigbo but also for other Nigerians.

Family and Education in Nigeria

In this section, I will discuss informal education—education in Nigeria before the arrival of Western/formal education—and the Nigerian family while paying attention to the extended family structure. I will also discuss formal education—schooling—and the Nigerian family, specifically the arrival of Western or formal education and its consequences on the role of the family in the education of children.

Family Structure

The nuclear family (wife, husband, and children) is not the important unit in the African traditional setting. Rather, the extended family or the kin group is the most essential unit or cultural ideal (Oke, 1986; Ohuche, 1991; Ogbaa, 2003). For example, Oke (1986) points out that the extended family has wide acceptability and practice in Nigeria. A typical extended African family, made up of several nuclear families (Nwa-Chil, 1984, p. 7), might include the maternal and paternal uncles, aunties, grandparents, cousins,

---

3   The Igbo word *Ndigbo* (a term I will often use in this study) simply refers
     to the Igbo people. It is a combination of two Igbo words, namely, *Ndi*
     meaning *people* and *Igbo*, the ethnic group and their language (Reynolds,
     2004; Ebelebe, 2007).

nephews, and nieces from both sides of one's parents. Mbiti (1990) includes the dead as members of the extended family; he designates them as the living dead, because they are still interested in the well-being of the living (p.104). In other words, for most Nigerians, the family is much larger than the nuclear family. The extended family system that emphasizes interpersonal relationship values, such as cooperation, connectedness, and interdependence (Smith, 1997), is involved in all aspects of the life of the members, even in the choice of a spouse, which is a collective responsibility (Obidi, 2005, p. 24). It is not a surprise then that the families, along with the community, guide and direct the informal education of children.

Informal Education: Education before the Arrival of Western Schooling

Every society, whether simple or complex, has its own unique system of education (Fafunwa, 1991, p.15), which is a way of transmitting accumulated knowledge from one generation to the next (Nzekwe, 2007, p. 21). This is the case in Africa before the advent of the Western system of education (Fafunwa, 1982, 1991; Ozigbo, 1999), and it continues in addition to formal schooling. Ozigbo (1999), while discussing the Igbo society of Southeast Nigeria and education, has this to say: "Europe or Christian missions did not bring the concept and practice of education to Igboland. What the Europeans brought was the Western type of education" (p.119). "Education" here is understood as

> the aggregate of all the processes by which a child or young adult develops the abilities, attitudes, and other forms of behavior, which are of positive value to the society. It is a process for transmitting culture in terms of continuity and growth and for disseminating knowledge either to ensure social control or to guarantee rational direction of society or both. (Fafunwa and Aisiku, 1982, p. 11)

The above definition encompasses the intellectual, physical, social, and emotional aspects of development and education. It targets the child and young adult with the purpose of socialization, transmission of culture and knowledge, and the development of skills primarily for the good of the individual and society. This means "education in old Africa was an integrated experience" (Fafunwa, 1991, p.16). The subsequent definition by Fafunwa (1991) summarizes the goals and methodology of informal education:

> African education emphasized social responsibility, job orientation, political participation, spiritual and moral values. Children learnt by doing; that is to say, children and adolescents were engaged

in participatory education through ceremonies, rituals, imitation, recitation, and demonstration ... (p.16)

To further illuminate these informal educational goals, Fafunwa and Aisiku (1982) list the seven cardinal objectives, which are as follows: to develop the child's latent physical skills; to develop character and to inculcate respect for elders and those in positions of authority; to develop intellectual skills; to acquire specific vocational training; to develop a healthy attitude toward honest labor; to develop a sense of belonging; to encourage active participation in family and community affairs; and to understand, appreciate, and promote the cultural heritage of the community at large (pp.11–12). From this list, one can distill its basic attributes, which include student centeredness, family and community involvement, curriculum, and objectives. Clearly, African traditional education intimately ties into social life, hence its multivalent character (Fafunwa and Aisiku, 1982, p.10). Nevertheless, informal education differs from formal education in some respects.

Ozigbo (1999), in a brief comparison with formal education, noted that the traditional educational system had no fixed schools, professional teachers, classrooms, grades or daily schedules or academic calendars, or intervals, like holidays or standardized textbooks (p. 119). While it lacks a formal systematized structure, informal education does not lack educational objectives, philosophy, curriculum, and methodology.

In summary, education in the old Africa or precolonial Igbo society aimed at nurturing the whole child to adulthood and beyond. A child did not have to demand education from the family or the community; it is a cultural process embedded in the rearing of children, and it occurs seamlessly as children participate in their cultural and social context. As a process of the integral development of the child, it emphasizes the participation of all members of the community.

Family and Informal Education

Parents and family play vital roles in informal education. The structure of the extended family is the backbone of informal education. Informal education is ongoing—continuous with everyday activities of the community. Each stage of life presents its challenges and, accordingly, its particular curriculum. Though student centered, other aspects of its process, like the design of the curriculum, instruction, management, and assessment are the collective responsibility of parents, family, and community. For example, knowledge is transmitted orally through parents, relatives, peers, and acquaintances to the young, adolescents, and adults (Ozigbo, 1999; Ogbaa, 2003). Skills are taught through practice with parents, family, and other community members, who act as mentors and supervisors. Fafunwa and Aisiku (1982) neatly tie informal education together with the role of family as follows:

> It takes the form of informal lessons on ethics, acceptable codes of conduct and behavior, values, history and family genealogy, basic agricultural practices, socialization through family, clan and peer group, different initiation ceremonies, moonlight stories (which have moral lessons) in the village square by elders or at the home by parents and grandparents. (p.10)

The centrality of parents, the extended family, and the community in the education of the child gave rise to the often-quoted African saying, "It takes a village to raise a child." Some cultures, including the Igbo, take it a step further by saying that "a child belongs to the community." With ownership comes responsibility, meaning that the community also shares in the responsibility of raising the child. For some cultures, like the Borana people of southern Ethiopia and northern Kenya, the word "orphan," as understood in the Western sense, virtually does not exist. Even when a child loses both biological parents, the community assumes the responsibility of bringing up the child. For Ndigbo and other Africans, it is safe to say that there is a very thin line between the raising of a kid and education. Mbiti (1990) aptly expresses this notion:

> Nature brings the child into the world, but society creates the child into a being, a corporate person. For it is the community which must protect the child, feed it, bring it up, educate it, and, in many other ways, incorporate it into a wider community. (p. 107)

Family, Informal Education and Modern Society

The strength and relevance of the extended family in the education of children is daily tested by the prevailing capitalistic ideology that permeates all global thinking and sociopolitical economic activities. It is left to be seen how the extended family system, the informal education, and the traditional values, structures, and cultures it nurtures will survive the current brand of capitalism, competition, individualism, and technology-driven globalization. With regard to the education of children in present-day society, Nwa-Chil (1984) is of the opinion that parents and families are ill equipped to do the job alone in the current changing society.

> With rapid technological changes and the growing economic diversification and occupational specialization, which modern society demands, a point has been reached at which preparation

for adult life cannot be left to parents alone, not only because they may not have the knowledge or the time, but also primarily because the rate of change has reached such a momentum that each coming generation must be better equipped for the challenges posed by these societies. (p. 52)

The position of Nwa-Chil can hardly be contested because of the fact that the process of education is dynamic. Education "serves as the prime fashioner of individual growth and a progressive democratic society" (Walker and Soltis, 1997, p.13). In other words, it evolves with the society to serve its needs. Simply put, as civilization marches on, traditional education seems no longer adequate to prepare children for active participation in the modern society. Besides, the coming of Europeans to Africa brought about a different society and culture. Family alone cannot transmit the new culture that is still evolving. Transmission of new cultures (in this case, Western forms of cultural ideas and processes) is a duty family now shares with formal schooling (a new institution introduced by missionaries and colonizers). Furthermore, Western education serves as a springboard to national development that leads to active participation in the global community. Here again, parents and family cannot singlehandedly cope with preparing their children for the new demands of society, such as national development and globalization. Schooling accordingly has become an integral part of education—the process of preparing children for responsible adult life in the society. As a result, Aluede (2006) locates the importance of schooling in the present-day society in this way; "schooling to modern society is what initiation rites were to traditional societies" (p. 54). Initiation rites integrate the postulant into the society, and accordingly, schooling helps the individual to navigate and find footing in modern society.

Today, formal education is widespread and seems to be the norm. For example, UNESCO says that 63 percent of Nigerian children of primary school age are in primary school.[4] Informal education, however, occurs alongside and intertwines with formal schooling. Adamu (2003) argues that today education takes place not only in schools but also within families, communities, and society. He does not see education as compartmentalized into informal and formal processes; rather, each flows into the other. After all, both have the same basic objectives. Education is a process that starts at home, is formalized at school, and then continues on in the larger society (Ohuche, 1991). Nzekwe (2007), while not disagreeing with Adamu and Ohuche, calls

---

4   This is primary school net enrolment/attendance (%) for 2000–2007. UNESCO (2006). Retrieved November 30, 2009, from http://www.unicef.org/infobycountry/Nigeria_statistics.html

for the incorporation of some of the strengths of informal education strategies to enrich the overall education of children. He notes in particular that the effective roles of parents, grandparents, siblings, peers, and age groups in informal education is something that would enrich the new face of education in Africa, including Nigeria (p.114).

The Entrance of Formal Education

The arrival of Western education issued forth a new age with a new face of teaching and learning in Nigeria, with the corresponding consequences on culture and society. The new face of education redefined the role of parents, the family, and the community in the education of children.

Although Africans never invited Western schooling, they embraced it after some measure of resistance. It was an aching embrace that left Africa at a crossroad of Western socialization and self-definition. Africa lost some aspects of its educational system in order to accommodate the philosophy and methodology of Western education. The result is that Western education ended up dominating education in Igboland and indeed Africa, thus giving rise to a crisis of identity in education. While some African nations are still searching for an appropriate system of education, others have changed their systems and philosophies several times, thus jeopardizing continuity. This might help to explain why Africa is at the bottom of the world's educational league (Obanya, 2002). Lagging far behind, almost being left behind near the bottom of the educational heap, further explains why Africa seldom gets a seat at the table of world affairs.

Christian missionaries and European colonialists, who brought schooling to Nigeria and Igboland, each had their own self-serving purposes for education. For example, according to Obidi (2005),

> "Apart from the purpose of using education for [religious] conversion, the missionaries placed emphasis on bookish education rather than on the acquisition of practical skills because of the demand from commerce and government for educated persons" (p. 169).

The missionaries, who later added acquisition of certain types of skills to the curriculum, did so at the request of the colonial administrators and traders—that is, to meet the needs of colonial administration, which is to train people to work in their enterprise.

Formal Education and Family Participation

The colonial masters and missionary groups, who were the agents of formal education in Africa, were never invited. They came on their own accord and, in their parlance, imposed "civilization" on the people, using formal education (schooling) as a major strategy to do so. There was no input from the people in formulating their programs of "civilizing the people." Their relationship with their "hosts" at best was that of master-servant. Anya (2004) illustrates this point using the Nigerian experience as an example:

> The pattern of colonial intrusion into the area that became Nigeria never afforded the opportunity for the consultation of the indigenous peoples on their governance or their expectations or their future aspirations as individuals and as peoples. (Anya, 2004)

In addition, the agents of Western education focused primarily on their own interests, serving their immediate purposes. For example, the missionaries in the early stages emphasized reading the Bible and evangelization. Later, the traders and colonial administrators, in collaboration with the missionaries, upgraded the curriculum to provide clerks, interpreters, preachers, and errand runners with the skills necessary to serve their purposes (Nzekwe, 2007, p. 8). This, in effect, made formal education look like a production line for the workforce of their choice; in the case of the Christian missionaries, this took the form of primarily bolstering proselytization.

The Disconnect Between Formal and Informal Education

The obvious consequence is that the early missionaries and colonizers failed to build their brand of education on the already-existing traditional educational frameworks. As a result, the colonialists deliberately succeeded in colonizing the educational system too. For example, the agents of Western education erroneously believed that the natives, the Igbo of Southeastern Nigeria, had no worthwhile past, history, no culture, and no system of education (Nzekwe, 2007, p. 39). The lack of involvement or consultation with the locals led to suspicion of the colonial masters and, in some places, brought about some level of resistance. The lesson is obvious, namely, that the introduction of a new element—Western schooling—into a culture should not discount that culture's factors. New ideas should not blind one to the values inherent in the traditional practices (Obidi, 2005, p. 261).

By this approach, the missionaries and colonialists, who introduced Western education to Igboland and the rest of Nigeria, succeeded in contradicting an important principle of development. Development, according to Ake (2003), cannot be received. It has to be experienced by participation with the process that brings about the development. People need to be the agents, means, and the end of their own development (p.140). With the arrival of formal education, the parents, family, and community, who had been the pillars of informal education, became the "receivers of development" through Western education, meaning that Western education failed to build on one of the strengths of informal education. Parents were no longer central agents in the education of their children. The consequence is that formal education in Igboland developed without encouraging parental involvement in the education of children. There are efforts to reverse the mistake. For example, the Dakar Framework for Action[5] recommends that education in the developing nations should build on the already-existing mold (Peppler-Barry, 2000).

The coming of Western education also resulted in a shift of focus, from being student centered (informal education) to being teacher centered. Nzekwe (2007) points out that the teacher-centered brand of Western education is one of the reasons for Igbo children dropping out from high school. Such teacher-centered curriculum made teaching and learning boring (p.101). All these factors account for the diminished roles of parents and family involvement in formal education compared to the informal education prior to the introduction of Western schooling. The diminished role of parents and family is akin to the belief by some that the responsibility of educating children has been entrusted to educators (Swap, 1993, p. 28).

Nzekwe (2007) is also aware of the consequences of making educational decisions without involving parents and families. Focusing on finding a solution to Igbo-Nigerian children dropping out from high school, he recommended that "decisions should not be made in isolation from parents and communities" (p.118).

It is part of the mission of the Universal Basic Education Commission (UBEC)[6] to reverse this trend, hence its slogan: Education for All is the

---

5   The Dakar Framework for Action is the product of a world education forum that took place in Dakar, Senegal, in April 2000. Like previous conferences, its mission was about meeting education for all (EFA) goals and target for every citizen and for every society (Peppler-Barry, U. [ed.] (2000). World Education Forum Dakar- Senegal 26-28 April, 2000. *Final Report*, Paris, France: UNESCO).

6   Nigeria is a signatory to Universal Basic Education, which is one of the Millennium Development Goals (MDG). UBEC is the commission charged with the implementation of the Nigerian Universal Basic Education program.

Responsibility of All (UBEC, 2005b). This is a reminder that education in the past was the responsibility of the family, parents, and community; and it ought to continue to be so, in spite of its new face, the fusion of the informal and formal aspects of education.

The background information on history, culture, family, and education constitute a base from which Igbo families in Chicago and their children pursue a new life in a new environment. In the subsequent section, I will endeavor to answer the question, why (and how) did Nigerians, particularly the Igbo, immigrate to United States? I will then describe the Igbo community in Chicago.

Nigerian Immigration to the United States and the Igbo Community in Chicago

In this section I will present a short history of Nigerian immigration to the United States. I will also discuss the Igbo community in Chicago, their orientation toward education, and their challenges as immigrants.

Igbo-Nigerian Immigration to the USA and Chicago: A Historical Perspective

In discussing Nigerian immigration to the United States and using Nigerian independence in 1960 as a reference point, Ogbaa (2003) distinguished four phases or waves: the early colonial period (1925–52), the late colonial period (1952–60), the postcolonial period (1961–70), and the postbellum period (1970–present). While maintaining four waves of immigration, I use a different reference point, namely, the thirty-month Nigerian civil war, also known as the Nigerian- Biafran War (1967–1970). This event has become both the foundational and defining, the before and after event in the history of Ndigbo (Igbo people). Instead of Ogbaa's fourth wave (the postbellum period), the period of the US government's Diversity Visa (DV) Lottery Program will be used. Therefore, the four different periods of the Igbo-Nigerians' arrival in the USA that I will discuss include (a) pre-independence to 1967–immigration before the civil war; (b) during the Nigerian-Biafran War (1967–1970), (c) after the civil war (1970–1980), and (d) immigration in the 1980s to the present day. These four waves of immigration are referred to as Nigerian immigration to the United States "in the modern era" (Sarkodie-Mensah, 2000), thus distinguishing it from the era of slave trade. During the several hundred years of slavery, several thousand individuals from present-day Nigeria were brought to America. Ogbaa (2003) estimates that one out of every four Africans brought to America in chains came from what is presently Nigeria (p.113). The modern-era immigration is more pertinent as a focus for this study.

Motivations and Waves of Immigration

With regard to Igbo-Nigerian immigration to the USA, there are diverse motivations associated with immigration (Djamba, 1999, p. 210). The primary motivation for Igbo-Nigerian immigration to the United States has been the quest for education (Akyeampong, 2000; Reynolds, 2002; Ogbaa, 2003). In fact, the first Nigerians came to the United States essentially for higher education (Sarkodie-Mensah, 2000, p. 10). Secondary motivations include socioeconomic and political threats to survival (Akyeampong, 2000; Reynolds, 2002; Ogbaa, 2003). Takougang (2003) notes precisely that "the severe economic difficulties increased poverty and political instability that have plagued many African countries in the last two decades [referring to 80s and 90s] have resulted in large-scale migration of Africans to Europe and the United States" (p.1). Major American cities like New York, Houston, Los Angeles, Chicago, Dallas, Atlanta, Baltimore, and Washington DC are among the priority destinations for Nigerian and Igbo immigrants (Djamba, 1999, Takougang, 2003).

What follows is a summary of each wave, noting the predominant motivation for each era.

Before the Beginning of the Civil War in 1967:
Pre-independence and Political Turmoil

According to Sarkodie-Mensah (2000), in 1926, the New York–based Institute of International Education reported that there were three documented Nigerian students in American universities. The number increased to twenty-two students in 1944. It is also known that Dr. Nnamdi Azikiwe, the first president of Nigeria, arrived by boat in 1925 and was a student in Storer College, Lincoln University, and Howard University (Sarkodie-Mensah, 2000). Almost all Nigerian immigration to different US cities before the Nigerian independence and the Nigerian-Biafran War was for the sole purpose of pursuing one or another form of education (Reynolds, 2002; 2004). Reynolds (2004) calls this group the "primary immigrants" (p. 165). Some were those who came under the auspices of a US government scholarship program, whose purpose was to help train Nigerians to fill the vacuum created by colonial bureaucrats and technocrats who left Nigeria after the independence. Others were Nigerian civil servants on study leave in the United States, sponsored by the newly independent Nigerian government. Still, others were sponsored by their families or clans (Sarkodie-Mensah, 2000). With so many job opportunities at home, it was not surprising that most students returned to Nigeria after graduation to supply the workforce urgently needed by the new government to build the nation (Akyeampong, 2000; Sarkodie-Mensah, 2000; Reynolds, 2002; 2004; Ogbaa, 2003; Takougang, 2003).

This was to change in the newly independent country as the hope of improved economic and social conditions waned and political tension and instability mounted. Hence, some graduates, not sure of their future in the politically tense Nigeria, chose to settle in some United States cities, thus setting the ball rolling for Nigerian settlement.

In summing up, the handful of early Igbo immigrants in US cities, including Chicago, came primarily for education, with no intention to settle. But as their homeland began a political and economic downward spiral, settling in United States became an attractive option, if not an imperative. Unfortunately, to date, the bad socioeconomic situation in Nigeria has not changed; rather, it has become worse.

During the Nigerian-Biafran War (1967–1970): Fleeing for Life

At the start of the thirty-month Nigerian civil war (Nigerian-Biafran War 1967–1970), most Nigerians, especially the Igbo, Ibibo, Efik, Ananag and other ethnic groups from southeastern Nigeria (who were already in the United States), were unable to go back, because their homeland was a theatre of war. Other Nigerians, especially the southeasterners studying in other parts of the world, found America to be a safe haven and thus immigrated to various US cities. Some chose particular cities, especially if they had relatives residing there. Some luckier individuals, because of their qualifications, readily found jobs in teaching and other professions and thus settled into their new environment. Some married Americans and raised children. On the other hand, those who were not able to find work and who could not return home became undocumented immigrants. Amnesty granted to undocumented immigrants in the 1980s changed their status for the better (Takougang, 2003; Rong and Preissle, 2009). It is safe to say that the main motivation for Igbo immigration during this period was survival (*osondu*—running away from the theater of war and seeking refuge in American cities). The quest for education as the primary reason for immigration regained its place in the early 1970s, after the war ended.

After the Civil War (1970-1980): Reunion and Boom

Immediately after the civil war, some Ndigbo (Igbo people) in different parts of the United States, who had been separated from their families, wanted to reunite with their loved ones. Some Ndigbo encouraged and invited members of their families to apply for visas and to immigrate to the United States (Ogbaa, 2003). Though the number of successful immigrants in this period may have been relatively small, it eventually contributed to a swelling the of Igbo-Nigerian community in US cities.

There is another track of Nigerian immigration to the United States during this period. According to Ogbaa (2003), religious-humanitarian relief organizations, such as the American Catholic Relief Services, Caritas International, and the World Council of Churches, played a role in Igbo immigration to the United States during this period. Supplying relief to Biafra during the war gave them first-hand knowledge of the ravages and devastation of Biafra and its people. This moved some of them to sponsor Igbo immigration to the United States. The relief organizations also played significant roles in reuniting families separated by the war. Their role, though on a much smaller scale, is comparable in recent times to what some organizations have done in helping some Sudanese immigrate to the United States. Nevertheless, the quest for education that triggered Igbo-Nigerian immigration to the United States continued during this era.

Then in the 1970s, Nigeria enjoyed an increased level of prosperity due to the oil boom. Before and during this time, Nigerian universities were few, and limited space could not meet the increased demand for tertiary education. With the increase in disposable income resulting from the oil boom, some Nigerians could afford an American education for their children and relatives. Consequently, many young Nigerians traveled to the United States to pursue a much-desired postsecondary education. Their numbers were significant enough to merit Nigeria a place among the top six countries of the world that sent postsecondary students to United States in the 1970s and 1980s (Sarkodie-Mensah, 2000).

1980–Present Day: Brain Drain and New Immigration Policy

This is the period that has experienced the highest number of Igbo-Nigerians' immigration to cities in the United States (Reynolds, 2002) due to the multiple motivations for immigration that characterize this era. These factors include economic and political problems, the brain drain, the quest for better higher education, the US immigration policies of the 1986 Immigration Reform and Control Act (IRCA), and the 1990 Diversity Visa Lottery Program (DV Lottery Program).

After almost five decades of independence, most African countries are still afflicted by grinding poverty, endemic corruption, high rates of unemployment, the collapse of political institutions, and war and destruction (Takougang, 2003). For most Africans, especially professionals, optimism and the hopes of independence, such as self-governance, freedom, economic prosperity, and improvement in social and economic life, have been dashed. The seriousness of these social, economic, and political problems of the 1980s led to brain drain, not only for Nigerians but for the African continent on the whole (Akyeampong, 2000; Sarkodie-Mensah, 2000; Reynolds, 2002; 2004; Ogbaa, 2003; Takougang, 2003). The phenomenon led to the massive exodus of professionals and highly skilled workers from the African continent to Europe, the United States, Canada, and Australia, seeking a calmer political climate and better working conditions (Reynolds, 2004). Most of these professionals who studied in Europe and America found themselves returning to their former host countries in search of greener pastures. Akyeampong (2000) suggests that it is difficult for an impoverished economy, such as that of Nigeria, to provide job opportunities for its labor force, whether skilled or unskilled. Furthermore, the slumping economy in Europe that necessitated tighter immigration policies in countries like Britain and France, which were traditional destinations for African immigrants, made the United States an even more attractive option to Africans, who were eager to emigrate (Takougang, 2003).

Apart from political corruption, military rule during this period contributed equally to the brain drain. Autocratic military rule, corruption, and the abuse of fundamental human rights drove many Nigerians to seek refuge outside the country (Ogbaa, 2003, p. 10).

The 1986 Immigration Act made it easier for undocumented immigrants or those whose immigration papers had expired to regularize their papers or obtain a permanent residence status (Takougang, 2003).

Above all, the US Immigration Act of 1990, otherwise known as the Diversity Visa Lottery Program, provided increased opportunity for Igbo-Nigerians to immigrate to the United States. "The act makes available fifty thousand permanent resident visas annually to persons from countries with low rates of immigration to the United States" (USDS-Bureau of Consular Affairs, 2006). The Diversity Visa Lottery Program opened the door to many Nigerians, both professionals and nonprofessionals, to immigrate to the United States. This program accounts for the substantial number of Nigerians living in the United States today. For example, the 2007 Diversity Visa Lottery Program result indicates that Nigerians won 9,849 (about 20 percent) visas of the fifty thousand available to all qualified countries (MyUSGreenCard, 2007).

Although there are various reasons why Nigerians emigrate to the United States, a quest for education is primary. Over the years, socioeconomic and political reasons have become part of the motivations for immigration. The US Immigration Act of 1990—the Diversity Visa Lottery Program—is an immigration opportunity many Nigerians have utilized. Now I will focus on Igbo-Nigerians in Chicago.

Nigerians in Chicago: Demography and Patterns of Residence

About one-third of black African immigrants in the United States came from Nigeria (Djamba, 1999, p. 211). Chicago, along with other cities like New York, Houston, Los Angeles, Dallas, Atlanta, Baltimore, and Washington DC, are among the priority destinations for Nigerian and Igbo immigrants (Djamba, 1999, Takougang, 2003). More than one million Nigerians are presently living in the United States (Ochu, 2009). With an estimated thirty thousand in Chicago, Nigerians constitute the largest African community in Chicago (Cogan and Ibe, 2005). While the Igbo and Yoruba groups form the majority of Nigerians in Chicago, other ethnic groups, such as Efik, Hausa, Fulani, Ijaw, Ibibio, Igala, Tiv, and Edo, also live in Chicago. Nigerians own and patronize several African stores both on the north and south sides of the city. The fact that these stores do relatively good business is a sign of a large Nigerian presence in Chicago (Cogan and Ibe, 2005). These stores carry popular Nigerian foods, such as dried fish, bitter leaf, *egwusi* (melon seed), plantain, palm oil, yam, cocoyam, and other familiar products. They are more than a place to shop; they also "provide a place for new arrivals to make acquaintances" (Cogan and Ibe, 2005).

Nigerians living in Chicago belong to various associations and organizations, based on their ethnic groups, states, or towns of origin. Members have more allegiance to these organizations than other more broadly focused Nigerian organizations for the most part. In fact, it is hard to find a functional Pan-Nigerian organization in Chicago. This is not surprising because Nigeria is a country where ethnicity is much more important than nationality. Even in the diaspora, one's ethnic or tribal identification is very apparent in the interactions of Nigerians.

That notwithstanding, most Nigerians, including the Ndigbo, reside mainly in the north side and far south side of Chicago (Cogan and Ibe, 2005). In addition, those of similar ethnic groups tend to reside in close proximity to each other. There are, however, some Ndigbo, mainly professionals, who have recently moved into the middle class and the affluent suburbs of Chicago (Reynolds, 2004).

The Igbo Community in Chicago

Here I will briefly describe the Igbo community in Chicago—their demography, residential pattern, cultural orientation toward education, and, finally, challenges they face as immigrants.

Igbo Families in Chicago: Demography and Residence Pattern

One of the difficulties in determining the number of Ndigbo in Chicago is that the US Census and the Immigration and Naturalization Services (INS) figures consider only race and nationality, rather than ethnicity, like the Igbo ethnic group (Reynolds, 2004, p. 183). That notwithstanding, Reynolds (2004) estimates that there are about five thousand Ndigbo living in Chicago and the suburbs, with many residing on the north side and the south suburbs of South Holland and Calumet City. Reynolds (2004) bases her figure on a "personal count of Igbo network members in three large immigrant associations in Chicago taken between 1997 and 2001" (p.183). Today, almost ten years later, this would be a conservative estimate of the Igbo in Chicago. In addition, one has to take into account the American-born children of Igbo heritage during these years.

Town Unions and State Organizations

Takougang (2003) points out that as the population of African immigrants increase and the people begin to adapt to their new environment, they are no longer interested in simply making money. They are also concerned with building stronger communities, which may also include the formation of ethnic-based organizations, such as town unions and organizations similar to what they had experienced in Nigeria prior to emigration. These town unions, apart from being platforms for meetings and interactions, also become support and welfare organizations (Reynolds, 2002). Another aspect of these organizations and unions, according to Akyeampong (2000), is to maintain cultural, economic, social, and political ties with the homeland. For example, most Igbo prefer to be buried in their homeland. It is one of the responsibilities of these organizations to arrange for the transport of the body of a deceased member home for the funeral and burial. Most Igbo in Chicago belong to their homeland town or state organization or both. There are several of these, such as the *Enumbra* Foundation, *Anambra* State Association, Chicago-USA (ASA-USA-Chicago), *Enyimba* Association, *Okigwe* Association, *Ngwa* National Association of Chicago, *Anambra* Women United, and the *Mbaise* Cultural Association. These state or town unions, each with an independent constitution and leadership, form a federation of the Igbo community in

Chicago, which serves as the platform for common Igbo feasts or events, such as the annual Igbo fest or *Iri-ji Ndigbo*, the annual New Yam festival.

A recent development in the Chicago Igbo community is the Igbo language and cultural school. The school has two campuses, located on the northwest and south sides of the city. Its main objective is to teach the ancestral language and culture to the American-born Igbo children. Both campuses of the school are staffed by volunteers and are in session throughout the school year except during the summer, when they organize soccer clinics for children.

Religious Affiliation

Ndigbo in Chicago, like those at home, are predominantly Christian, with Catholic or mainline Protestant churches in the majority (Reynolds, 2002). A few Ndigbo belong to Pentecostal Christian communities. Igbo Catholics in Chicago, for example, though registered with the parish in their neighborhood, usually gather one Sunday a month in a designated Catholic parish to celebrate mass in the Igbo language. There is also an occasional Christian interdenominational service for Ndigbo.

Profession and Occupation

Ndigbo in Chicago are engaged in diverse professional occupations, such as research scientists, physicians, computer and civil engineers, teachers, pharmacists, nurses, college professors, accountants, bankers, lawyers, and entrepreneurs (Reynolds, 2002, p. 276). This does not mean that there aren't any poor and unskilled Igbo in Chicago (Reynolds, 2002). Some of the recent immigrants, especially the beneficiaries of the Diversity Visa Lottery Program, find it difficult to make ends meet and cannot find jobs with the skills they acquired at home. As a result, most go back to school for retraining or they begin new careers.

Education and Ndigbo in Chicago: Cultural Orientation toward Education

Education is a life experience that starts at home, is formalized at school, and continues during the individual's experience in the larger society (Ohuche, 1991). Schooling is a key component of the educational process (Dodd and Konzal, 2002), although informal activities at home and in the community are also evident. Even with the incorporation of schooling into the Igbo educational process, the purpose of education remains basically the same. For Ndigbo, education in the past stressed work orientation, political participation, social responsibility, and spiritual/moral values, serving as a channel for preparing children for adult life as well as inducting them into society (Ohuche, 1991, p. 4). As a community, the Igbo are aware that education is crucial and imperative for the success of an individual and society and gives a nation a seat at the table of world affairs. This explains the centrality of education among Ndigbo in raising children (Ohuche, 1991).

Back in their homeland, Nigeria, the strategy of Christian missionary evangelization through formal education paid off. Ndigbo have the highest literacy rate in Nigeria today (Ketefe, 2006). "The Igbo spirit of enterprise and competition, their remarkable attraction to novelty, and their desire for social mobility" (Ebelebe, 2007, p. 161) were instrumental in their welcoming of Western/formal education with open arms. However, the speed with which Ndigbo embraced schooling does not obviate their caution in embracing novelties.

Ndigbo's desire for education is passed on from one generation to the next. Even in the diaspora, the love of education is manifested by their ubiquitous presence in educational institutions not only in Nigeria but all over the world. The Igbo "primary immigrants" (Reynolds, 2004, p.165) in Chicago today are parents and grandparents. As dutiful seniors, they especially have the inclination to pass on to their children and grandchildren the value of education and its necessity for success in society and to become a responsible citizen. Reynolds (2004) is amazed at the educational background of Igbo immigrants in Chicago, noting that the majority of Ndigbo she encountered in the Organization of Ndigbo (ONI) have either completed postsecondary education or are in the process of doing so (p.163). Her amazement has to do with the preconceived notion that immigrants from a poorer and less developed area of the world are less likely to be educated and possess fewer skills (Fukuyama, 1993; Reynolds, 2004). In spite of her amazement, which suggests a deficit attitude, she argues that the Igbo immigrants of Chicago form part of the migratory Nigerian middle class—the brain-drain group, the educated professionals who leave their countries of origin in sufficient numbers to harm the economy and change the social life of the homeland (Reynolds, 2002, p. 274). Nevertheless, some Igbo have come to learn that qualifications alone do not guarantee employment in one's area of specialization. Hence, some Igbo in Chicago work as cab drivers, parking-lot attendants, or nursing assistants while upgrading their skills and qualifications, or retraining in various fields (Takougang, 2003). Another reason why some of these professionals opt for jobs outside their field of training has to do with pressure to support family both here and at home. Searching for a job can take a long time and, thus, becomes very challenging, as they need to eat and take care of their family in the meantime.

Igbo Children in Chicago: Schools, Careers, and Professions

This section will seek to answer two questions: what kind of schools do Igbo children attend and to what professions and occupations do they aspire?

Igbo children attend a variety of schools. Reynolds (2002) finds it interesting that most Igbo families would prefer to send their children to Catholic parochial schools or faith-based private schools. Rong and Preissle (2009) confirm Reynolds' findings, stating that there is a high probability of Nigerian immigrant children being enrolled in faith-based private schools (p. 191). Reynolds (2004) notes that 10 percent of the National Merit Scholars list from St. Ignatius College Prep High School in Chicago are Igbo children (p. 277). Another reason why these parents prefer faith-based private schools, according to Ogbaa (2003), is that some who were born before the Nigerian civil war attended one mission school or another (p.144). Because of their good educational experience, they endeavor to make the same opportunity possible for their children.

Like some American families who move to the suburbs so their children can attend better schools, Igbo families in the suburbs like to send their kids to good and strong public schools (Reynolds, 2002, p. 277). The standard of education and security in these suburban schools satisfies most of the Igbo families who choose this route. There are, however, a few Igbo families who, despite the high property taxes they pay that fund public schools and the high standard of education in these suburban schools, still prefer to send their children to private Christian faith-based schools.

Ekpere nne na nna o bula bu ka nwa ha karia ha. "The prayers of every parent—mother and father—are that their children will be greater or better than them." It is the dream and wish of every Igbo parent that their children will accomplish more in life than themselves. This is not just a prayer but also a philosophy that guides Igbo parents as they raise and educate their children. Today, education among Ndigbo, including those in the diaspora, has become an expression of that philosophy. In addition, children among the Igbo are a kind of life insurance and retirement savings. Ndigbo believe that children will always take care of their parents in their retirement and old age. Thus, the desire to have a happy and fulfilling retirement helps to explain why Igbo parents invest a lot in their children.

Many Igbo parents encourage their children to go into medical, legal, pharmaceutical, or engineering professions (Ogbaa, 2003). These professions are traditionally associated with prestige and fame. Most parents also believe that such professions would guarantee job security for their children.

Education is central in raising their children (Ohuche, 1991). It has priority in their lives in Chicago. But what kind of challenges do they face as immigrants and also as they raise their children?

Challenges Ndigbo in Chicago Face as Immigrants

Regardless of the motivation and destination, immigration poses a distinct challenge to the immigrant. Immigration requires adaptation to a new and unfamiliar environment that is socially, politically, and culturally different. It has a tendency to generate a high level of uncertainty (Sharlin and Moin, 2001, p. 405). Ndigbo, like other Nigerian immigrants, come with some cultural, family, and ethnic values that sometimes clash with aspects of the American way of life (Ogbaa, 2003, p. 39). Therefore, the challenges in these areas result from the fact that for most Ndigbo, Chicago is new and a different environment. However, understanding the details of the impact of the new and different environment on parental involvement in the education of their children is one of the main points of this research.

Igbo immigrants in Chicago face varying challenging responsibilities, such as supporting family members at home (Nigeria), meeting certain expectations from home, adapting to their new environment, and dealing with racism.

Supporting Family Members at Home

Most Igbo immigrants in Chicago support members of their families in Nigeria partially or wholly through financial remittances.[7] Some even become the financial backbone of the family at home (Reynolds, 2004, p.174). Apart from this support, they are often in communication with their family and friends in Nigeria, thanks to the improvement, though still marginal, of the Nigerian telephone system. The cultural obligation to support families and other relations back home and communicate with them regularly adds extra pressure on Igbo immigrants in Chicago. The result is that some individuals have two jobs, or they work extra hours to meet their financial obligations in Chicago as well as at home. In addition to supporting the extended family, some may also have to care for children left by deceased siblings. For this

---

7   World Bank 2009 record indicates that in 2008 Nigerians in diaspora remitted a total of 10 billion dollars, making her among the top ten recipients of migrant remittances among developing countries (Ratha, Mohapatra and Silwal, July 2009).

reason, some travel to Nigeria once or twice a year, which further creates a financial burden.

Family ties are very strong among Ndigbo no matter how great the geographical distance (Ogbaa, 2003). Because of the attachment of a husband to his nuclear and extended family at home and perhaps in the diaspora, there is sometimes a tense relationship between an Igbo husband and his American wife or between an Igbo wife and her American husband. For all Igbo couples, there is often the problem of whose extended family should be prioritized, the husband's or wife's.

Perception of African and Nigerian Immigrants

African immigrants experience discrimination as do their African-American brothers and sisters (Takougang, 2003). In addition, the Igbo belong to what Ogbaa (2003) refers to as "double minority—black and foreign-born" (p. 73), those who come from the so-called "dark continent" (p.106), which is perceived only as war torn, disease ridden, and poverty stricken. This psychological burden constitutes another challenge to Ndigbo and other African immigrants in the United States. For example, Sarkodie-Mensah (2000) says that the mention of Nigeria to an average American conjures up images of jungles, disease, war, poverty, and children living in squalor. Though the American media is partly to be blamed (Sarkodie-Mensah, 2000), Igbo immigrants in Chicago have to deal with being perceived as lazy, criminal, dishonest, or even violent people. Should an Igbo have "all the right American values of hard work and education and have embraced assimilation into the mainstream American culture" (Takougang, 2003, p.5), he/she will still be perceived negatively or as an object of philanthropic works of charity. Besides, immigrants, especially those from poorer and underdeveloped countries, are often seen as bearers of foreign, less desirable cultural values (Fukuyama, 1993). They are also the first to be blamed whenever things begin to go wrong in their host country. Most Igbo, faced with the burden of countering this and other unsupported perceptions and labels, have to work extraordinarily hard to excel in school and at work, with the hope that their children and grandchildren will have a better experience. In addition, the accent with which most Igbo people speak English adds to this already negative perception.

Expectations of Immigrants

The reality is that immigrants arrive in their host country with certain expectations, whether they be right or wrong, positive or negative. Igbo immigrants in Chicago, especially the new arrivals, generally face the challenge of dealing with misconceived notions about the United States, especially regarding personal wealth. Relatives back home also have their own expectations, which unfortunately prompt unhealthy expectations on the part of immigrants, who are expected to send money back to Nigeria regularly; otherwise, they would be regarded as a failure (Ogbaa, 2003). According to Akyeampong (2000), it does not take long for a new arrival to realize that American streets are not paved with gold nor do dollars grow on trees. Soon after arrival, the reality begins to dawn on immigrants that they have to work very hard to earn a living in the United States, even though it is a very rich country. The slogan "there is no such thing as a free lunch in America" becomes very real. This is, then, the challenge of changing unrealistic expectations and fashioning more realistic aspirations in order to meet them. The willingness to learn from the experiences of those Igbo people, who are already longtime residents and citizens, can ease the various difficulties the new arrivals may face. It also depends on the willingness of those who have been here for a long time to share their experiences and provide guidance to the new arrivals.

Traditional Family Structure and Values

As is the case with other Nigerian ethnic groups, the traditional Igbo family organization is the extended family (Oke, 1986; Ohuche, 1991). It is a challenge for most Igbo families to continue to maintain the extended family structure (where extended family members might be in Nigeria) in an environment that strongly emphasizes the nuclear family structure and individualism. Despite the difficulties Igbo families experience in adhering to the extended family structure in their new environment, the mutual support and conviviality extended to families partially explain why they have not been totally abandoned.

On the socioeconomic level, families have to cope with the fact that they can hardly survive on one income, typically that of the husband, the traditional breadwinner. Both spouses are compelled to work to make ends meet. In some cases, the wife, the traditional homemaker, actually works more hours than the husband does. This translates into more income from her, which is psychologically difficult for some Igbo husbands to accept. The patriarchal nature of Igbo society makes it difficult for some Igbo husbands, who find themselves in this situation. But the husband has no choice because that is one of the realities of this new environment. The effect of this is that the social structures of Igbo families are changing. It is not uncommon nowadays for an Igbo husband and wife to share work traditionally reserved for women, such as looking after the children, preparing their breakfast, or carrying and feeding infants during public gatherings.

American-Born Igbo Children

Igbo tradition requires children to be obedient to their parents and other adults; they are to be respectful when communicating with elders and should never contradict them (Sarkodie-Mensah, 2000). But American-born Igbo children grow up in an environment with different social norms from those of their parents and grandparents. They know the value of dialogue and like to express their opinions. They also know their rights and the limitations of their parents' relationship with them. Thus American-born Igbo children, more like native-born American children, are usually not afraid to engage their parents or elders in a dialogue or an argument. It is a challenge to parents, if not embarrassing, considering how they themselves were brought up. Therefore, some Igbo parents, especially the new arrivals, have to face the challenge of how to deal with children being more assertive and not traditionally subservient.

Finally, in the midst of all these challenges, the ability to speak and understand English gives Igbo immigrants some leverage as they navigate through the maze of life in their new environment. Nigeria adopted English as its national language after its independence from Britain in 1960. Hence, English is taught right from primary schools as a second language. English as the official language of Nigeria makes it possible for more than 250 different ethnic groups in Nigeria to communicate among themselves (Ogbaa, 2003), and it enables easier integration into the broader English-speaking world.

Conclusion

What I have presented here is a description of some of the contextual influences experienced by Igbo families beginning a new life in Chicago. According to Ogbaa (2003), this context acts as a wellspring from which they draw strength to survive and make their unique contribution to American life (p. 18). As this study seeks to understand how these Igbo families in Chicago are involved in the education of their children, I will, in the next chapter, present and examine the theoretical framework of the study.

CHAPTER 3

The Dynamics of Parental Involvement

In this chapter, I will first present, explain, and analyze both Epstein's theory of overlapping spheres of influence and Bronfenbrenner's ecological systems theory (EST), which form the theoretical framework of this study. Though these theories are presented separately here, I use them together as a unit. The application of both theories, therefore, as a dyad will become more evident in the course of this review (and study).

In the second section, under the title "Parental Involvement: Theory and Practice," I will discuss the theoretical framework—the two theories— in relation to the perceptions and practices of parental involvement while highlighting the importance of context. The third part of this chapter discusses communication as a very essential element in the practice of parental involvement. Parental involvement essentially is a form of relationship between the family and school in the education of children, and therefore, the need for mutual communication is central. The fourth section will discuss challenges that school communities[8] sometimes face in the practice of parental involvement.

Theoretical Framework of Parental Involvement

The purpose of this section is to present and analyze the two theoretical frameworks that are essential in understanding the concept of parental involvement used in this study. The two theories are Joyce Epstein's (2001) theory of overlapping spheres of influence and Urie Bronfenbrenner's (1977, 1979, 1986, and 1989) ecological systems theory (EST).

At this juncture, it is important to understand why a link was made between the two theories and the reason for applying the two theories as a unit.

---

8   A school community, as used here, refers to the agents involved in the education of children—family/parents, school/educators, and community.

While Epstein's theory posits that parents, family, community, and school exert overlapping influences on the education of children, Bronfenbrenner's EST asserts that the development and life activities of individuals do not occur in a vacuum. Rather, they occur in a context, and that context influences the way the individuals live and function. Therefore, the link between the two theories is that the overlapping spheres of influence of parents, family, school, and community on the education of children occur in specific contexts. Similarly, the specific contexts in which parents, families, community, and school function shape the nature of the overlapping influences they exercise on the education of children in the community.

Used together as a tool, the two theories help to understand the dynamics of the relationship between family, school, and community as they influence the education of children. The theories together offer a fuller explanation as to why diversity in contemporary perception and practice of parental involvement shouldn't be a mystery. However, to understand these concepts better, I will examine the two theories separately.

The Theory of the Overlapping Spheres of Influence: Understanding Parental Involvement

The education of children takes place in the following environments: home (family), school, and community (Epstein, 2001). Because the lives of children take place in all these three settings, Epstein (2001) argues that these institutions or agents should optimally work together for the integral development and education of children.

The theory of overlapping spheres of influence posits that none of the environments can adequately educate children alone. School and family cannot afford to work separately if both are to achieve the objective of raising responsible citizens, who will contribute meaningfully toward a better society. Epstein (2001) further argues that for any school-aged child, there is no "pure" time out of school or home since time spent in either affects what happens in the other (p. 33). Fullan (2001) lends credence to the above argument by asserting that in the postmodern society, you can no longer accomplish educational goals unless forces are combined, because education has become too complex for any one group (like teachers) to undertake (p. 197). To Fullan (2001), "forces" refers to parents and other community members, who are not only crucial but also are largely untapped resources necessary to the task of educating children (p.199). Since none of the agents can adequately do the job alone, both school and family must become allies in the education of children.

Thus, the imbrications of the sway of these environments on the education of the child are what Epstein (2001) describes as the overlapping spheres of influence. It is essential to mention that the theory did not say precisely that there are only two or three environments for the education of children. Rather, it focuses on home and school as "the two major environments that simultaneously affect children's learning and development" (Epstein, 2001, p. 31). Swap (1993) refers to these prominent agents as the principal stakeholders in children's education (p. 28).

From this theoretical perspective, parental involvement means the various instructional and non-instructional activities through which parents show commitment and exercise influence over the education of their children. It involves the exercise of influence in spheres that include social, cognitive, psychological, moral, physical, and spiritual development and education of children. So far, this section has provided an insight into the nature of the influences on the children's education by parents, family, school, and community.

What follows is a brief description of how the theory of overlapping spheres of influence works.

The Mechanics of the Overlapping Spheres of Influence

This section will attempt to answer a simple but important question: what are the underlying forces in the workings of the theory of the overlapping influence?

Epstein (2001) describes the theory by distinguishing the external and internal structures of the model. Here, "external structure" refers to the forces that influence the interactions of the social institutions that come from outside the agents, such as school, family, and community. They are internal when the forces that impinge on the agents are from within.

External structure: As shown in figure 4, the model of overlapping spheres of influence consists of three overlapping and nonoverlapping circles representing the family, school, and community in the education of children (p. 27). The degree of overlap is under the control of four forces, namely (a) time, (b) experiences in families, (c) experiences in schools, and (d) experiences in community, which she designates as forces A, B, C, and D respectively. Force A, which is depicted as a horizontal arrow in figure 4, represents the "developmental time and history line for students, families, schools, and communities" or simply an "individual and historical time" (p. 27). Force A for a child, for example, will include his/her chronological age, grade level at school, and the sociopolitical conditions of the period in which the child is at school. Forces B and C represent experiences, philosophies, practices of family (B) and school (C) respectively. Force D represents the experience, philosophy, and practices of the community. All these forces determine the degree of the overlap of the spheres of influence in a school community and consequently help to set the boundaries of influence or the overlapping and nonoverlapping spheres of the agents. What can be seen here is that the practices and philosophies of parents and teachers and the pressure they put on each other while exercising influence on the education of children all determine the degree of overlap.

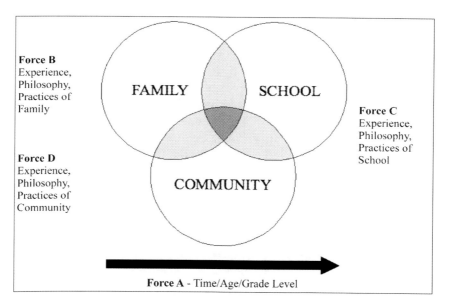

Figure 4. Overlapping Spheres of Influence of Family, School, and Community on Children's Learning (External Structure of Theoretical Model).

Source: Epstein, J.L. (2001). *School, Family and Community Partnerships*. Boulder, CO: Westview Press, (p. 28).

To illustrate how the model works, Epstein (2001) compares the education of a handicapped child with that of a "normal"—without physical, mental, or emotional challenges—third-grade child. She explains that the degree of overlap of the spheres of influence in the case of a handicapped child's education will differ based on forces A, B, C, and even D. She argues that a handicapped child is likely to experience more overlap because "parents [home] and special teachers [school] may begin a highly organized cooperative program to benefit the child" (p.29). In other words, there are a lot more issues that are likely to bring the two social institutions together for the benefit of the handicapped child than the normal child. As well, school and home may be compelled to tailor their interactions according to the needs of the handicapped child's education.

In the same breath, a high level of overlap of home and school influences in preschool and early elementary children would be expected. In such circumstance, the point of intersection (figure 4) of family and school will be equally large. But there can be occasions of great overlap in all grades due to forces B and C—varying philosophies, policies, practices, and pressures of family and school (p. 29).

The "internal structure" (figure 5) is a term that describes the dynamics of interpersonal relationships within both the family and school (intra-institutional interaction) and between the family and school (inter-institutional interactions). These interactions, which revolve around the child, include various types of communication between the family and school and within each of these social institutions. Epstein (2001) uses lowercase and capital letters to differentiate the types of interactions—intra-institutional and inter-institutional interactions. For example, intra-institutional interactions—family (f) and school (s) and parent (p) and teacher (t)—are those that occur separately as parents, children, members of the extended family, or other relatives conduct their family life and personal relationships. Similarly teachers, principal, and other school staff create school policies or conduct school or individual activities without reference to other agents of children's education (p. 30).

On the other hand, inter-institutional interactions—Family (F) and School (S) and Parent (P) and Teacher (T)—are those that occur as members of the two institutions interact for the education of children. The Child (C) or (c) in this model has a central place in the interaction and influence, which is always part of intra-institutional and inter-institutional interactions.

The external and internal structures do not work in isolation from each other. Rather, they are intimately related. A hypothetical example of the dynamics of overlapping spheres of influence vis-à-vis external and internal structures would be a parent transferred to another state by her company. Before moving to the new location, the parent is compelled to commute weekly to her new assignment. The external factor would be the new assignment while the internal factor is the limited interaction she has regarding the child's education. Nevertheless, Epstein (2001) does not hesitate to point out that there is never a complete overlap because both families and schools maintain some functions and practices that are independent of each other (p. 29)[9]. For example, the choice of a family to have more children is independent of the school.

---

9   Notice that the nonoverlapping sections of figures 4 and 5 are much more prominent than the overlapping portions.

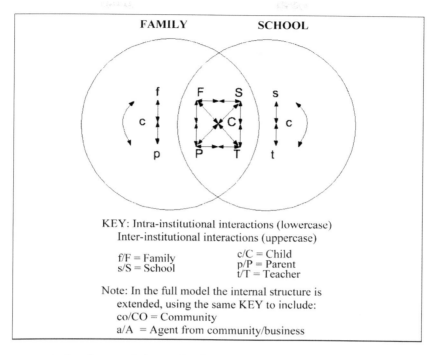

KEY: Intra-institutional interactions (lowercase)
Inter-institutional interactions (uppercase)

f/F = Family
s/S = School

c/C = Child
p/P = Parent
t/T = Teacher

Note: In the full model the internal structure is
extended, using the same KEY to include:
co/CO = Community
a/A = Agent from community/business

Figure 5. Overlapping Spheres of Influence of Family, School, and Community
on Children's Learning (Internal Structure of Theoretical Model).

Source: Epstein, J.L. (2001). *School, Family and Community
Partnerships.* Boulder, CO: Westview Press, (p. 28).

In summary, the theory of overlapping spheres of influence explains that family, school, and community not only work together to accomplish a common educational mission for the benefit of children and society but that the influence of their work also overlaps. But in the theory of overlapping spheres of influence, Epstein did not fail to establish a link between perception and practice. Attitude and beliefs are essential for any successful educational practice (Constantino, 2003).

Link Between Perception and Practice in Overlapping Spheres of Influence

The purpose of this section is to understand the link between the "perception" and "practice" of parental involvement in the education of children as seen through the theory of overlapping spheres of influence.

Epstein (2001) further suggests that the attitudes of professional educators toward the children in their care influence how they relate to the students and families. Educators and parents can perceive pupils primarily as either students or children; such perception has important consequences for the practice of parental involvement in a school community (Epstein, 2001). When children in school are viewed simply as students, there is a tendency to separate the family from the school, thus making the child's education isolated and, in effect, incomplete. But when they are viewed as children, both parents and teachers can see the opportunity to share the responsibilities.

Epstein (2001) paints hypothetical scenarios that reflect the perceptions of educators and families about children either as students or as children. Educators that approach children as students will likely make a statement like, "If the family would just do its job, we could do our job." And families will say something like, "I raised this child, now it is your job to educate her" (p. 405). With such mind-sets, the spheres of influence and the practice of parental involvement can hardly overlap.

On the other hand, treating youngsters as children will reinforce the idea in educators that families and schools should work together for the education and development of children. Educators having such a perspective may reflect the following example: "I cannot do my job without the help of my students' families and the support of community." Family members may well present something of this statement: "I really need to know what is happening in the school in order to help my child" (p. 405).

School-Like Families and Family-Like Schools

Epstein (2001) coined the two terms "school-like families" and "family-like schools" to further demonstrate the relationship between perception and practice in the overlapping spheres of influence in the education of children.

Parents who run their families like schools are characterized as school-like families. Due to their perceptions, they create school-like environments with academic schedules for studies, homework, and activities that foster learning. Children are rewarded based on individual efforts in these kinds of environment. In such families, parents more often treat any child as a student (p. 405) in need of opportunities to learn.

In family-like schools, individual attention is key in the family dynamics. This pattern recognizes each child's individuality and makes him/her feel special and included (p. 405).

Therefore, it is safe to say that overlapping spheres of influence can be effective when both parents and educators perceive students primarily as children, who are in search of learning. The opposite situation would likely present a conflict to the child, as there is "no pure time" for the child in either home or school. These are the choices before the family and school. Whichever choice is made goes a long way in influencing the nature of the relationship between families and schools with regard to the children's education. Ultimately, perceiving the "kids" as children will maximize the influence both parents and school bring to children's education. Such a choice, when made, requires some fundamental shifts in the attitude of both educators and parents in order to achieve purposeful parental involvement.

In summary, the theory of overlapping spheres of influence explains why family, school, and community should work together to accomplish a common educational mission for the children and society. Despite the theory's insights of parental involvement and how it elucidates the issues of perception and practice, there are certain aspects of the theory that raise further questions. Before the next section, which deals with the strengths and weaknesses of the theory, I offer a brief reflection on perception and parental involvement.

Perception and Parental Involvement

Attitudes and beliefs, according to Constantino (2003), are essential building blocks in a relationship between parents and schools (p. 11). "Perception" here means the parents' belief, attitude, and understanding regarding parental involvement. It all starts in the mind. Practice flows from perception. For example, Lopez (1999) notes that some teachers see parents as "partners" only when they subscribe to a predetermined "school agenda," regardless of parents' involvement outside the "school agenda" that promotes children's education (p. 220). Such teachers' view is narrow and consequently measure parental involvement based only on the "set of prescriptive practices" (p.214) of the school. However, parents in the study (Lopez, 1999) have a broader view of parental involvement and acted accordingly. They perceived "involvement as teaching children the value of education through the medium of hard work" (p. 219). There is another link between perception and practice of parental involvement. Dauber and Epstein (1994) noted that the attitude of most parents in their study, who believe their children attend a good school and that their teachers care about their children, directly affects the manner they work with the teachers in the education of their children (p. 56). On the other hand, Epstein (2001) suggests that the attitudes held by professional educators toward the children in their care have a significant influence on how they relate to students and families.

Critique of Epstein's Theory of Overlapping Spheres of Influence

This section, which offers a critique of the theory of overlapping spheres of influence, will examine the strengths and weaknesses of the theory. The goal of the critique is to understand the theory, better highlighting its power to shed light on the phenomenon of parental involvement in the education of children.

Strengths of the Theory

The strengths of the theory will be examined under three themes: inclination, the common mission of duty to children and society, and education as a lifelong process.

Inclination

One of the basic assumptions of the theory is that the education of children takes place in the following environments: home, school, and community (Epstein, 2001). This permits the home, school, and community to play complementary roles in the education of children. Lightfoot (1978) suggests that the family's role is critical in both the child's development and successful schooling. Furthermore, even in modern society, the home continues to be an important milieu for educating children (Barbour and Barbour, 1997). Epstein (2001), Lightfoot (1978), and Barbour and Barbour (1997) suggest that because children live their lives in all three environments, it is reasonable to assume that they can work together for the education and development of the children.

In effect, the theory explains and reinforces how family, school, and community work together in the schooling and, ultimately, the education of children. For example, for a family in rural Borana, Ethiopia, family or community involvement in the education of children, according to the theory, should not be viewed as a foreign imposition or phenomenon, but rather, an intrinsic role and duty that parents, family, and community owe to their children and society. After all, "parents everywhere love and care for their children, and they want to be involved in all aspects of their children's development, including education" (Epstein and Sanders, 1998, p. 392). Besides, as Bronfenbrenner (1979) noted, it is hard to find a parent of any socioeconomic status, ethnic group, or type of family who is not deeply committed to ensuring the well-being and development of children (p. 849).

To sum up, a family's interest in and influence on the education of its children is as natural as the inclination to be actively involved in their education. Nevertheless, the impetus for this kind of collaboration can be a weakness of the theory, to be discussed further in the section on the weakness of the theory.

Common Mission

The theory of overlapping spheres of influence presumes that family, school, and community share a common mission in the education of children. Having a common mission implies sharing mutual responsibilities and participation in their children's learning and development. Because of these shared goals and responsibilities, all parties should become allies in a common educational mission, the integral and quality education of the children.

The theory of overlapping spheres of influence further implies that none of the institutions alone can adequately educate children. Family and school cannot afford to work separately if they are to achieve the objective of raising responsible, self-supporting citizens, who can contribute meaningfully toward a better society and world. The theory considers the resources of family and community to be indispensable in the education of children, not optional or a footnote to the process (Swap, 1993). It is also in the light of pursuing the same goal for the benefit of the child and society, that Obidi (2005) regards school as "an extension of the family—*in loco parentis*—in the place of a parent" (p. 234). This explains the theory's emphases on coordination, cooperation, and mutual interaction of families, schools, and community. This notion of common mission and shared responsibility strengthen the belief that common messages, such as the importance of school, hard work, thinking creatively, and helping one another, that are equally reinforced by family, school, and community are more likely to positively impact children's education (Epstein, 2001, p. 404).

The education of children becomes a shared responsibility when common mission and collaboration are valued by participants; it is then that education becomes indeed "the responsibility of all" (UBEC, 2005a).

Education as a Continuous Process

An additional strength of the theory is that it rightly portrays education as a continuous process. The theory affirms the belief that education is a lifelong process that does not occur only in school. The family's educational influence on the child starts from birth and continues throughout schooling and beyond. Before a child begins formal education, the family already has completed a great deal of basic informal education in the areas of intellectual, social, and psychomotor development (Nwa-Chil, 1984; Ohuche, 1991). The alliance between school and family converge as the child begins schooling, and this alliance should continue throughout life (Nwa-Chil, 1984; Henderson, Marburger and Ooms, 1986: Ohuche, 1991).

The Spanish-born American philosopher, George Santayana, once asserted that "a child educated only at school is an uneducated child" (Hawaii State Department of Education (2007). Santayana implies that schooling alone cannot provide the holistic education needed by children to survive in society and contribute to its advancement. In addition, isolating schooling from the home has significant consequences for the behavior and the development of children (Bronfenbrenner, 1979, p. 848). In fact, total isolation of home and school is not possible because a child brings family influence to school just as issues from school are bound to manifest themselves in the child's behavior at home. Lightfoot (1978) maintains that "as children enter the classroom, their families also come with them" (p. 10). She further argues that there is both an invisible and pervasive presence of families in a child's classroom, which cannot be ignored.

To sum up, the theory of overlapping spheres of influence underscores the inherent inclination for parents and families to be involved in the education of their children. Furthermore, it explains why family, school, and community can work together to accomplish a common educational mission, a lifelong process, that benefits the children and society. Despite the illumination that the theory of overlapping spheres of influence brings to the understanding of the family-school relationship, there are certain weaknesses in the theory I could spot. These weaknesses raise some questions that call for further discussion.

Weaknesses

The potential of the theory of overlapping spheres of influence to generate conflict and disagreements among stakeholders in education over its applicability cannot be underestimated. What follows is a discussion of the tensions that might arise with the theory under the following themes: inclination, delineation of duties and power play, incongruent home and school values, meaning of educational success, and responding to the influence of an ally.

Inclination

The theory takes it for granted that the home and community naturally have roles to play in the education of the children. However, some educators and parents are not persuaded that families have something to contribute to the schooling, ultimately the education, of children. One educator, Sarni (Lightfoot, 1978, pp.107ff), typifies this opinion. According to Lightfoot,

Sarni is an outstanding elementary schoolteacher, who has an "uncomplicated and unambiguous" (p. 108) view about parental involvement, namely that "parents should not become involved in the educational process within the school; neither should they criticize [nor] undermine the efforts and values of the teacher" (p.108). "Parents [family] should be seen, [and] not heard" (p. 108). In addition, Sarni expects parents to relinquish control over their children, offering them to the teacher, whose judgment and wisdom they should trust and whose skills and competence they should greatly admire (p. 116). These are some of Sarni's beliefs about parental involvement, which counter the theory of overlapping spheres of influence. Unfortunately, there are other educators out there like Sarni for whom the theory is not plausible and therefore will not find it useful in their relationships with parents. On the side of parents, there are some who hold a "restaurant approach[10]" to their children's schooling and education.

Delineation of Duties and Power Play

Family, school, and community, which have a common mission, share the following functions in the education of children: socialization, cultural transmission, leadership training, health, knowledge acquisition, discipline, moral, and cognitive development (Fafunwa, 1967, 1991; Obidi, 2005; Ezeani, 2005). Sharing a common goal does not diminish the need for a division of labor among the agents.

Shared functions can also introduce tensions, particularly in situations where expectations of family and school are not clearly delineated, resulting in what I refer to as the "blame-game syndrome." Educators might accuse parents or family of not doing their part, not influencing enough or too much (Swap, 1993), while parents can level the same kind of accusation on the teachers or educators (Lightfoot, 1978, p.114). A blame game can also arise in a situation where the child is not performing at the expected level. Lack of communication can also cause the family and school to blame each other equally. Another reason that can set off finger wagging could be the inability of educators to investigate the forces that impinge on the child and family (Lightfoot, 1978).

The issue of discipline is another potential source of the blame game. Most principals and teachers want to hold the parents and family responsible if a child has discipline problems, meaning that parents and families are

---

10   "Restaurant Approach" is a term I learned from the principal of the school where I did my educational leadership internship. She uses it to describe parents who, rather than being involved in the education of their children and believing that they have paid for their children's schooling, expect the school and teachers to serve them the "menu of schooling and education."

perceived as failing in their duty regarding the education of the child at home, not the teacher.

The issue of power can be a weakness of the theory. Olivos (2006) questions how much influence the family or parents can have in a family-school relationship equation, bearing in mind the dominant influence of school in the education of children. He noted that in some circumstances, the influence of the school is so overwhelming that parental involvement ends up being solely school centered or prescribed activities in which parents and families often assume secondary roles to teacher.

Incongruent Home and School Values

Epstein's theory does not acknowledge that the values, which schools teach, are not always in agreement with those of the students' families or communities. Where such incongruence exits, tension is bound to mount over which values take precedence. The values that should be taught to children can become an object of contention between home and school.

Children, as they begin schooling, naturally acquire new knowledge and behaviors that may not only conflict with the cultural knowledge and values embedded in the habits of home (Weisner, 2005), but may also pose a source of confusion to the child. The case of Thandi (Coll, 2005, pp. 158-168) and her family illustrates this situation very well.

Thandi Hong is a fourth grader and the youngest daughter of Sak and Maryyna, Cambodian immigrants who live in a small northeastern American city. Sak and Maryyna came to the United States from Cambodia as refugees in the late 1970s during the Khmer Rouge regime. Both parents still maintain many aspects of their Cambodian culture, in spite of the many years they have lived in the United States. Thandi laments her inability to connect school and home experiences. "When you come home from school, everything changes. You have to be really quiet and really sensitive to things, be a good girl ..." (p. 160) Thandi was born in the United States, but her parents, especially her father, want her to be rooted in Cambodian culture. Apart from the bits and pieces of the Cambodian world she experiences at home, all she has known, lived, and experienced so far outside of her family's influence is the mainstream American culture. Thus, she is torn between the American influences and values she learns at school and the Cambodian cultural values her parents want to inculcate in her or even impose on her.

For Thandi there are two separate, if not opposing, environments for her education. These two prime environments, which can hardly be described as having overlapping influence on her education, lack communication. The situation certainly does not help her schooling and education, and that explains her frustration: "When you come back from school, everything changes." Thandi's family and school are at odds with respect to Thandi's education—a shared responsibility and duty of the home and school.

The Meaning of Educational Success

The theory of overlapping spheres of influence assumes that home, school, and community will have the same understanding of educational success or students' achievement. This is another weak side of the theory, as family, community, and school could possibly disagree on what constitutes educational success. Such disagreement is likely to affect the usefulness of the theory in understanding the family-school relationship in the education of children. What constitutes a successful education of the child, one may ask. The opinions of Laosa (2005) and Monke (2006) are insightful.

First off, both Laosa (2005) and Monke (2006) agree that educational success does not consist solely of skill acquisition and cognitive development (Laosa, 2005; Monke, 2006). There are other qualities and elements that make the education of children successful and complete. For Monke (2006), success in education includes qualities such as hope, stability, respect, compassion, a sense of belonging, moral judgment, community support, and parental care (p. 22), while for Laosa (2005), it includes social and emotional development (p.77).

In essence, the education of children includes both instructional and non-instructional activities, and neither of these is the sole preserve of family, school, or community. It is only when the pursuit of academic excellence is meshed in a purposeful manner with the social, emotional, and moral education of the child that one can begin to think of educational success.

Responding to the Influence of an Ally

Not all educators believe that families and community have overlapping spheres of influence in the education of children. Such belief is bound to influence their response to a family's involvement in the education of its children. How the family, school, or community, having these beliefs, each respond to the influences of the others in the educational process could be a potential source of disagreement. Henry (1996) believes that a school's response to home influence can be either negative or positive (p. 94). When negative, it might result in cultural discontinuity for children between home and school. When positive, it will bolster children's education (p. 94). In sum, Epstein's model only works if a school community welcomes and appreciates the importance of the three environments—family, school, and community—in which the education of children takes place and recognizes the need for their collaboration.

Conclusion

To conclude this critique of the theory of overlapping spheres of influence, I restate that the education of children takes place in the home, school, and community. These environments are not compartmentalized or isolated from one another because the child lives and grows within the influence of all three. When they work together and complement each other, they provide quality education for the children. Epstein (2001) explains that the roles of these environments should overlap and most often do. The overlapping influence, though desirable, can also create tensions among the several agents of child's education.

Parents, family, school, and community each have their own context. The ecological systems theory, which I will discuss in the next section, further explains the nature and constituents of these contexts or environments and the interactions that result in a child's development and learning.

Ecological Systems Theory: Parental Involvement and Context

Here I will present and discuss Bronfenbrenner's ecological systems theory. In the course of the discussion, it will become more apparent why the theory and the context it explains is essential to this study.

Understanding the Ecological Systems Theory

Bronfenbrenner's (1977, 1979, 1986, and 1989) ecological systems theory (EST) is about how context influences human development. A question posed by Bronfenbrenner that helps to clarify the import of the theory is, "what are the specific characteristics of the person and of the environment that are to be regarded as both the products and producers of development?" (Bronfenbrenner, 1989, p. 191) Bronfenbrenner answers the question through the EST he proposes.

EST posits that a person's individual world, the ecological system, is made up of several layers, otherwise known as subsystems (Weiss, Kreider, Lopez and Chatman, 2005, p. xiii) or sub-contexts. The constituents of these subsystems include social, economic, geographical, historical, cultural, and political elements (or institutions). In the case of the developing child, family and school are primary.

Layers of the Ecological Systems Theory

"Ecology" ordinarily means "the study of the relationships between living organisms and their interactions within their natural or developed environment" (Encarta World English Dictionary, 1998-2005). This definition does not differ much from its usage here. "Ecological system" here refers to the natural or developed environment of an individual.

The EST (figure 6), which is represented visually as a set of concentric circles surrounding the child (center of diagram), illustrates the complexity of these multiple levels of EST and helps to explain the mechanism through which children and their families are influenced (Weiss, et al., pp. xiii-xiv).

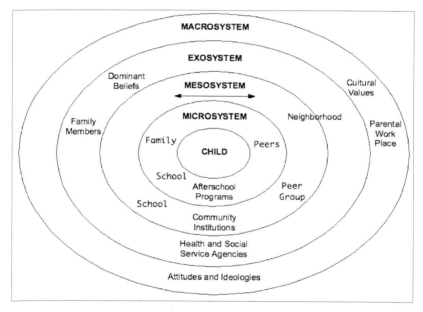

Figure 6. Ecological Systems Theory

Source: Weiss, H., B., Kreider, H., Lopez, M. E. and Chatman, C. M. (2005). Introduction: Preparing Educators in Family Involvement. In Weiss, H., B., Kreider, H., Lopez, M. E. and Chatman, C. M. (Eds.) *Preparing Educators to Involve Families: From Theory to Practice*. Thousand Oaks, CA: Sage Publications Inc., (p. xiv).

Starting from the innermost circle, Bronfenbrenner (1977, 1979, 1986, and 1989) delineates five layers of the environment that form a child's world in terms of development and education. The essence of the delineation is to distinguish the immediate from other layers and their corresponding interactions and consequences on the developing individual.

I will summarize the classification and describe these five layers (subsystems or sub-contexts), namely, microsystem, mesosystem, exosystem, macrosystem, and chronosystem.

Microsystem

This is a layer of complex associations between the developing person and the environment in an immediate setting containing the individual (Bronfenbrenner, 1977, p. 514). It is the environment closest to the child. Its constituents include family, home, school, and peers. The microsystem, because of its closeness to the developing child, is the most potent influence on the child's development, and so family, parents, and school are the prime stakeholders in the education of the children or, in the opinion of Lightfoot (2003), "the primary institutions for socialization of children"(p. xxiii).

Mesosystem

Mesosystem is the interrelationships of the microsystems of the developing child (Bronfenbrenner, 1977, p. 515). This is where the constituents of the subsystem home, school, and peers interact and therefore impact the development and education of the child. Simply put, "the mesosystem represents the degree of connection, coordination, and continuity across a child's microsystem" (Weiss, et al., 2005, p. xiv). That is, the more the interrelationship, the more consistent the influence is likely to be.

Exosystem

According to Bronfenbrenner (1977), this is an extension of the mesosystem that embraces other specific structures that are outside the microsystem and mesosystem layers and, as such, do not exert direct influence on the developing child. The influence of the exosystem on the developing child is relayed through other layers of the systems. The elements of this larger system, which indirectly influence the development of the child, include the parents' workplace, the media, governmental agencies (local, state, and federal), the distribution of goods and services, and communication and transportation facilities (Bronfenbrenner, 1977, p. 515). For example, a policy that directly alters the parents' work schedule is likely to indirectly affect the child's development and education. Such a policy can precisely increase or decrease the attention and care parents devote to their children's well-being and development.

Macrosystem

The macrosystem differs significantly from other sub-contexts already considered. It refers not to the specific context affecting the life of the developing individual but to the general prototype existing in the culture or subculture, which sets the pattern for the structures and activities occurring at a concrete level (Bronfenbrenner, 1977). Elements that make up this layer include cultural values, religious beliefs, attitudes and ideologies, global economy, scientific discoveries, and national and international politics. Its overarching influence passes through all layers to influence the child. Good examples are the effects of industrialization or World War II on the society, family, parents, and, indeed, the education of children. The current globalization process is another good example. Globalization, as a component of macrosystem, is a prototype phenomenon affecting individuals and societies in varying ways.

Chronosystem

Another part of the EST usually not visually represented as a distinct layer is the chronosystem. According to Bronfenbrenner (1989), the chronosystem is that aspect of influence on developmental changes triggered by life events and experiences. This system represents the element of time (experience), both in the individual's life trajectory (e.g., life stages such as infancy, childhood, adolescence, adulthood, or events such as divorce, severe illness or death of a parent) and historical context (e.g., the birth of a sibling, entering school, and various rites of passage) (Bronfenbrenner 1989, p. 201). It is ever present in all other layers of the ecological system. The chronosystem can be external or internal experiences or events in relation to the individual. These events or experiences, whether of internal or external origin, are key in altering the existing relationship between the person and environment and, consequently, in initiating developmental changes (Bronfenbrenner, 1977, p. 513; 1989, p. 201). Consider, for instance, the reduced attention an only child often gets with the arrival of a second child in the family.

Next, the EST will be analyzed for its strengths and weaknesses.

Critique of Bronfenbrenner's Ecological Systems Theory

At this point, I need to reiterate that parental involvement is important because a child's home is an important context of the child's development and education. Secondly, to understand parental involvement, we need to understand the context of the family or home of the child. Furthermore, parental involvement as a human behavior cannot be exercised in a vacuum without reference to the school community's ecology.

Strengths of EST

The strengths of EST with regard to parental involvement in the education of children include establishing the role of context in the development and education of children. EST defines and delineates context and addresses the various degrees of influence. It spotlights the role of children in their development and education. Finally, EST explains why different varieties of parental involvement may exist.

Establishes the Role of Context in the Development and Education of Children

One of the major strengths of EST is its explanatory role of context in the development and education of children. As already noted, an individual's development does not take place in a vacuum. For a child to reach its potential, both the environment in which development occurs and the setting in which educational influence occurs are central. Lightfoot (1978) adds that in the complexities of family-school relations in the education of children, it would be misleading to disregard the cultural boundaries within which people live and function (p.176).

EST Defines and Delineates Context, and Addresses Various Degrees of Influence

EST not only clearly explains the importance of context in the education and development of children, but it also defines and delineates the context in a comprehensible manner. EST posits that the ecological systems of the child, his/her individual world of education and development, is made up of several layers or subsystems or sub-contexts.

A contribution of EST from this standpoint is that it presents a mental picture of the level of influence that each subsystem wields in the development and educational process of children. The essence of the delineation, as already noted, is to distinguish the immediate environment and larger contexts of the child and the corresponding consequences on the developing individual. The closer the layer is to the developing individual, the more the interaction and consequently the more potent the influence. In this regard, EST contributes to a better understanding and practice of parental involvement in the education of children.

The Place of Children in their Education and Development

Another important contribution of EST is that it highlights the role of children themselves in their education and development. Lightfoot (1978), notes that most often children are ignored in the equation of the family-school collaboration in their education. She questions the dyadic relationship between school and family, never mind that the child is the subject of the dialogue and interaction of that relationship. She further wonders if by such a dyadic stance, parents and educators are really projecting "their needs to feel competent and successful as parents and teachers" (p. 84). In reality, an effective parental involvement relationship ought to be a triadic relationship, taking the interests and concerns of the child, school, and family into consideration. EST deserves credit for emphasizing the role of the individual in the development process. Likewise, in the case of parental involvement, the theory highlights the place of the child in the process.

The developing individual is not a passive recipient of development and educational stimuli but an active participant in the process and is indeed part of the parental involvement equation. It is the interaction of the individual and the environment—different layers of the context and their constituents—otherwise known as "producers," that leads to the process of the development of the individual, the "product" (Bronfenbrenner, 1989, p.191). Simply put, education and development (of children) are the function of both the environment—the producers and the developing individual, the product.

EST Explains Why Varieties in Parental Involvement Exist

Bronfenbrenner (1989), in addition to noting that there is no context-free development process of the individual, also points out that the settings in which all people live and function are not the same. For example, the ecological systems of a Hispanic family of six who lives in inner-city Chicago will most likely be different from that of a Nigerian immigrant family of three, who reside in an affluent suburb. According to EST, these differences in the families' environment are bound to influence their day-to-day activities and accordingly influence their involvement in the development and education of their children.

Constantino (2003) does not hesitate to remind educators and other stakeholders that each school community is unique: "whatever their commonalities, no two school communities will be exactly alike—nor should they be" (p.11). Similarly, the means of achieving the same basic goal of parental involvement may differ because of the different contexts in which families live and function.

In conclusion, EST gives conceptual insight into the nature and dynamics of the context in which education of children takes place. It further sheds light on the complex relationship between family and school in the education of children. Because of the different contexts in which families, schools, and communities live and function, varieties of parental involvement should not come as a surprise to anyone. However, despite these strengths, EST also has certain weaknesses, which I will discuss in the next section.

Weaknesses

The weaknesses of EST include the erroneous assumption that the delineation of EST will fit every culture; the assumption that EST does not acknowledge the changing meaning and structure of family; the fallacious assumption that family, school, and community always work together in the education of children; and the generalization that children always respond to the influences of the environment, including educational and developmental stimuli.

Configuration of EST May not Likely to Fit Every Community and Culture

The delineation of the ecological systems by Bronfenbrenner might not fit every community and culture. For instance in figure 6, Bronfenbrenner places extended family as a constituent of the exosystem. By placing this important agent (extended family) in the exosystem sub-context, far from the immediate environment of the developing child, it suggests that extended families have a lesser influence on the development and educational process of the child.

Therefore, a different delineation is necessary in those cultures and communities where the extended family system is as important as the nuclear family. According to Oke (1986), the extended family has wide acceptability and practice in Nigeria. For the Igbo people of Southeast Nigeria, the extended family culture is still strong and as important to the child as members of the nuclear family. For this reason, it should be part of the microsystem of the child's ecological system.

Another element Bronfenbrenner did not take into account is the power of information technology in today's world. The media and information technology, which are conspicuously missing in this important subsystem (microsystem), can have a direct and profound influence on children's education, similar to the constituents of the microsystem of the child's ecological system. Information technology today is highly advanced and is readily available to the child. Plenty of information is at the fingertips of many children, which many of them can independently seek and use for either positive or negative purposes and ultimately impacts their development and education. In addition, it is no secret that some children are more savvy in the use of information technology than their parents.

EST Does not Acknowledge the Changing Meaning and Structure of Family

Related to the above issue are the different ways people construe the word "family" today. Gestwicki (2004) shows how the family has experienced profound changes in the past century, giving rise to single-parent (mother or father) families; stepfather, stepmother, and stepchildren homes; and teenage-mother (children bearing children) single-family homes. She further shows that while the traditional family model may be diminishing, other forms are rising, which may include people not related by blood or hereditary bonds such as those created by adoption (p. 463). As the society evolves, so will the structure and meaning of the family. EST did not take into consideration the evolution of the family in terms of new meaning and structure.

Will Family, School, and Community Always Work Together for Children's Education?

EST assumes that family and school will work together to "produce" development. This is what Bronfenbrenner (1989) refers to as the interactions of the "producers" of development (p.191), meaning that elements of the microsystem, like the school and parents, interact in order to produce development. By definition, parental involvement involves collaboration and mutuality. Effective parental involvement may elude a given school community, where family attitudes or beliefs or unwelcoming school structures or attitudes may not favor or promote parental involvement.

According to Swap (1993), some parents or families believe that the job of educating children has been delegated to schools and educators, and anything more amounts to interference. Such a narrow understanding is indicative of a kind of compartmentalization of the process of educating children and can emerge by equating schooling to education. Families with such beliefs and attitudes, in the words of Sergiovanni (1999), are simply not ready to do things differently (p. 153) nor will they be ready to work together with other stakeholders in the education of their children. Factors such as fears, negative feelings, and other emotions related to parental involvement education can create a distance between family and school in the job of educating the children of the community (Becher, 1984). Mistrust of family involvement developed by educators over the years can equally distance family and school in the education of children (Constantino, 2003), negatively impacting the entire dynamics of parental involvement and ultimately of the education of children in a given school community.

The inability of some schools to look beyond their institutional perspective (of parental involvement) (Finders and Lewis, 1994) or reexamine the standardized notion of parental involvement can also create a distance between family and school. The obvious consequence of such an attitude is the failure on the part of educators "to reach out to the hard-to-reach low-income families" (Olivos, 2006, p.17). This is more pronounced in some school communities, where "showing-up behaviors" (Nderu, 2005) or "specific scripted school activities" (Lopez, 2001, p. 416) constitute the mainstay of parental involvement.

The existence of a conventional approach to managing schools, which "emphasizes hierarchy, individualism, and technology rather than dialogue, relationship, and reciprocity" (Swap, 1993, p. 17) is another indication that school and family may not be working together for the education of children. Swap (1993) further argues that because teacher-preparation programs follow this traditional approach (in school management), hierarchical and authoritarian principles are more likely to govern the schools' relationships with families and communities (p.17).

Family and school occupy the same microsystem of the developing child and, as producers of development, are supposed to interact with one another in the mesosystem. Unfortunately, some educators and families do not believe that they can work together for the education of children or interact as producers of development, and that further complicates the problem.

Will Children Always Respond to the Influence of the Environment?

It is possible that while family and school fulfill their roles effectively in the education of children, it is not guaranteed that children will respond accordingly. There are a number of factors that might hinder the child from responding to, and interacting with, school and family in ways that promote his/her education and development. Samuel Sava cites a lack of a better childhood as an element that can hinder a child from responding to appropriate education and development stimuli: "It's not better teachers, texts, or curricula that our children need most; it's better childhoods" (Swap, 1993, p.15). Lack of a better childhood includes children engaging in activities or situations that distract them from their educational and developmental processes.

Some families explicitly or implicitly deny their children a better childhood by making them work to augment the family income. Children subjected to such experience are inadvertently prevented from growing in proximity to the necessary adult influences. In Nigeria, for example, a good number of kids spend their days on the street, hawking one ware or another. These unfortunate Nigerian kids, who spend several hours a day away from home, are not growing in close proximity to their parents. They are being denied a better childhood and the opportunity to benefit from positive educational and developmental influences within their environment.

Nevertheless, there are some occasions where bringing children to work has had educational benefits. The Longoria family (Lopez, 1999) alluded to the above assertion while explaining why they bring their kids to the field (work). On their part, Mr. and Mrs. Longoria bring their children to work in order to teach them the importance of hard work and responsibility (Lopez, 1999, p.166).[11] Despite its weaknesses, EST is still a good tool that sheds light on the issue of variations in the perceptions and practice of parental involvement.

The Link between the Ecological Systems Theory and Parental Involvement

Lightfoot, (1978; 2003) Bronfenbrenner, (1989) and Epstein (2001) agree that family and school are the most important institutions in the education and development of the children. What challenges scholars of parental involvement, among other issues, are the "how" and the "level / how much" of the phenomenon in a given school community (Comer, 1984; Chavkin, 1998; Mattingly, Prislin, McKenzie, Rodriguez and Kayzar, 2002). Bearing in mind that a context-free discourse and practice of parental involvement is not realistic (Bronfenbrenner 1989), facing the challenges of deciphering the how and how much should include understanding the impact of the psychosocial climate and other environmental factors so as to create an optimal learning environment for children (Comer, 1984, p. 323). This approach is consistent with the wisdom that, in resolving educational questions rather than decontextualizing the issue in question, there is a need to pay attention to its social context (Feinberg and Soltis, 2004).

Fullan (2001) wonders why certain forms of parental involvement produce positive results while others seem wasteful or even counterproductive (p. 198). More recently, Olivos (2006) wonders why, despite the long history of parental involvement in American education, the public school systems have not made headway in establishing an authentic relationship with the communities they serve, particularly the "hard-to-reach" parents and families, which are African Americans, Latinos, immigrants, and low-income families (p. 17). Both Fullan's (2001) and Olivos's (2006) questions are very illuminating, especially when put in dialogue with the interest of this study, namely to understand the parental involvement of Igbo parents in Chicago in the education of their children. Equally instructive are the opinions of Feinberg and Soltis (2004),

---

11   We will learn more about the Longoria family in the section on parental involvement: theory and practice.

that there is a strong tendency to overlook social, political, and cultural factors in resolving controversies in education (p.10). The social, political, and cultural factors enumerated by Feinberg and Soltis form the major components of sub-contexts and the entire ecological systems Bronfenbrenner posits. The position of Feinberg and Soltis (2004) finds support in the statement that decontextualizing the school problem, which has a long history in educational literature and policy, often results in a haphazard approach to educational issues (Olivos, 2006, p. 25).

Based on the insights from EST and the advice of Feinberg and Soltis (2004), the search for an answer to Fullan's and Olivos's questions begins by examining the role of context in parental involvement. Just as context largely determines the nature of children's development, the ecological systems of family, school, and community shape their involvement in the education of their children.

After enumerating the myriad difficulties that parental involvement can face—such as the structure of the family, cultural, social, and economic issues—Henderson, Marburger, and Ooms (1992) wondered why many reports on educational reform neglect these issues (p. xv). According to EST, the issues listed by Henderson et al. (1992) are factors that influence the day-to-day activities of the child, family, community, and school in their respective ecological systems.

In the same vein, while acknowledging the challenges of establishing family-school partnerships in school communities serving families with low-income and new immigrants (e.g., blacks, Hispanics, and American Indians), Comer (1984) considers the understanding of the social, economic, and historical issues that influence day-to-day activities in such communities (p. 323) to be essential. Epstein (2001) corroborates this by noting that "good programs will look different at each site, as individual schools tailor their practices to meet the needs, interests, time and talents, ages, and grade levels of students and families" (p. 408). To further emphasize the role of context in the perception and practice of parental involvement, Wright and Stegelin (2003) cautions the would-be constructors of family-school relationship, noting that some strategies are common across groups while others are chosen to fit the specific needs of the child, family, and community (p. 60). Constantino (2003) does not hesitate to remind educators and other stakeholders that each school community is unique. He writes, "whatever their commonalities, no two schools will be exactly alike—nor should they be" (p.11).

The above opinions and assertions are different ways to underscore that context and time, the ecological systems, are vital in fashioning the perception and shaping the dynamics of parental influence on the education of children. Unfortunately there is a tendency to overlook the importance of ecological systems in the attempt to resolve educational issues. Such neglect could, from time to time, be counterproductive or lead to wastefulness (Fullan, 2001) in school-family relationships in the education of children.

Now with the tendency to overlook context in resolving educational questions, one does not have to look very hard to find the answer to Olivos's question concerning the inability of public school systems to establish parental involvement among low-income families. For example, Lightfoot (1978) notes that while educators blame these families for inadequate attention to their children's cognitive needs, they fail to explore the structural and institutional forces that impact the lives of these low-income families and shape their relationships with their children (p. 13).

Context has its dynamics too. It is not static. Context changes with the movement of time (chronosystem). Likewise, parental involvement shifts with the ebbs and flows of the context. "Parental involvement for a new century" is a feature article authored by Jacobi, Wittreich, and Hogue (2003). The underlying assumption of this article is that the dawn of a new century has engendered a new context, raising up new expectations for parental involvement (Jacobi, Wittreich and Hogue, 2003, p.11). The authors assert that parental involvement in the new century ought to respond to the needs of the new environment with its new attributes, such as information technology, globalization, migration, immigration, etc.

Summary

In the final analysis, parental involvement is about the relationship that links family, school, and community with the aim of providing a better learning environment and educational experiences for children. Like all human behavior, parental involvement happens in a context. As a dyad, the theories in sum identify home/family and school as the most essential elements of the environment in which a child's education occurs. Families and schools each have their unique ecological systems that govern their day-to-day activities. These unique environments that are subject to vagaries of the larger ecological systems shape and reshape the overlapping spheres of influence family and school exert on the education of children. That is to say, the perception and practice of parental involvement cannot be divorced from the Ecological systems of the school community.

The next section puts the two theories in focus in the practice of parental involvement in education.

Parental Involvement: Theory and Practice

I have presented and analyzed the two theories that are fundamental to understanding the dynamics of parental involvement. The broad aim of this section is to discuss what we know about contemporary parental involvement in education as represented in scholarly research.

First, I will present various typologies of parental involvement and appraise them. Using examples from research, I will show how context influences the understanding and practice of parental involvement, especially those outside the traditional practices. The last part of this section will highlight the role of communication in parental involvement.

Typologies of Parental Involvement

There are various practical expressions of parental involvement. In scholarly literature, various typologies are generated from an analysis of the various ways that parents are involved in education; as such, they reflect the experiences of a particular school community. What necessitates and inspires a particular variety of involvement can be a school community's culture, history, politics, geography, educators, community members, school district policies, etc., or simply the Ecological systems of the school community. To examine these various types is simply to look at the patterns in which parental involvement is expressed in concrete ways in a given school community.

Lopez (1999) analyzed twelve popular parental involvement typologies presented by some of the most respected individuals in the field. Epstein, Hoover-Dempsey, Chavkin and William, Henderson, Marburger and Ooms, Gordon, Delgado-Gaitan, Comer, Henry, Swap, Berger, Olmstead, and Greenwood and Hickman (Lopez, 1999) developed these typologies. Each scholar proposes a different array of activities that parents and families should engage in to influence their children's education. These typologies range from Comer's and Olmstead's three types of involvement to Henry's twelve ways that parents can be involved in the education of children (Lopez, 1999). With the exception of Gordon's typology developed in the 1970s and a few in the threshold of the 1990s, the majority of these typologies emerged in the 1990s.

While acknowledging that these are not the only typologies extant in literature, Lopez (1999) notes that they are a fair representation of the popular typologies in parental involvement discourse (p. 49). From the collection of various typologies, Lopez (1999) outlined seven activities, which I will summarize. They are as follows:

Parents as Volunteers or Paraprofessionals in Schools

This activity is a belief and behavior whereby parents assist the school in a wide range of activities, which includes assisting teachers and administrators, helping organize social events, guiding excursions, or helping in the lunchroom and playground during break. Some parents are rewarded financially for these services, depending on the arrangement in the school community. In such circumstances, parents are known as paraprofessionals, although not all paraprofessionals are parents.

Parents as Teachers of Their Own Children

This is an activity where parents are involved directly in the teaching and learning processes either at school or at home. Activities here include helping with homework, reading to children, telling stories, reviewing previous lessons, and helping in other ways that promote the cognitive development of children.

Parents as Learners

This type of parental involvement is expressed when families and parents attend various conferences, seminars, and workshops, with the aim of improving their parenting skills on the best ways to create education-friendly environments for children. Some school communities offer English as Second Language (ESL) adult programs to help parents fit into the larger society and be better involved in the education of their children.

Parents as Audience and School Supporters in School Functions

Parents, as a way of being involved in the education of their children, attend student performances (e.g., plays, concerts), sports, or social events. Through this attendance, parents also support and promote school functions.

Parents as Providers of Basic Student Needs

The basic needs of children include health, clothing, food, shelter, and, above all, care and love. These essentials not only help in ensuring regular attendance but also engender a better learning and teaching atmosphere for the benefit of the children and the entire school community.

Parents as Decision Makers on Governance Boards

This is a way parents are involved in the governance and decision making in the education of children. The culture of having a school board is widespread in the United States, and often, parents and family members are elected to these boards. The amount of power they can wield can be anybody's guess. The PTA is another platform through which parents participate in governance and influence school decisions. It is also not uncommon to find parents as members of different education committees in the school community, including local governance councils.

Parents as Interlocutors/Conduits for School-Derived Information

This type of parental involvement emphasizes the importance of communication in school-family relationships. Both agents are obliged to share vital information that would enhance children's education. For an effective school-family partnership, a two-way communication needs to be established. Through a two-way communication, parents and educators express their expectations and values and discuss and monitor children's progress and needs. School policies are also made known to families through this channel of communication.

Having outlined various activities that form practice of parental involvement extant in literature, I will now appraise them against the background of the theoretical framework of this study.

Appraising Typologies of Parental Involvement

Some issues arise from the typologies of parental involvement. One is that these typologies are often construed as benchmarks for parental involvement (Lopez, 1999; Nderu, 2005; Olivos, 2006) and inadvertently have become, for some, a manual or a dos-and-don'ts handbook or a prescription guide for parental involvement. However, it should be noted that such an attitude will not remove the effectiveness of these typologies when used in the right climate and context.

That these typologies, when used in the right environment and with the right intentions, have proven to be beneficial to the school community does not imply that they will equally answer to the needs of all families and school communities. Though families and school communities might appear similar, they still have their own unique ecological systems. A better understanding of such unique environment as Comer (1984) suggests would boost parental involvement practices, create a better learning environment, and ultimately enhance children's education in the community. Lightfoot (2003) notes that one size does not fit all. She nevertheless points out that there are lessons in each context that delineate sound principles and good practices that are applicable to a variety of settings and situations (p. xxix).

For example, I witnessed, during my educational leadership internship in a Chicago urban Catholic school, a group of parents who organized an art fair in their school community. The exhibition, which usually takes place during the last weeks of the school year, was a forum where students' art works are organized and exhibited for parents and other members of the school community. The two parents who coordinated and organized the art fair were not members of the staff of the school nor were they members of the faculty. However, they had the approval and the cooperation of the school and community to put on the show. The activities of these two parents, though worthwhile, would be difficult to duplicate, for example, in a rural Borana, Ethiopia, school community, which has a totally different ecological system. Nevertheless, Borana family and community, as I experienced them, were equally involved in different but meaningful ways in the education of their children. For example, most parents undertook the teaching of Borana customs and way of life to their children through a hands-on approach. Another issue with typologies is the question of who sets the agenda or defines the activities.

It is not uncommon for schools to define and set goals, identify the values and practices outside the school that would contribute to school success, and invite parents, families, and communities to participate (Swap, 1993, p.30). Such typologies, which either collectively or individually favor the school apparatus (Lopez, 1999), constitute a "school-centered definition of family and community involvement" (Olivos, 2006, p.18). In addition, these school-centered activities often require that parents or families must show up on school premises. Nderu (2005) refers to this as "showing-up behaviors" kind of parental involvement, which includes activities like volunteering, attending school events, parent-teacher conferences, and PTA meetings (p. 2). Lightfoot (1978) remarks that some of these activities are "ritualistic occasions that do not allow for real contact, negotiation, or criticism between parents and teachers" (p. 28). But even for "showing-up behaviors," parents and families are required to seek and follow guidelines set by the school. Olivos (2006) identifies school-centered activities or showing-up behavior as a narrow band of behaviors and attitudes, which school districts and schools tolerate as legitimate forms of parental involvement (p. 18). This questions the parents' overlapping spheres of influence in the education of children. Certainly, parental involvement, such as overlapping spheres of influence, cannot mean simply following prescriptions for school-family collaboration written basically by the school.

The unwritten rule that makes the views and practices of the members of the upper echelon of the society a reference-point is another issue to consider in appraising typologies of parental involvement. "Because American society places greater worth on the cultural and social capital of middle- and upper-class whites" (Olivos, 2006, p. 48), it is not uncommon to perceive and express parental involvement through the lenses of and the activities of families of the higher echelons of society. In fact, Lareau (1987) notes that schools' standardized views of the "proper" role of parents in schools tend to reflect the culture and lifestyles of the upper middle class (p. 82). The cultural capital of parents, she adds, determines the level of their response—that is, their compliance to the school expectations (p.73). It is safe to say that most parental involvement typologies are middle- and upper-class biased. Unfortunately, such an attitude tends to place low-income families on a deficit pedestal, essentially making them victims of deficit's perspective (Auerbach, 1989; Swap, 1993; Finder and Lewis, 1994; Epstein, 2001; Olivos, 2006).

That families and parents, because of circumstances of poverty and a poor educational background, might not be able to meet the parental involvement expectations set by the school does not mean that they cannot be involved in the education of their children. Lopez (1999) demonstrates that migrant families, who are perceived through the deficit lenses, can be positively involved in their children's education in nonstandardized methods. His findings show the narrowness of such a standardized perception and praxis of parental involvement in the education of children.

As already noted, the above typologies have proven successful in some contexts; they also have limitations, namely, they are not capable of responding to the needs of every family and community involvement in the education of children. This kind of limitation is significant and should attract the attention of all those interested in addressing school-family relationship issues. Yet there is the temptation to prescribe or transplant these typologies from one successful school to other school communities without considering the existing ecological system. Such transplantation or "prescription" amounts to the decontextualization of educational problems and planning. In turn, such attempts may fail due to a type of "immune rejection," leading to a wasteful, counterproductive exercise. Nonetheless, since these typologies can be modified for use in other localities, school communities can learn and adapt what is necessary to their own localities (Weiss, et al., 2005, p. xx); but certainly, nothing should be imposed on any community.

In conclusion, there is nothing wrong with these typologies, especially in situations where they respond to the needs and meet the expectations of parental involvement of a given school community. What becomes problematic is to use any of these typologies to judge the level of parental involvement in a different ecological system. It is always important to ask how parents, families, and communities can exercise their overlapping responsibilities in the education of children based on their Ecological systems and funds of knowledge. Such a question not only expands understanding and practice, but it also increases the repertoire of practices beyond these known typologies.

Context and Parental Involvement: *Aligning Perceptions and Activities*

In this section, I will use some scholarly studies of parental involvement outside the mainstream to highlight the importance of context in the perception and practice of the concept.

The Council of Chief State School Officers' (CCSSO) 2006 report noted that parental involvement signifies a broad continuum of education-related parent activities (p.5). The officers, while acknowledging that parental involvement has clear benefits, called for specific strategies for involving culturally diverse and low-income families, especially during the early grades (CCSSO, 2006, p. 5). Embedded in the CCSSO 2006 report is the recognition of the unique environment in which these low-income and culturally diverse families live and function. It is also a call that challenges educators and parents alike to be creative in developing strategies that will allow these families to influence the education of their children effectively (Chavkin and William, 1990, p. 248).

Seven years earlier, before the CCSSO's 2006 report, Lopez (1999) studied the perception and practice of parental involvement among some migrant families with the aim of uncovering other effective parental involvement methods outside of institutional practices. These migrant families no doubt have their respective ecological systems, which consist of a life dominated by high-mobility, temporary seasonal employment, long and gruesome hours of work with low pay, societal marginalization, vulnerability, and limited English language skills (Lopez, 1999; Lopez, 2001; Lopez, Scribner, and Mahitivanichcha, 2001).

One of the outcomes of Lopez's (1999) study is the distinction he made between traditionally sanctioned and nontraditional ways of parental involvement. Lopez (1999) notes:

> Parental involvement is manifested in specific/legitimated practices, signified through certain modes of interaction, and ritualized through performance-like "scripts," which necessitate particular modes of behavior and interaction. (p. 9)

The above definition, often found in the American educational landscape, excludes the unknown ways that many low-income parents and families, who value education, support and are involved in their children's education. Though most of such families will devote significant time and energy in search of the basic needs of life, such as food, clothing, and shelter, some, at the same time, are still involved in the education of their children in ways that yield positive academic performance and a healthy social, cognitive, and moral development. Some of these parents might not be directly involved in the acquisition of technical skills[12], for instance, or other legitimated practices but are directly involved in other aspects of learning and instilling qualities that make for a successful education. In any case, the acquisition of technical skills and knowledge alone does not define educational success as Monke (2006) pointed out. Other components of educational success, such as respect, moral judgment, discipline, hard work, compassion, etc., are often what families, parents, and community bring to bear for the benefits of the children's holistic education.

Of the three migrant families Lopez (1999) studied, two did not follow the pathway of traditional parental involvement practices—ritualized performance like "scripts"—which necessitates particular modes of behavior and interaction yet were effectively involved in the education of their children. These families influenced the education of their children by bringing to bear those other components of what makes for successful education. Below is an excerpt of his conclusion:

> The three families in this study all had a different understanding of traditional "involvement" pursuits. The Padilla and the Longoria families were not involved in the "traditional" sense: having little formal interaction with the school personnel and never having reinforced particular class lessons with their children at home. Yet both families strongly believed they were "highly" involved in their children's education by taking their children to work and instilling in them a strong work ethic. Mrs. Salinas, on the other hand, did perform many formal involvement rituals, but her reasons for being "involved" in this way had more to do with a belief in a work ethic (i.e., making sure her children were "working" and not slacking off in school) as opposed to being involved for "democratic" or "participatory" reasons. In this regard, Mrs. Salinas's understanding of involvement extended beyond the school grounds to make sure her children understood the value of work at home, at school, and on the job. As a whole, all the parents in this study understood "involvement" as something broader than scripted roles to be

---

12   By "technical skills," I mean an explicit school curriculum, such as reading, writing, and math. These are not the only things that are taught or learned in a child's educational process. There is more to education than what teachers explicitly focus on.

"performed"; involvement, for these families, engendered teaching children the value of education through the medium of hard work. (p.206)

It is obvious that the Padilla and Longoria families did exert positive educational influence but perhaps in ways not recognized by the institutional perspectives (Lopez, 2001). Mrs. Salinas used a combination of both recognized and unrecognized types of parental involvement. Lopez's (1999) findings independently validate the confessions of Finder and Lewis (1994), that some parents of other unfamiliar environments within the constraints of their contexts do indeed influence the education of children but, unfortunately, are rarely recognized by educators, who are largely influenced by the mainstream understanding of parental involvement.

In the final analysis, Lopez (1999) calls for an expanded definition of the current repertoire of parental involvement outside the boundaries of the traditional understanding. He further recommended the search for creative ways to get the most out of these and other unrecognized understandings of involvement (p. 224). In sum, "these findings not only challenge discursive/ hegemonic understandings of parent involvement, but also open up new avenues for research and practice" (Lopez, 2001, p. 416).

Another example of a parent who is involved in her children's education in a nontraditional way is Dixie. Dixie is one of the seven women who participated in a study of the role of parents in Singaporean education authored by Lana-Khong (2004). Dixie is a single parent, who runs a successful business that leaves her with little or no time for direct involvement in her children's education. She believes and recognizes "the importance of education today, seeing her mothering role as providing her children with education as a foundation in life" (p. 97).

In spite of her unique Ecological systems (tight business schedule and the highly competitive Singaporean society), Dixie neither lost interest nor betrayed her sincere intention to support and "be involved" with her children's education. She had to work hard to provide for her family and children. Furthermore, despite her childhood, which was devoid of parental support in education (why she herself didn't go far in education), she was still very involved in her children's education in terms of providing them with a very conducive learning atmosphere. She believed that she was really involved in her children's education, though not perhaps in the manner of other mothers in the study, who either stopped working or who worked part-time in order to devote more time to their children's education. Dixie's involvement was primarily hiring a team of tutors and maids, who would provide a conducive educational atmosphere for her children. Dixie's mother was also a member of this team, and she provided other needed support, leaving Dixie to focus on her business, the sole source of income for her family.

For Dixie, parental involvement meant being an inspiration agent to her children, providing financial and material support and creating a good home-learning environment. Through these steps, Dixie belongs to the class of the families identified by Constantino (2003) as those who contribute significantly to the education of children by providing the most positive and enabling home environment. Dixie, who hardly showed up at school for any activity, represents another strand of parental involvement that falls outside the traditionally recognized form of parental involvement. Dixie deserves credit for being creative in being involved in the education of her children, despite the nature of her ecological system.

There is yet another example of parental involvement that does not fit the usual pattern. In what seems like more of a reaction to the dominant view of the parent's role in the education of children, here is an opinion given by a Somali parent[13]:

> I've seen a guy who one time said that educators are the few who educate the student, and I said, "[They] do only half; the other is the parent." He said, "No, parents don't do anything. It is only the teachers." I don't agree. You ... found him in the classroom. Who prepare[s] him to come here? Who prepare[s] to make sure he eats? Who prepare[s] ... his clothes, prepare he can sleep well, and do the homework [sic]. I mean, you can't ignore parent's role in education. It's obvious! (Nderu, 2005, p. 73)

The Somali parent cited above was convinced that though he might not be able to show up at school for any activity, he was nonetheless deeply involved in the education of his child. This parent believed that his duty—half of the duty of educating children—which unfortunately is not recognized, perhaps from the standpoint of deficit perspective as parental involvement, complements the work of educators in the school. The parent made it clear that without such a complementary role, it is doubtful whether children would be successfully educated. The duty (involvement) of the Somali parent indeed overlaps with that of the school and community.

The above examples highlight the difficulties surrounding not only the definition of parental involvement but also its practice. Different contexts, or rather what Lana-Khong (2004) simply calls the situation of the school community in which parents operate, plays a key role in the perception and practice of parental involvement, thus giving rise to numerous and varied faces

---

13   The study was conducted among an immigrant Somali community in Minneapolis, MN.

of parental involvement and "broader than scripted roles to be performed" (Lopez, 1999, p. 206).

For Lana-Khong (2004), the rightness or wrongness of perception does not arise. What matters most is the outcome of the understanding based on the situation or context (p.66). It is for the same reason that there are calls for the expansion of the meaning of parental involvement beyond the traditional understanding and practices (Lopez, 1999; 2001) or to look outside its institutional perspective (Finder and Lewis, 1994) or to appreciate "the half of the duty" performed by parents, family, and community in the education of children (Nderu, 2005).

The foregoing discussion might give the impression that parental involvement is an amorphous phenomenon. Though it takes its shape according to the prevailing context, parental involvement still possesses essential elements. Mole (2005) calls these essential elements the essence of partnership, which includes communication, sharing power and responsibilities, and building mutual respect between schools and families (p.134). This essence of parental involvement form the basis for "activities [that] families and parents engage in to support their children's learning whether at home or in school or in community" (Weiss, Kreider, Lopez and Chatman, 2005, p. xii).

In the above examples of parental involvement outside the recognized models, there appears to be no official channel of communication between family and school. It is possible that the lack of acknowledgement of these efforts may be due simply to the lack of a clear communication channel between these agents of children's education. In the next section, I will discuss the role of communication in parental involvement.

Communication and Parental Involvement

By definition, there is a relationship among all of the possible actors who may exert influence on the education of children. This relationship can only be realized through mutual communication. The purpose of this section is to underline the importance of communication in parental involvement.

Communication as a Fundamental Aspect of Parental Involvement

Merriam-Webster's Collegiate Dictionary (1999) defines "communication" as a "process by which information is exchanged between individuals through a common system of symbols, signs, or behavior." This process is complex because of so many variables, which include the sender's voice and body language, the message itself, and the receiver's expectation and reaction (Berger, 2000, p.188).

A popular saying goes thus: "Communication makes or mars a relationship." The implication for parental involvement is that communication is central in home and school relationship for the sake of children's education (Dodd and Konzal, 2002). The success of a relationship existing within the overlapping spheres of influence depends on the level of exchange between family, school, and community (Sanders, 2006). That is to say that there is an absolute need for both family and school to communicate and interact on a regular basis in order to coordinate and manage the healthy development and education of children (Davis-Kean and Eccles, 2005, p. 57).

The experience of Marilyn Brown, both a teacher and a parent, demonstrates this point further. "It All Comes Down to Communication" is the title of her experience describing an encounter between her and her son's teacher (Dodd and Konzal, 2002, p. 32). It is hard to miss the point of that caption with regard to parental involvement practices.

Brown's son, a kindergartener, did well academically and socially. He was able to tie his shoes, though not quickly. Brown, oblivious of the fact that a kid's ability to tie his/her own shoes is indeed a classroom benchmark and expectation, bought her son a pair of sneakers with Velcro closures. Her intention was that since her son is not quick in tying his shoes, it would be one less problem the teacher would have to worry about. However, she was surprised to find in the report card that there wasn't a check mark in the box for "Able to tie own shoes." Regrettably, she says, "Had I known that tying shoes was on the report card, I would have made sure that he had shoes to tie." Reflecting on this incident, Brown realized the importance of teachers letting parents know classroom benchmarks and expectations up front. In this occurrence, she uses her experience as a teacher and a parent to show how communication can give insight to a murky situation and how it can help to forge a better relationship between the teacher and the parent for the benefit of children's education and society.

Parental involvement, as already indicated, is not an end; rather, it is a means to an end. Likewise, communication is not an end in parental involvement but a means to an effective collaboration of home and school that ultimately leads to shaping a better educational landscape that promotes teaching and learning.

Consider a situation where there is a change in teaching and assessing mathematics, but parents have not been informed about the benchmarks of evaluation, yet they are still required to assist their children with math homework (Ford, Follmer and Litz, 1998). Effective communication between school and parents would avert any potential confusion and frustration that the above situation might create. It is against this background and to forestall such potential frustration that the National PTA (2000) made effective and meaningful communication one of the standards of school-family collaboration in the education of children. The standard reads, "Communication between home and school is regular, two-way, and meaningful" (p. 25). To further emphasize the centrality of communication in a school-family relationship, the association notes that this is the basis on which all other standards are built. "When parents receive frequent and effective communication from the school or programs, their involvement often increases, their overall evaluation of educators improves, and their attitudes toward the programs are often more positive" (National PTA, 2000, p. 25).

There is another potential gain that communication brings to parental involvement that has to do with efficiency. Effective and meaningful communication can even save time. Effective communication can result in parents becoming more cooperative, and as a result, the principal spends less time mediating between angry and frustrated parents and teachers (National PTA, 2000, p. 26).

All Have Information to Share

Communication is a fundamental component of family-school relationship (Epstein et. al., 2002), because both home and school are primary institutions for children's education (Lightfoot, 2003, p. xxiii). Fullan (2001) believes that families do have vital information that is not available to anyone else (p. 199). For the benefit of children's education, such information must be shared.

The willingness and openness to share such information for the benefit of children's education is essential. That is, communication between family and school has to be productive (Lightfoot, 2003, p. xxix). Sharing information in school-family relationships, especially in this era of differentiated education, is crucial. For most teachers in the classroom, differentiated instruction would mean focusing on whom they teach, where they teach, and how they teach, with the primary goal of ensuring effective learning for varied individuals (Tomlinson and McTighe, 2006, p.3). Knowing whom the teachers teach or discovering the particular intelligences with which a child is blessed is a joint task of both parents and teachers. However, unfortunately, parents sometimes tend to be secretive, cautious, and indeed hesitant to share any information they think might reduce their children's competitive advantage (Lightfoot, 2003, p. xx).

Information is not just important in any collaborative responsibility, but the issue of whether collaborators have access to it is vital. Equally important is how to make use of the information shared. For example, the information a parent shares with a homeroom teacher can be the key to helping the children overcome learning or discipline challenges. Equally, a teacher might share information with a parent that would help a parent best to assist a child at home. My experience as a school director in rural Borana, Ethiopia, taught me that families and parents need not be literate or highly educated in order to share information that will enhance children's education and development. Again, they were cautious in the kind of information they shared

Different forms of communication include report cards, parent-teacher conferences, newsletters, school websites, classroom newsletters, phone calls, personal correspondence, home visits, attending village/community meetings, or announcements in churches, mosques, synagogues, or temples, etc.

Summary

Communication is the oil that lubricates the wheels of the overlapping spheres of influence wherein parents, family, community, and school are involved in the education of children. It is the foundation of a successful family-school relationship (Sanders, 2006). This is because they have vital information, which boosts children's education, to share. Unless there is an effective channel of communication between home and school, the overlapping spheres of influence on the education of children might be counterproductive. In order to reap the benefits of parental involvement, communication must flow between home, school, and community. Besides, parents must speak and be heard in an essential issue like the education of children (Hanhan, 1998, p. 107), because family and school are two primary institutions of their socialization (Lightfoot, 2003, p. xxiii).

Finally, just like the overall influence is defined by the ecological system, so is the nature of communication in a given school community shaped by its environment. There is no single recipe or set of discrete rules for constructing productive parent-teacher communication (Lightfoot, 2003, p. xxix). But what are the likely parental involvement challenges a given school community might face?

Challenges to Parental Involvement

In this section, I examine the challenges a given school community is likely to face in the understanding and practice of parental involvement. Challenges basically arise when parents and family are unable or are hindered from exercising their intrinsic influence on the education of children.

Various challenges to parental involvement have been identified and categorized (Swap, 1993; Henry, 1996; Lopez, 1999; Molnar, 1999). Swap

(1993) identifies the following challenges: changing family demographics, school practices that do not support family relationships, limited resources supporting parental involvement, and lack of information about how to establish partnerships as sources of challenges (p. 13ff). Molnar (1999) used the three categories of Schaeffer and Bertz to discuss some of the challenges of parental involvement: human nature, communication, and external factors. While Henry (1996) identified one broad barrier—institutional—Lopez (1999) discussed challenges from three perspectives, namely, school-based, home-based, and cultural-based barriers. These other categorizations of challenges of parental involvement are basically similar to Swap's more broad-based classification, which I will use in the subsequent discussions.

Changes in the Traditional Meaning and Configuration of Family

The fact that family is changing both in structure and meaning is no surprise. The speed with which the change is taking place is not only astonishing, but has also left most families grappling with the task of living up to the demands of the ever-changing meaning and structure of family. Important trends in society, such as increasing numbers of working mothers, the rising number of single parents (mother or father), marital instability, a decreasing family size, stress in modern living, development of a child-centered society, mobility and urbanization either as a sole factor or a combination of factors, introduce lasting changes in family structure and meaning (Gestwicki, 2003, p.17). The National Center for Health Statistics (1991), cited by Swap (1993), paints the picture of changes in the family in terms of figures and degree of change, thus

> 70 percent of mothers of school-aged children are now in the workforce compared with 30 percent in 1960. Almost half of all marriages end in divorce. There are more single-parent families: 25 percent, double the figure in 1970. A third of all marriages are now remarriages, and one out of four children has one or more stepparents. The number of children having children has increased dramatically in the last decade, particularly among children under fifteen. (p. 14)

Some critics might call these changes an unprecedented revolution, while for others it's simply a transformation. Regardless of the name, these changes have a profound impact on the dynamics of homes. Changes in the structure and meaning of family affect its role in the integral education of children. To say the least, it makes educating children nowadays more challenging than ever.

Reflecting also on the impact of changes in family configuration, the National PTA (2000) offers the following thoughts:

> The last half century is the first time that children are not growing up in close proximity to their parents and people in their primary social network. And high mobility has decreased the numbers of relatives, friends, and concerned adults in the lives of children. Thus, while children need more help than before in handling the usual inner stimulation related to growth and increased external stimulation, they have less adult support. (p. viii.)

In some situations, the poor performance of children—that is, their inability to learn at their grade levels—has been traced to these changes in family structure and its effect on parents' role. For example, the trauma of divorce may remain with a child for a long period and consequently affect his/her educational development (Wright and Stegelin, 2003, p.160). Wright and Stegelin (2003) went on to argue that divorced and blended families remarrying after divorce are indeed part of the subsystems of the child's Ecological systems (p.161). The comment of Samuel Sava, the executive director of the National Association of Elementary School Principals, suggests yet another challenge with regard to family structure and parental involvement in the education of children.

> This family revolution is the greatest single cause of the decline in student achievement during the last twenty years. It's not better teachers, texts, or curricula that our children need most; it's better childhoods, and we will never see lasting school reform until we first see parent reform. (Bacon cited in Swap 1993, p.15.)

The point of the above statement is unambiguous, namely, that parents and families are failing in their educational duties. Though its validity can be contested, the fact remains that a "family revolution" has explicitly impacted family-school relationships. Interestingly, there are parents who have the "restaurant approach" to the education of their children. These include some parents, whose Ecological systems requires them to work several hours and jobs in order to meet their financial obligations. For lack of time and the compelling need to meet their financial responsibilities, such parents entrust the entire educational process to the school. These disengaged parents are negative examples of the theory of overlapping spheres of influence. Similarly, such families make it possible for their children to grow distant from their influence. Such parents are so absorbed in their work that they have little or no time to exert the expected influence on their children's education or create the kind of home environment that promotes education or actions and inspires love of learning.

Sava's opinion about the unfortunate situation of some children, who lack better childhoods, has some connection to conditions of poverty. Poverty, as a consequence of limited financial resources, can be obvious as well as subtle (Fuller and Tutwiler, 1998, p. 258). And as a possible part of a family's ecology, poverty is also an enemy of both the child's education and the entire household (Fuller and Tutwiler, 1998, p. 257).

Gestwicki (2003) counsels that changes in family structure and meaning "are not necessarily bad or worrisome, unless one insists on clinging to the past, maintaining the exclusive rightness of bygone ways" (p.17). This implies that these changes are inevitable, and as such, one should not simply surrender to them but be open to make the best out of the situation so as to have some positive influence on the educational process. Simply, these changes in family structure and meaning call for creativity and innovation in how parents, family, community, and school can exercise positive influence effectively on the education of children. However, the creativity of Longoria (Lopez, 1999) and Dixie (Lang-Khong, 2004) families, as we already saw, are examples that change should never be used as an excuse to shirk the duty parents owe to their children and society or, with regard to children's education, remain a disengaged parent.

Such changes and challenges notwithstanding, families are still the engine of economic and social development and should continue to be part of the equation when establishing policies and priorities for economic and social development programs, including education (Adesina, 1999, p. 53).

School Practice and Structure That Do not Support School-Family Relationships

By nature, parental involvement calls for collaboration and mutuality in planning and decision making; "mutuality" implies shared responsibility and sharing information. However, these are not easy to come by due to what Henry (1996) referred to as institutional barriers (p. 93), such as unwelcoming school structures and closed attitudes to parental involvement. Institutional barriers have two levels, the organizational structure and the human side.

Molnar (1999) notes that the distancing begins in the mind, leading to the skepticism of the school staff toward parental involvement. Skepticism in itself, she concludes, is a major barrier to parental involvement in schools since it discourages any effort in that direction, thus lowering the window for parent-school collaboration, if not slamming it shut completely.

Again, at times educators relate to low-income families from a deficit perspective (Auerbach, 1989; Swap, 1993; Finder and Lewis, 1994; Epstein, 2001; Weiss, et al., 2005; Olivos, 2006), "which in itself becomes a barrier to family involvement" (Weiss, et al., 2005, p. xvii). This is common where parental involvement is prescriptive or offers no more and no less than "specific scripted school activities" (Lopez, 2001, p. 416). In such a situation, it is presumed that parents, who are perceived by schools to be inadequate, are unable to meet the prescribed school activities, and consequently, others perceive them as not making any worthy contribution toward the education of their children.

Furthermore, conventional approaches to managing schools that emphasize "hierarchy, individualism, and technology rather than dialogue, relation, and reciprocity" (Swap, 1993, p. 17) add to the challenges that parental involvement might face in a given school community. Swap (1993) adds that because teacher-preparation programs follow a traditional approach to school management, hierarchical and authoritarian principles also govern the schools' relationships with parents (p.17). This helps to explain why some American schools still have some elements of a protective model of parental involvement (Swap, 1993). The protective model illustrates the situation where parents or family may believe or may be forced to believe by the culture and climate of the school that the job of educating their children has been delegated to schools and educators; anything more than that would amount to interference (Swap, 1993). The barrier to parental involvement from this perspective is that some schools, families, and communities, in the words of Sergiovanni (1999), are not yet ready to do things differently (p. 153). For example, over the years some educators have developed a basic mistrust of parents visiting classrooms, which negatively impacts the relationship between family and school (Constantino, 2003, p. 92).

Another form of institutional barrier arises when schools are unable to look beyond the institutional perspective of parental involvement (Finders and Lewis, 1994) in order to reach the hard-to-reach low-income families (Olivos, 2006). This is more pronounced in some school communities, where "showing-up behaviors" (Nderu, 2005) or "specific scripted school activities" (Lopez, 2001) constitute the mainstay of parental involvement. The barrier here reflects the inability of educators to reach out to those parents and families (such as the Longorias or Padillas mentioned earlier), who, due to their unique ecological system, can hardly show up in the school premises or are unable to meet the school's narrowly defined requirement of parental involvement.

Finally, for some parents who are already reluctant to participate in the life of the school, a little resistance from the teacher would confirm their fears, and consequently, they may pull back and give up.

Avoiding Conflicts

Some conscious effort by the school to avoid getting into conflicts with parents and families could inadvertently forestall positive and beneficial parental involvement (Swap, 1993, p.18). Under normal circumstances, parents or community members don't go out of their way to purposely seek conflict for the sake of it. But the fact of life is that conflicts are not unexpected in an important relationship, such as school-family collaboration for the education of children. It is natural for parents to bring concerns into the school-family relationship. Moreover, difference inevitably provokes tension, as there is the possibility of misinterpreting other people's intentions, background, or culture (Swap, 1993).

But conflicts are not always all negative. Depending on how conflict is managed, it can be a blessing in disguise. In some cases, where parties are open to its resolution, conflict can be revealing or insightful. It can even accelerate the maturation process. Hence, conflict resolution can be a tool for improving the management of school and indeed creating a stronger school-family relationship for the education of children.

But the reality is that in most school communities, the attitude toward conflict is different, if not completely negative. It is construed as a portent of uneasiness and disruption to the life of the school, hence the urgency to avoid conflict in toto (Swap, 1993). Preserving the status quo and tradition becomes the preferred option. It would not surprise me if administrators who are skillful in avoiding conflicts are even sometimes rewarded (Swap, 1993). Avoiding conflict includes efforts to keep parents at arm's length. This, by implication, consists of shutting off the resourcefulness parents and family would bring to bear on the life of a school community and its duty to children and society.

In addition, deliberate efforts of excluding parents for the sake of avoiding conflict create an unnatural vacuum in the life of a school community. To make up for this gap in the life of a school, Swap (1993) says that schools engage in ritualized parental involvement (p.18). These ritualized encounters are choices of involvement, which do not allow for authentic contact, negotiation, or criticism between parents and educators (Lightfoot, 1978, p. 28). Lightfoot (1978) further argues that these ritualized encounters are institutionalized ways of establishing boundaries between insiders (teachers or educators) and outsiders or "interlopers" (parents) under the guise of polite conversation and mature cooperation (p. 27).

Limited Resources to Support Parental Involvement

Swap (1993) noted that teachers participating in a workshop she offered identified time and finances as among "the issues and constraints that kept them from reaching out to parents" (p. 22). In any given school community, instruction usually is the target of these resources—time and money—and rightly so. Most schools do not have all the finances needed for school programs, which basically come down to instruction and administration (Swap, 1993). A family involvement program is hardly a top priority in a tight school budget. The available resources are usually devoted to taking care of personnel, programs, and supplies. Schools and teachers believing that better school instruction is the sole engine that drives student achievement usually will spend little time and money on parental involvement programs. Even when resources are budgeted for parental involvement, the figures are tiny. For example, school districts that received more than $500,000 per year in Title I funding are required to reserve no more than 1 percent ($5000) for parental involvement activities (Moles, 2005, p. 133). So obviously, parental involvement is not a priority when it comes to allotments of this type. Most schools (public, but especially private) would have to depend on the generosity, time, and funds of parents and other stakeholders to implement a school-family relationship program.

The current culture of testing (Meisels, 2005; Strauss, 2006) (a bedevilment for education today), which puts a lot of pressure on principals and teachers, is another reason why little or no resources are allocated to parental involvement programs. Unfortunately, testing culture presents an irresistible motivation to teach what is in the tests (Meisels, 2005), and as a result, teaching and learning are gradually being reduced to preparation for tests. The dire consequences of sanctions due to poor test performance is simply scary. Moreover, in public schools, students' performance is generally linked to the level of funding schools receive from the government (Meisels, 2005). To make sure that students' achievement test scores are high enough, school resources are devoted to preparing for tests, to the determent of other programs like parental involvement.

Time specifically is a scarce commodity, considering the pressure on families, administrators, and teachers alike to meet many other daily commitments. Lightfoot (2003) notes for instance that "the traditional two parent-teacher conferences each year is nowhere near enough time for teachers and parents to stay in touch or communicate with one another productively" (p. 237). She recommends more time and frequent contact while noting that meeting such a demand would be challenging, requiring a major shift in the value that both families and schools place on family-school relationship (p. 237).

The challenges of time and resources to parental involvement especially require that school communities be continually innovative in parental involvement practices.

The Gap between Theory and Practice

Chavkin (1998) brings up another challenge facing parental involvement, namely, the gap between theory and practice:

> "Educators need to go further than just finding out if school, family, and community partnerships are helping education. We need to know how, when, and which partnership are improving education" (p.10).

Constantino (2003) agrees with Chavkin: "there still exists a great chasm between what we know and what we do" (p. 53). The great chasm can also lead to what Epstein (2001) refers to as a "rhetorical rut," a situation in which educators express support for family-school collaboration without taking action (Epstein, 2001, p. 407).

Rhetoric as a Challenge to Parental Involvement

Though the evolution of parental involvement continues to date, there is a widespread belief among educational stakeholders that there is value in parental involvement or the family-school collaboration in the education of children (Lightfoot, 1978; Swap, 1993, Henderson & Berla, 1994; Henry, 1996; Fuller and Olsen, 1998; National PTA, 2000; Epstein, 2001; Fullan, 2001, Constantino, 2003; Lightfoot, 2003; Olivos, 2006). Epstein and Salinas (2004) put it eloquently: "... students do better when their parents and teachers are partners" (p.13).

Al Gore (1997), while challenging stakeholders in American education on the issue of parental involvement, noted thus:

> The most promising approach to improving our schools may be the oldest and most obvious: getting families more involved in their children's education. I agree with Secretary Riley[14] ..., that [the] American family must be the rock on which a good education is built. (Gore, 1997)

With all these nice words about parental involvement, one would naturally like to know what the actual practice is like.

Mattingly, Prislin, McKenzie, Rodriguez and, Kayzar (2002), in

---

14   Richard Wilson Riley was secretary of education under President Bill Clinton and Vice President Al Gore.

Evaluating Evaluation: The Case of Parent Involvement Programs, described the likes of the above positive statements as "rhetorical support" for the phenomenon. Epstein (2001) is of the opinion that teachers, administrators, students, and families would all like to involve parents in the education of their children but simply lack the knowledge of how to go about it (p. 3). Because of the gap and yearning to fill it, most educators end up in a "rhetoric rut" (Epstein, 2001, p.407).

Motivated by the desire to establish empirical support that family-school relationships are indeed beneficial and to reduce the rhetorical rut, Mattingly et al. (2002) embarked on a parental involvement evaluation project. Their conclusions were the following:

> We do not claim that parent involvement programs are not effective but point out glaring flaws in the existing evidence upon which academic and political support for these programs is sometimes based. Most serious among the flaws is the fact that evaluation designs and data collection techniques are often not sufficiently rigorous to provide valid evidence of program effectiveness. (p. 571)

Despite its lack of empirical evidence, the authors (perhaps on a conceptual level) still found value in parental involvement in the education of children. Their belief is rooted in the conviction that parents and the home environment play a significant role in children's intellectual, social and emotional development (Mattingly, et al., 2002, p. 552). It takes a joint effort to achieve successful education of children. However, Mattingly et al. (2002) also suggested pathways for improvement in terms of research methodologies.

With regard to the gap between theory and practice of parental involvement, Gore's (1997) opinion should be of interest to all who are involved in the selling of parental involvement in school communities. In order not to misinterpret him, I quote his exact words:

> Tipper [Gore's wife] and I hosted our sixth national conference on family policy this summer in Nashville on the topic of "Families and Learning." We learned that one-third of all students say their parents don't know how they're doing in school. We learned that 80 percent of families say teachers and parents need to do a better job of working together …

Gore's observation further confirms that there is a missing link between the rhetoric of parental involvement and the actual practice. Despite the issue raised by Gore (1997) and Mattingly et al. (2002), the phenomenon of school-family collaboration has always found a place in the American educational history.

The "confession" of Finders and Lewis (1994), who are both educators and parents, is instructive with regard to parental involvement rhetoric. They acknowledged that it was only when they started talking to parents of different communities that they were forced to examine their own deeply seated assumptions about parental involvement (p. 50). Based on these revelations and in order to overcome the deficit approach, broaden the knowledge and practice of parental involvement, and, in due course, narrow the gap between rhetoric and practice, Finders and Lewis (1994) suggested that it has become imperative to look outside of the institutional perspective of school-family partnership (p. 50). Looking outside the traditional forms of parental involvement and, in the long run, closing the gap between rhetoric and practice begins with considering other environments in which children and that of those who influence their education live and function. Such environments often do not fit into mainstream society.

There is no doubt that parental involvement has become a high priority among politicians, educators, researchers, and parents, a paucity of research-based practice notwithstanding (Chavkin, 1998; Mattingly, et al., 2002). With the growing interest in the field and research centers springing up, the trend is changing. The lack of information about how to establish parental involvement is still a challenge to scholars and practitioners alike.

Likewise, the need to move parental involvement from rhetoric to reality is a primary challenge that families, schools, and communities face (Christenson, Godber and Anderson, 2005, p. 21). Steps toward addressing this issue would include addressing the question raised by Fullan (2001) or Olivos (2006) on why some parental involvement programs are successful, others wasteful and counterproductive, or a total failure. The task facing educators and other stakeholders is to present compelling evidence that parental involvement enhances students' education and ultimately benefits the society, thus reducing the gap between rhetoric and practice.

Finally, despite the challenges, parental involvement is still a value and a necessity that cannot be ignored in the education of children. Ignoring the phenomenon would mean ignoring the essential influence parents bring to the integral education of children. These challenges of parental involvement as discussed above are not insurmountable. Some parents and families, as we have seen, have risen up to the challenges posed by their distinctive Ecological systems and creatively exerted a positive influence on the education of their children.

Conclusion

I began this chapter by examining the two theories that form the theoretical framework for this study and its implication in the perception and practices of parental involvement. In the course the discussion, the importance of context in the understanding and practice of parental involvement was considered. Both parents and school have vital information about the education of children to share. Therefore, communication as an essential element in parental involvement was discussed. I concluded the chapter by discussing the various challenges that parental involvement face.

The presentations in chapters 2 and 3—background information on Igbo people and theoretical framework and its analysis—so far are in relation to the study's focus on how Igbo parents in Chicago are involved in the education of their children. Hence, in the subsequent chapter, I will describe how I conducted the study.

CHAPTER 4

Research Design

In this chapter, I will lay out the blueprint or research design for this study on the parental involvement of Igbo families in Chicago in the education of their children. First, I will articulate the research problem and the purpose of the study and then state the questions this study seeks to answer and its contribution to parental involvement scholarship. I will present my methodology, narrative inquiry, and offer reasons for my choice. I will also explain how I recruited participants, collected the data, and analyzed it. This chapter will end with a discussion of quality and ethical considerations.

Research Problem

The Igbo community in Chicago, as compared to the Irish, German, Polish, or Italian immigrants that preceded it, is a newer immigrant group of which little has been written (Bayor, 2003). For immigrants who have come to begin a new life in the United States, adapting well and thriving in the new environment requires them (and their children) to tread the path of education (Rong and Preissle, 2009). While there are shared experiences across all immigrant groups, there are also important differences. Parents and families everywhere, whether minority or immigrants, care about their children and play a fundamental role in their education (Epstein and Sanders, 1998). How they navigate and negotiate relationships with the schools is shaped by their own histories and cultural meaning systems.

The research problem is that there is a lack of knowledge about Igbo parents' perception of and their own involvement in the education of their children, of what actually constitutes parental involvement activities, and the challenges they face in their day-to-day engagement in the education of their children in Chicago. There is a need to hear their stories.

Purpose Statement

The primary purpose of this study is to understand how Igbo parents in Chicago engage in the education of their children and how they make meaning of that experience. Understanding the support they have and the challenges they face as they influence the education of their children are also what this study seeks. All immigrants are not the same, and knowing about Igbo experiences will enable scholars and educators to recognize commonalities and differences with other immigrant communities from Europe, Asia, the Caribbean, the Middle East, Latin America, and Africa.

Research Questions

The research questions are as follows:

1. What are the Igbo parents in Chicago perceptions of parental involvement?
    a) What is the relationship of parenting and education in the Igbo community?
        i) How do they define what their responsibility is in terms of being involved in their children's education?
    b) How do they understand the school's expectations of and assumptions about parental involvement in schooling and education?
        i) What do parents think the school expects of them?
        ii) How do schools support the involvement of parents in education beyond schooling?
        iii) How do schools impede the involvement of parents in education beyond schooling?
2. What forms of activities constitute parental involvement?
    a) What kinds of parents' interactions and activities in the education of their children do the parents engage in?
    b) How, beyond schooling, are parents involved in their children's education?
    c) What is the nature of communication between family and school?
        i) How does communication relate to forms of involvement parents engage in relating to the education of their children?
        ii) How does communication relate to challenges and support their involvement?
3. What are the challenges of parental involvement that Igbo parents in Chicago face?

4. How does the immigrant experience interact with their involvement in the education of their children?
5. How have parents' perceptions and views of parental involvement changed over time?

Importance of the Research

This qualitative study will help us to know more about the Igbo population in Chicago relative to the education of their children. In addition, it will provide insight into how Igbo parents and families, given their context, understand and engage in the education of their children. From the perspective of the Igbo community in Chicago, this study will help to broaden the body of knowledge regarding parental involvement to include information about the Igbo population in Chicago—a minority immigrant community.

Having stated the problem this study seeks to address, its purpose, and significance, I will now explain how I conducted the research and also offer reasons for my choice in the subsequent section.

Methodology

There are "different ways of researching the world" (Crotty, 2003, p. 66). Narrative inquiry, which falls into the broader qualitative approach, is my chosen methodology for this study. Qualitative research seeks to uncover meanings and perceptions on the part of the people participating in the research, viewing their understandings against the backdrop of their overall worldview or culture (Crotty, 2003, p. 7). The fundamental premise here, as in most qualitative approaches, "is that reality is constructed by individuals interacting with their social worlds—that is, making sense of the world through their individual experiences of it" (Lana-Khong, 2004, p.15). In other words, as Schram (2006) argues, it "proceeds from the assumption that ideas, people, and events cannot be fully understood if isolated from the circumstance in which and through which they naturally occur" (p. 9).

Creswell (2003) further affirms my choice of qualitative approach in this study. He argues that qualitative inquiry is the methodology of choice when "… not much has been written about the topic or the population being studied, and the researcher seeks to listen to participants and build an understanding based on their ideas" (p. 30). Not much has been written about the Igbo community in Chicago. There is a need to hear their stories. Narrative inquiry will enable me to hear and learn from their experiences in relation to their engagement in the education of their children.

Narrative Inquiry

Having been a priest of the Catholic Church for over eighteen years, I have used stories, both real and fictional, to preach, teach, minister, and counsel people. What informs my frequent use of stories in ministries is what I regard as the power of story.

Fundamentally, stories are about life experiences that are shared (Clandinin and Connelly, 2000). Narrative inquiry becomes a channel of disseminating the stories of participants as analyzed by the researcher. Stories have the power to communicate complicated messages in a simple but profound manner and consequently help people to internalize enduring lessons of life. Whenever I hear a story, I imagine myself in it, and the story becomes a tool for reflection of life. Simply, stories lived and told educate the self and others (Clandinin and Connelly, 2000, p. xxvi). Stories of Igbo parents' involvement in the education of their children will educate me and others.

Phillion (2002) identifies another power of story. According to her, narrative, which is rooted in the present, reaches out to the past and turns an eye to the future (p. 20). One of the reasons I use stories in my ministry is because they help the audience connect life activities of the past, present, and future. In other words, a listener listens to the past, applies it in the present, and looks forward to or prepares for the future (Clandinin and Connelly, 2000). Thus, standing in the present to tell and reflect on the stories (lessons of the past embedded in their stories) of Igbo parents' involvement in the education of their children becomes a way of preparing for their future engagement in the education of their children.

Another power of story lies in its ability to provoke the mind. Stories provoke thinking, stretch the mind, raise questions, and suggest answers. For example, after using stories in preaching, I have often been asked by some members of the audience what happened to a particular character in the story. This tells me that the individual was not only listening attentively but also thinking and developing a relationship with the characters in the story. We reaffirm stories, modify them, and create new ones (Clandinin and Connelly, 2000). Through reflection and analysis of the stories of Igbo parents' involvement in the education of their children in this study, new stories will emerge.

Furthermore, the link between narrative, context, and experience in research is another reason for my choice of narrative inquiry. Narrative inquiry aims at how people structure the flow of experience to make sense of events and actions in their lives—that is, how people contextualize experience and knowledge (Schram, 2006, p. 104). It is hard to separate experience and narrative (Clandinin and Connelly, 2000); consequently, narrative inquiry provides me a good platform to understand the experience of Igbo parents in Chicago relative to their involvement in the education of their children. One of the realities of life is that

> [p]eople do not deal with the world event by event or sentence by sentence. Instead, they frame these events and sentences in larger structures—narratives or stories—that provide context for interpreting the meaning of these parts. (Schram, 2006, p. 105)

The experience of parental involvement of Igbo families in Chicago in their context and based on their own meaning is what this study seeks to understand. The theory of overlapping spheres of influence assumes that parents and families of every background exert influence on the education of their children. I am interested in hearing first-hand stories—experiences—of how Igbo parents feel they influence the education of their children in their respective ecological systems so that we can better understand the meaning and practice of parental involvement in this immigrant community.

Methods

In this section, I present how I recruited participants and collected and analyzed data. Parents constitute the prime source of data for this study. I interviewed participants to elicit their stories of parental involvement and analyzed them to provide answers to the questions this study seeks.

Criteria for Selection of Participants

Participants must be residents of Chicagoland, who are either an Igbo mother or a father or a non-biological caregiver/guardian, who plays a parental role in the life of a child or children. (All such caregivers will be termed "parents" in this study). In addition, such parent (as defined above) must have one or more children attending a public or private elementary, middle, or high school, but they must not be homeschooled. Parents with children in lower grades of elementary school are prioritized to be chosen as participants. This is because parental involvement tends to be more active and more explicit in lower grades of schooling (Epstein, 2001; Lightfoot, 2003). In addition, a participant must have been a Chicagoland resident for over a year, and their children must have completed at least one school-year cycle in Chicagoland, thus offering parents of such children the opportunity to experience a school year in its entirety so that they have sufficient experience to discuss.

Number of Participants

Qualitative inquiry generally focuses on small samples, which makes for in-depth understanding of the subject of a study (Patton, 2002). I interviewed ten parents—six females and four males—for this research. My choice is also informed by the fact that other studies closely related to mine interviewed participants ranging from three to eight (Lightfoot, 1978; 2003; Lopez, 1999; He, 2002a; Lana-Khong, 2004; Smith, 2008).

Recruiting Participants

Recruiting participants for this study involved the following:
1. Using e-mail and phone calls, I contacted those parents (those who I am acquainted with or were recommended to me by some DePaul students who know about my research topic) who meet the criteria as potential participants. I know some Igbo parents because of my participation in the Igbo community in Chicago. My strategies of selecting participants I am familiar with or who were recommended to me is known as snowball sampling (Patton, 2002). An advantage of snowball sampling is using known social networks to select potential rich-information participants or cases (Patton, 2002).
2. Using a phone script for recruiting potential participants, I called these prospective participants to explain the study and invite them to participate in the study. Through this step, I was able to recruit the required number of participants for the study and scheduled for the time and venue of the interview. I used e-mail and telephone calls to confirm the time and venue for interview.

Data Collection

Parents are the primary source of data for this study, although I anticipated that participants may volunteer some archival data. Since none was volunteered, parents selected for the interviews became the only source of data.

Interviews

According to Rubin and Rubin (2005), interviews operate for qualitative researchers like night-vision goggles. It not only permits them to see what ordinarily is not in view but also examines what is often looked at but seldom seen (p. vii). In addition, it enables the researcher to enter into the participants' perspectives and gather their stories (Patton, 2002, p. 341).

I conducted in-depth interviews with ten parents. Each interview lasted between 63 to 104 minutes.

I used a semi-structured interview guide. Instead of closed or leading questions, I used broad, open-ended questions that were designed to encourage participants to share their own personal experiences and views as they determine appropriate and pertinent (Creswell, 2003; DeCuir-Gunby, 2007). It also allowed the participants to have or share control over these discussions; after all, it is their stories that are the focus of the interviews. Follow-up (probing) questions were used to maintain focus on the topic of this study and to explore more deeply pertinent themes as they arose.

I recorded all the interviews using a digital tape recorder and with an audiotape recorder as a backup in case of technical difficulties. I transcribed the interviews verbatim.

Language Used for Interviews

All the interviews were conducted in the English language because all the participants are fluent in English language. It is also the language of communication in their new community (United States). The English language is Nigeria's national language. The participants, like me, also are all fluent in the Igbo language. However, there were a few occasions during the interview when some participants switched from English to Igbo and Igbo to English or used Igbo sentences or proverbs to make a point. In such cases, I transcribed those sentences in Igbo, wrote them in italics, and used the transcribed excerpts in this book. I translated those sentences into English language and most often explained them where necessary.

Schedule and Venue of the Interview

In scheduling the interviews, I followed what was convenient for participants. Few of the participants were gracious enough to call and requested for a reschedule. Seven of the ten interviews took place in the homes of the participants. Others were in a room of a neighborhood university, in a high school classroom after class, and in a Starbucks. All interviews took place between February 28, 2010, and April 22, 2010, approximately one interview per a week.

Interview Process

The questions in the Interview Guide (which I developed) served as the compass for interviewing the parents. The questions revolved around the following themes: background information of the participant, parents' perception of involvement in children's education, and the child's home environment and the parents' experiences of involvement in the education of children. Other themes include the nature of interaction between parent and the school of his/her children, the nature and channels of communication and challenges. I used follow-up questions to clarify the participants' positions on issues raised. I made it known to the participants that there is no wrong answer to the questions.

Archival Data

Although I left it at their discretion, none of the parents in the study offered any archival data, such as report cards, school newsletters, letters (communications between family and school), and school websites.

Research Journal

I kept a journal during the research process to record my research procedure (audit trail), thoughts, questions, feelings, emerging analytical ideas, and any other things that may have been helpful in developing analyses and interpretations. The entries of the journal became part of the sources for writing the biographies of participants (see chapter 5) and the methodological reflection at the end of the study.

Data Analysis

Data analysis moves from raw data (interviews) to evidence-based interpretation. It entails classifying, comparing, weighing, and combining materials to extract the meaning and implications, to reveal patterns, or to stitch together descriptions of events into a coherent narrative (Rubin and Rubin, 2005). Through this process, the researcher constructs informed, vivid, and nuanced reports that reflect what the interviewees said—the opinions and policies expressed in the archival data that respond to the questions the researcher seeks to answer (Rubin and Rubin, 2005).

I used the following steps to analyze the data: (a) listening to and transcribing audio tapes, (b) coding and sorting the data, and (c) creating a visual analytical scheme.

Transcribing the Interviews

The first step in transcribing was to upload the interviews from the digital recorder to the computer and label them. While using a foot paddle to control the speed of playback, I listened and typed the interviews on paper word for word. Replaying of the tapes several times afforded me the opportunity to go deeper into the minds of the interviewees and thereby added to the quality of the data available to me.

Coding, Sorting, and Analysis

According to Emerson, Fretz, and Shaw (1995), coding and sorting are systematic processes of sifting through many pages of data of discrete and often loosely related incidents (stories). Coding allows the researcher to sort statements by content of stories, concept, theme, or event rather than by the people who gave the information or the archival data (Rubin and Rubin, 2005). An additional reason adduced by Emerson et al. (1995) for coding is the need to produce a coherent and comprehensible analysis for readers, who are not directly acquainted with the social world of the participants (p. 142). I read the transcribed material and then manually coded the data. I then sorted the coded data into themes related to the research questions and other issues that emerged during the interview.

After coding and sorting concepts and themes, I visually represented the data. One of the aims of this is to establish links between the themes and concepts that emerge during sorting and coding. This process helped to deepen the analysis.

Storing Data

I stored the data in a secure place, in a locked cabinet at home accessible only to me, and in my password-protected personal computer.

Research Considerations

Broadly, there are two main research considerations, namely, quality and ethical issues. From these arise some pertinent questions: did I, the researcher, maintain integrity both methodologically and ethically all throughout the study (Schram, 2006)? Are the researcher, the data I collected, and the product (the result of the research) credible and consistent with standard research principles? Or in the words of Lofland, Snow, Anderson and Lofland (2006), did I provide the reader "with a clear description of systematic and theoretically warranted processes of data collection and analysis" (p.170)? Did the researcher have the interest of the research participants at heart (Schram, 2006)? In this section, I will discuss the quality and ethical considerations of a qualitative study.

Quality Consideration: Establishing Trustworthiness

Lincoln and Guba (1985) articulate the issues at stake with regard to quality consideration: "How can an inquirer persuade his or her audiences that the findings of an inquiry are worth paying attention to, worth taking account of? What arguments can be mounted, what criteria invoked, what questions asked, that would be persuasive on this issue" (p. 290)? Besides, how did I, the researcher, address these challenges and enhance the credibility of my study and conclusions (Schram, 2006, p. 173)? My discussion of quality will be in two parts: first, the criteria for judging the quality of the study and, second, the strategies I will use to address its trustworthiness as indicated above.

Criteria for Establishing Trustworthiness

The four criteria for judging the soundness of a qualitative research—trustworthiness—that Guba and Lincoln posit are credibility, transferability, dependability, and confirmability (1985; Patton, 2002; Shenton, 2003).

Credibility—Are the Findings of the Research Plausible?

Credibility as a criterion for establishing the trustworthiness of research seeks to convince the reader that the researcher presents a "true picture of the phenomenon under scrutiny" (Shenton, p. 63). The burden is on me, the researcher, to prove that the interviewees, my representation of participants' stories, and the analysis of them are believable or credible.

Transferability—Can the Result Be Applicable or Relevant to Other Contexts?

At the heart of the issue of transferability is the question, "how might my inquiry contribute to an understanding of similar issues in other settings" (Schram, 2006, p. 59)? It is important to note that the responsibility of transferability rests with the reader. My responsibility as a qualitative researcher is to do a thorough job of providing sufficient detailed information (thick description of the phenomenon and assumptions) in ways that will help the reader relate to the experiences and then make a judgment about transferability (Shenton, 2004). That is, readers consider if these dynamics are possibly relevant in settings you are familiar with.

Dependability—Do the Data Have the Same Meaning as the Researcher Asserts?

Lincoln and Guba (1985) established a link between credibility and dependability, noting, "there can be no credibility without dependability" (p. 316). From this perspective, dependability has to do with whether the data I will report are actually saying what I meant to say. Can a reader depend on the meaning I ascribe to the data I present in the study? Do the data I report have the same meaning as what I am asserting?

Another aspect of dependability has to do with research as a systematic process. Therefore, dependability as a criterion for judging the trustworthiness of a research is to ask whether the researcher followed the step-by-step process of research systematically (Patton, 2002, p. 546). Another way to think about this is to ask whether the data are skewed or influenced by the way the research was done or by any other external influences.

Confirmability—What Is the Extent of the Researcher's Bias, Interest, or Neutrality?

The following questions articulate the issues of confirmability: Are the findings of the study grounded in data? Or are themes, categories, and inferences derived logically from the data? Irrespective of my bias or interest, can others confirm my findings?

It is not uncommon for qualitative researchers to have certain assumptions and perspectives about a research project. Confirmability as a criterion focuses on the degree to which the researcher's bias, interest, or motivation influence the result of the study. In essence, confirmability ensures that the result of the study is the experiences and ideas of the participants, rather than a reflection of researcher's preferences and motivation (Shenton, 2004).

In sum, I have presented the four criteria—credibility, transferability, dependability and confirmability—with which to evaluate the trustworthiness of my qualitative study; what remains is to outline the strategies I used to affirm the soundness of this study—that is, how I applied these four criteria.

Strategies for Establishing Trustworthiness

I will discuss various strategies I used for establishing the four criteria of trustworthiness. There are some overlaps of strategies for these criteria, as particular strategies may address multiple criteria. Lastly, I will present myself—my positionality—in relation to the research.

Thick Description

What I have already presented under the section methods—data collection and analysis—are, in part, strategies for establishing the trustworthiness of the study. "Thick description" implies using a detailed descriptive language as a strategy for promoting credibility, transferability, dependability, and confirmability of the study pertaining to data. I used the words of the participants in my reporting and analysis (see chapters 6–11). I provided the background information of the participants, which I elicited during the interviews (see chapter 5). Such information helped to convey the actual situation and thus added to the trustworthiness of the study. Primarily, the application of thick description enhanced the transferability and credibility of this study.

Adopting an Established Research Procedure

Research is a systematic process. I followed acceptable qualitative and narrative inquiry research steps. Such includes selecting participants, using interview guides, conducting and taping in-depth interviews, transcribing, coding, analyzing, and reporting the interviews. The steps that I took have been proven successful in previous studies related to mine. Following a standard research procedure added to both the credibility and transferability of this study.

Audit Trail

Ordinarily, an audit trail refers to a record of communication or transaction. As already noted, research is a systematic process, and as such, I presented a step-by-step research process, which anyone interested in the study can follow. Since there cannot be an audit trail without a residue of records of the research process (Lincoln and Guba, 1985), the following materials are available for auditing the study: the participants' recruitment flyer, interview guide, commentary on the exact processes of doing the research (in the journal), and a clear write-up of the procedures and research experiences, including a methodological reflection. This audit enhances the credibility, dependability, and confirmability of the study.

Member Checking

Member checking is a strategy to determine the accuracy of the data and its analysis. It involves returning the data, analytic categories, interpretations, and conclusions to the interviewees, from whom the data were originally collected, for review to see how well it represents his/her understanding (Lincoln and Guba, 1985). I asked each participant to review the transcribed interview to ascertain the credibility of the data. For some participants, I did the checking over the phone, while for some, we met and went through the data line by line to make the necessary corrections. Among other advantages, Lincoln and Guba (1985) note that member checking will afford my participants the opportunity to correct any errors that might arise and equally challenge any perceived wrong interpretation (p. 314). Member checking strengthens the credibility and dependability of my research.

Peer Review

Creswell (2003) refers to peer review as "peer debriefing." It involves locating a person or peer, who will play devil's advocate for the study. The peer reviews and asks questions about the study so that the account will resonate with people other than the researcher. The uninterested peer probes and explores the researcher's biases and basis for interpretation. In sum, according to Lincoln and Guba, (1985), through the probing and exposing questions of the peer, it not only aims to keep the researcher honest but also helps him/her to be reflective about the past and future procedures of the research. The two people I asked agreed to be my peer reviewers[15].

The Researcher's Positionality and Background

To enhance the credibility of a study, Patton (2002) recommends stating personal and professional information—experience, training, and perspective—about the researcher, because such information may affect the data collection, analysis, and interpretation. It also helps readers to better interpret the research. He goes on to say that the essence of such step is that the researcher is the instrument in the qualitative inquiry (p. 566). Thus, I will first say a word or two about this research as a selective endeavor and then present relevant information about myself, the instrument of this qualitative inquiry.

Parental involvement in the education of children is a phenomenon that interests me. My experience in Borana, Ethiopia, as a school director and as an educational leadership intern in a Chicago Catholic school animated my interest in the role of family in the education of children. Hence, this research is a selective undertaking with the aim to understand the experience of the engagement of Igbo parents in Chicago in the education of their children.

---

15   One is currently a doctoral student; the second person, recently earned a doctoral degree. Both have had IRB training.

With this in mind and as a future educational leader, I looked forward to hearing the stories that Igbo families in Chicago will share with me.

I am a single male Igbo, who share a cultural background with the participants. I also come from the same geographical area, the southeast region of Nigeria, as the participants. However, we differ on some aspects of socioeconomic status.

I hold a Bachelor's Degree in Biological Sciences (B.Sc.) and Master of Arts in Theology (MA). As a Catholic priest, I have several years of pastoral and educational work in Nigeria and Ethiopia. Currently, I am a chaplain in a Catholic hospital on the northwest side of Chicago while pursuing a doctorate in education. These qualifications and experiences have given me a certain exposure and knowledge while obscuring others. I am not a parent or spouse, for example, and so have no personal experience as a parent.

My educational background, socio-religious status, and practical experiences are, at present, part of my being. One's personal biography is a primary lens through which the individual perceives reality. I monitored this fact by reflecting periodically during the research process, in a journal, on how my background is affecting my research work and vision. For the fact that I am not a parent, I expect that certain day-to-day parental issues might not come across to me easily; hence, I respectfully asked for explanations (without probing into the participants' privacy) for issues or things that might seem ordinary to parents.

Again, my educational qualification and experiences notwithstanding, fieldwork (the research process) was a learning opportunity for me. Hence, as a student (researcher) open to learning, I listened attentively to participants during the interviews and conversations. I considered no question too small for clarification during the interviews. I did not act as a teacher of the participants, but rather as their student. I allowed their stories to educate me. Their stories are the primary source of my data and text for my analysis.

The Igbo community in Chicago is almost 100 percent Christian but of different denominations. In addition to being a Christian, I am also a member of the Catholic clergy. The Igbo respect religious men and women, and priests are "in a position of power." Without denying my Christian identity and being a clergy, I presented myself primarily as a student. I stayed focused on the interview and did not go for interviews in my clergy habit or outfit. I recognized that the research and interactions with the participants was not an opportunity for religious activity or instruction or proselytization. Moreover, religious denomination is not one of the criteria for selecting participants.

Ethical Considerations: Did I Have the Interest of the Participants at Heart?

The main issues of concern here, as listed by Lincoln and Guba (2003), include doing no harm, obtaining fully informed consent, using no deception of participants, presenting reliable data, and protection of privacy and confidentiality.

Protection of Participants from Harm

The study does not pose any physical or psychological risks to the participants, except for personal time commitment for the interview. Each interview took between 63 to 104 minutes. All the interviews were completed in one session. None of the participants asked to split the interviews in two or more sessions. Since there are no wrong answers to the questions, a participant did not need to make special preparations for the interview. This, I believe, reduced the pressure on the side of the participants to prepare for the interview. In addition, the participants had the prerogative to choose the venue of the interview.

No Deception of Participants

This study seeks to understand how Igbo parents in Chicago are involved in the education of their children. The recruitment flyer and conversations during recruitment helped the participants know up front the purpose of the study and their expected role in the research. This was reiterated before the interview. The study is not about the private family life of the participants. It is also not about evaluating the performance of the children of the participants. Finally, I was open to answer any questions that any participant asked, especially with respect to the study.

Confidentiality—Protection of Participants' Identity

Confidentiality as an ethical consideration requires a researcher to keep the data—information about participants—confidential. I used pseudonyms for all participants and other people mentioned and locations in this research. The uploaded (digital) interviews were protected by the use of a password, while transcribed interviews appropriately labeled were always kept in one of my locked drawers at home. I am the only person that has the key to the drawers. I will delete the digital interviews and shred the transcripts after the study is completed following the requirements of DePaul's Institutional Review Board (IRB) regulations.

Privacy

Participants were invited to participate in the study without invading their privacy. The study is by voluntary participation. The purpose of the study, benefits, and the risks associated with being in the study were explained well to participants that helped them make informed decision about participation. Participants also had the prerogative to choose the venue and time of the interview.

Benefit

Right from the beginning of this research, I explained to the participants that they would receive no individual direct benefits. There might be an indirect benefit to the broader community and schools if this study is able to help raise awareness about ways families/parents are involved in the education of the children of the Igbo community in Chicago. I imagine that the participants enjoyed the experience of telling their stories and having the opportunity to be understood by educators. Participants thanked me for giving them the opportunity to participate in the study.

Risk

There are no foreseeable risks involved in participating in the interview beyond those experienced in everyday life. For one, the interview took participants' time and needed to rearrange their routine. I did not probe into areas that are emotionally sensitive. Furthermore, I made it known in advance that participation is voluntary, and any participant can withdraw at any time. None of the participants found any question emotionally sensitive or uncomfortable.

Informed Consent

The IRB-informed consent standards require that participants should understand the following issues: the purpose of the study, the benefits associated with being in the study, and the risks associated with being in the study. In addition to fulfilling the requirements of the IRB, I made sure that all participants knew that participation is voluntary. Participants can withdraw at any time during the research. I asked each participant to sign the participants' informed consent form before the interview after I made sure they understood the nature of the study and that they know what they are agreeing to. The time spent to go through the consent form by the participants varied. Some spent some time to read and signed it after a few questions.

Disclosure and Exchange

I explained to the participants that they have the right to know the results of the research. I offered each participant a transcribed e-copy of his/her interview to confirm whether it accurately represents his/her opinions or stories. I provided each participant with an e-copy of the study after defense and corrections. Again, as a public document, copies of my dissertation can be found in DePaul University library..

Conclusion

This study seeks to understand the experience of Igbo parents in Chicago with regard to parental involvement in the education of their children. In this chapter, I have presented a blueprint of how I conducted the research. I started by articulating the problem, purpose, and significance of the study. I did make known my methodology, narrative inquiry, and the reasons for such choice. I also presented how I recruited participants and collected and analyzed data. Finally, criteria and strategies I used to ensure that the study is methodologically and ethically sound were outlined and discussed.

I will next present the findings of the research, starting with the biographies of the participants.

CHAPTER 5

📖

Participant Biographies

In this chapter, I present the biographies of the participants in this study on how Igbo parents in Chicago are involved in the education of their children. In presenting the background of the participants, I took into consideration the fact that ours—the Igbo community in Chicago—is a community where most people know each other fairly well. Hence, my decision was to give only basic background information about the participants while omitting the details that would enable them to be easily identified.

Though the participants share some common characteristics related to their Igbo heritage, in some degree they differ in areas such as profession, family size, and the number of years they have lived in the USA. These differences make their stories unique and give color to their parental involvement experience. This goes a long way in enriching the Igbo collective experience of parental involvement in the education of their children in the Chicago area. The uniqueness of their stories will not come as a surprise to the average Igbo person because of the wisdom in the saying, *Ofu nne n'amu, mana ofu Chi anaghi eke.* "Though all the siblings of a particular family are born of the same mother, nevertheless their destinies are different." It simply denotes that siblings of the same parents, who have certain things in common and share basic family circumstances, differ in life experiences, stories, and destinies.

Most of the participants have a college education either here, in Nigeria, or elsewhere. A few have even acquired multiple degrees. For some, because they could not find a job with a college degree from Nigeria, it became necessary to obtain additional training or to go into a different field, where there are better chances of securing gainful employment after graduation.

The interviews, which ranged from one to two hours in duration, were conducted mostly in the homes of the participants. However, three were conducted in other places, such as a library. All the participants chose the venues, and the interviews were held at a time of day that was most convenient for them. For the interviews that took place at the homes of the participants, there was always the Igbo welcome rituals—*Icho Oji*[16]—upon my arrival.

Brief Biographies of the Participants

Here I will present brief biographies of the participants along with a description of some incidents that occurred during the interviews in order to provide a sense of the context in which to understand the participants better. These brief biographies of the participants, I hope, will be a window for the readers of the participant stories that I will present in the subsequent chapters. To preserve confidentiality, the names used here are not the real names of the participants or family member (spouse or children), and any details or information that would reveal their identity has been left out. My choice of these names is arbitrary, and in most cases, I have selected common Igbo female and male first names. Before presenting each participant's biography, I presented a synopsis of the participants (see table 1).

---

16   *Oji* or kola nut is a seed from a tree known biologically as *cola acuminate* if the seed has more than two cotyledons or *cola nitida* when the seed has only two cotyledons (Ugbala, 2003 and Ukaegbu, 2003). Cola acuminate, otherwise known as *Oji Igbo* or Igbo Kola Nut, which is planted and eaten in different parts of Nigeria, grows in different West African forests (Emenike, 2002 and Ugbala, 2003). Kola nut occupies a unique place in Igbo traditional life and rituals. *Oji* is used in Igbo welcome rituals. In fact, it is the first thing served to any visitor to an Igbo home (Emenike, 2002; Ugbala, 2003 and Ukaegbu, 2003). According to Ugbala (2003), "among the Igbo the kola is used according to tradition for rituals, for marriage ceremonies, title taking, offering or prayers at traditional ceremonies, to welcome visitors and to introduce a very important discussion and request." The kola nut in Igboland constitutes a remarkable social symbol of hospitality, life, peace, goodwill, kindness, reconciliation, and integrity (Ukaegbu, 2003). The centrality of *Oji* among the Ndigbo of Nigeria can be compared to the place of coffee ceremony (*Buna Qala*) among the Borana people of southern Ethiopia. Because the kola nut is not readily available in the homes of Igbo in the diaspora, Igbo custom allows for improvisation— that is, to use drinks, fruit, snacks, and even food in place of the seed for certain rituals like the welcome ceremony.

Name of Participant	Name of Spouse	Time in Chicago or the United States	Education and Occupation(s)	Number of Children, Age	Public or Private School(s)
Njideka (F)	Chijioke (Husband)	Born in the United States, arrived in Chicago in 1999	Medical profession	Four, ages 11 months to 7.5 years	Both local suburban private and public schools
Nsobundu (M)	Amaka (Wife)	30 years in the United States and 20 years in Chicago	Private business, self-employed	Four, ages 8–19 years	Public school and boarding school
Nkolika (F)	Okey (Husband)	2000	International relations degree from a Nigerian university, health profession, attending school to upgrade	Three, ages 22 months to 6 years	Private school (nonsectarian)
Nneka (F)	(Single Parent)	2001	Mass communications degree from a Nigerian university, media professional in Nigeria, retraining for a health profession	One, 6 years	Suburban faith-based private school
Nnamdi (M)	Uche (Wife)	28 years in the United States and 25/26 years in Chicago	MBA from a US university, self-employed	Three, ages 7–19 years	Public, private, and special schools

Name of Participant	Name of Spouse	Time in Chicago or the United States	Education and Occupation(s)	Number of Children, Age	Public or Private School(s)
Nneamaka (F)	Obinna (Husband)	25 years in the United States and 23 years in Chicago	Math/statistics degree from a Nigerian university, education master's degree, and certification in the United States	Five, ages 14–24 years	Faith-based private school and public school
Nebeolisa (M)	Chidimma (Wife)	22 years	Medical profession	Three, ages 2–7 years	Public school
Nonye (F)	Single Parent	10 years	Educator	One, 19 years (girl)	Private school
Nnaemeka (M)	Ijeoma (Wife)	30 years in the United States and Chicago	Self-employed	Five, ages 5–16 years	Private faith-based and public schools
Nwakaego (F)	Emeka (Husband)	11 years in Chicago	Medical lab science and technology degree from a Nigerian university, attending school to go into a new field, has a private business, helps her husband in his construction business	Five, ages 4–9 years	Faith-based private school and public school

Table 1: Outline of Participants' Biographies

Njideka

Njideka, or "Njide" for short, was born in a traditional Igbo home in a very strong Nigerian community on the West Coast of the USA. She has lived in other parts of the United States as a student. In fact, it was during the last years of her professional training in Chicago that she met her husband, Chijioke. She has been living in a western suburb of Chicago for more than ten years with her husband and four children. Njide and Chijioke are both in the medical profession. Her four children, whose ages range from seven and a half to eleven months, were all born in Chicago.

The choice of school for their children is always a big decision-making process for Njideka and her husband. Their children attend both local public and private schools. For example, the three-year-old attends a private preschool while the six- and seven-year-olds attend public school. Though she attended private faith-based schools from nursery through secondary school, Njideka and her husband had to consider many factors in choosing schools for their children. Academic factors top their consideration. Hence, they settled for local public schools for the older children over the faith-based private school in their neighborhood. They tapped into the experiences of other parents, who had been in the neighborhood longer before making their choice. However, as strong believers in moral and religious education, they believe that family religious practices and parish Sunday school are essential supplements to public school education.

Educating children is a complex phenomenon that involves home, school, community, church, and interactions with peers. It is a process that demands a lot, and it requires that parents give time with patience, gentleness, perseverance, dedication, and continuous guidance of the children.

Parental involvement to them means a serious commitment in investing in the children, their future, and that of the nation. Njideka says that no parents can afford not to, although people have different ways of going about it. Schools and parents have no option other than to work together in educating children to be responsible citizens. High standards for children must be set. Njideka believes that because her educational experience has gone well, she is obliged to provide the same, if not more, to her kids. Thus, she not only sets high standards and expectations for her children even at an early age but also does everything to ensure they meet those standards and expectations.

The interview took place in the basement of her home. Her husband took care of the kids during the interview, making sure that we were not distracted. After the interview, we went up into the living room and sat around the immovable marble kitchen table, where we had a nice conversation and dinner.

Nsobundu

Nsobundu came to the United States almost thirty years ago as a student. Since he arrived, he has lived in other parts of the country before settling in Chicago twenty years ago. He now lives in a western suburb of Chicago with Amaka, his wife of twenty-three years, and their four children, whose ages range from eight to nineteen. Nsobundu and Amaka had their tertiary education here in the United States. He is self-employed in the construction business. His children are at different stages of their education, from elementary and secondary school to college.

He does not bemoan the fact that his children are not in private school. In fact, he does not regret this because private schools are very expensive. Moreover, the majority of successful people in this country are not at all the ones that went to private schools. Many successful and well-educated Americans went to public schools, he noted, and then added that if a family can afford private school for their children, it's quite acceptable. His daughter, who is in a gifted program, went to public school. In addition, his eight-year-old son is not in a private school, but he already has the articulation of an adult. However, he suggests that there might always come a time when a child could need polishing in a private school. In general, Nsobundu is quite happy to have his children in public school. For him, the most important thing is to monitor his children's academic progress and work with the school on their educational development. It takes an ongoing collaboration between the school and home. He is of the opinion that the education of children requires time, patience, money, sacrifice—"you starve yourself to make sure your kids progress"—guiding them through the right career, which involves identifying what each child has a passion for and helping them to make good choices.

Nsobundu is blessed to have had parents who were involved in his education in Nigeria. His dad was an educator, and that made a big difference during his school days.

The interview was originally scheduled to take place on April 11, 2010, but was moved to April 14, 2010, at the request of the participant. Before the interview, which was to start at 8:00 PM, Nsobundu asked me to join all of them for dinner, an elaborate Igbo welcome ritual. Both the dinner and the discussion while eating were good pre-interview exercises.

Nsobundu asked his wife to participate in the interview, which started at 8:46 PM. About twenty minutes into the interview, a neighbor came "unannounced," interrupting us to thank Nsobundu for his support during his brother's funeral. I had to stop the tape to welcome the neighbor. Amaka invited the neighbor to the dining area, where she continued to meet with him. Meanwhile, we resumed the interview. The second interruption came when Nsobundu's youngest son, who was supposed to be sleeping by then, came down to complain about something I didn't quite understand. Nsobundu had to attend to him. A third interruption was a phone call from his son, who was in a boarding school in southern Illinois. Before these interruptions, Amaka would occasionally contribute to the interview, but she had to attend to the neighbor. After the interview, their neighbor and Amaka joined us for conversation.

Nkolika

The interview with Nkolika (Nkoli) took place in the kitchen of her home. We used the breakfast table while her three children were in the living room, which was next to the kitchen, watching their favorite Saturday TV kids programs. However, there were occasional pauses in the interview whenever Nkoli went to see what was happening when she hears crying or unusually high-pitched children's voices. These interruptions were understandable because her husband had gone to work, and she was the only one left there to supervise the children.

Nkoli was born in the United State but was raised in Nigeria. She came back to the United States after finishing her elementary, secondary, and tertiary education in Nigeria in 2000. Because she had gone back to Nigeria at an early age, it was not all that easy to adapt to the ways of the United States when she finally came back in 2000. She is married with three children, who were all born here in Chicago. Two of them are six and four years old, and she has a twenty-two-month-old baby. They reside on the north side of Chicago.

She was "forced" to go into health care because that is where she could easily find a job. This required her to go back to school to qualify for her newly chosen profession. Her husband is currently working in the health-care industry while he is going through retraining and upgrading his skills to become certified again for the medical profession.

The choice of school for her children really comes down to a matter of convenience. The public school in their neighborhood, though cheaper and having a good academic rating, did not suit her work schedule, so she had to settle for a private school that accommodated her work schedule. The education (including schooling) of her children dictates the pace of her life here in Chicago. This will continue until they become fulfilled and happy adults—her dream for her children.

She is happy with the school her eldest daughter attends, because of the way the teachers interact with parents for their children's education. She talked about how her daughter's teacher had discovered that her daughter lacked certain important social skills. Nkoli described to me how all three—parent, teacher, and student—worked together to improve them. She believes that it was the teacher's interest in the education of her child that brought about this discovery and its resolution. She sees herself as both a supporter and a partner with the school in the education of her children. On reflection, she said that she feels most to be a partner because, at the end of the day, education benefits everyone: her children, her family (husband, herself), and ultimately, the community.

In addition to the financial, emotional, and physical efforts involved in educating children, there is also the learning from other parents and the sharing of experiences with them that can take place. This is why sometimes Nkoli shares and learns from the experiences of her colleagues at work (especially those whose kids are of ages similar to hers). Nkolika uses the things she learned from her parents when she was in Nigeria in the upbringing of her children. She appreciates the support she gets from her husband immensely. She cannot imagine raising and educating her three children without him. She respects single parents who do it alone and sometimes wonders how they "make it."

Nneka

I met Nneka about six years ago in a christening ceremony—baptism ceremony of a child—hosted by an Igbo family. She lived briefly on the East Coast before joining her husband in Chicago in 2001. Her daughter Ogechi, who will soon be six, attends a faith-based private school in the western suburb where they live. Moral and religious development, academics, and security were all factors that influenced the choice of the school her daughter attends. Nneka's husband died soon after the birth of their daughter. Since then, she has been raising their daughter alone as a single parent. Though a professional with several years experience of working in a media organization in Nigeria, she is presently retraining to go into a health profession. Nneka had her elementary, secondary, and tertiary education in Nigeria before coming to the USA. She is very grateful to her parents for their involvement in her education and that of her siblings. Involvement in the education of her own child is more demanding in this country, but she is applying several things she learned from her parents about being involved in her daughter's education. It takes a lot to educate your child, she points out. It is not enough for your child to be a straight-A student. You must follow her every step of the way, keeping in mind that the school is the second eye of the parents. Educating a child is a challenge, but she faces it with joy. She is grateful for the immense support she receives from her neighbors, friends, faith community, and extended family in the overwhelming but fulfilling task of working with the school in the education of her child.

The interview took place in a private room of a university library in her neighborhood, and it lasted about ninety-seven minutes.

Nnamdi

Nnamdi is the first male I interviewed. The interview took place in a coffee shop on the north side of Chicago in the neighborhood where he lives. Nnamdi came to the USA about twenty-eight years ago to pursue a higher education. After his primary and secondary education in Nigeria, he worked in the financial sector in Nigeria before coming to the United States to go to the university. After two years of college in a Midwestern state university, he moved to Chicago to get his Master of Business Administration (MBA) degree in a private university. After that, he worked for corporate America for a while before setting up his own real estate and mortgage company. He is self-employed, which is why he can find time to be deeply involved in the education of his children.

Nnamdi is married with three children, all born here in Chicago, whose ages are nineteen, nine, and seven. Nnamdi's wife is attending graduate school while she works.

The primary influences in the choice of schools involve the talents of his children. Nnamdi looked for an institution that would work with him to develop his children's talents. For example, his daughter, who is inclined toward the arts, attends an alternative school where the emphasis is on art education. His eldest son is still attending both private and public schools with the goal of successfully developing his musical talents. There was also a financial consideration that constrained the choice of these schools.

Throughout the interview, Nnamdi narrated his stories more or less in the way of a philosopher. His criticism of today's schooling was interesting. For him, schools today are failing in the way they teach critical thinking and developing a sense of personal contentment, both which help an individual to develop personal responsibility and independence. He complains that schools are quickly becoming a place simply for preparing kids to take tests. In his way of seeing things, this means more work for parents in the education of their children. Despite this shortcoming, his children's schools are still very important to him, and he thinks that schooling should never be left to teachers alone. He sees himself as a partner and cheerleader but the one ultimately in charge of his children's education. He is the one who determines the foundation on which the school and society build the educational process for his children. For him, childhood education is a twenty-four-hour-a-day concern done at home, while driving to school, in the company of peers, and with school teachers.

At his request, we spent time talking on general topics—politics, theology, justice, and peace—before starting the interview. This pre-interview conversation, which lasted for more than forty minutes, was also an opportunity to get to know each other better since I had never met him previously. He was introduced to by my colleague at DePaul's Graduate School of Education, who knew about my research and interests.

Nneamaka

Being delayed by road construction, I called Nneamaka to notify her that I would be late. I was somewhat worried about this, but nonetheless when I arrived, the family—children, husband, and grandma—greeted me warmly. Nneamaka's husband, a good storyteller, warmed me up with some very interesting stories of his days at a university in the Deep South of the United States. His rib-cracking stories accompanied by the Igbo welcome ritual—*Icho Oji*—certainly eased any anxiety that I might have had before the interview began. The "entertaining interview preamble" was cut short when Nneamaka suggested that we move into a section of their big living room in order to start.

Nneamaka lives with her husband of almost twenty-five years in a south suburb of Chicago. She has five children—three boys and two girls. All of her children were born and raised in another part of the Chicago area, where they lived before moving to their present home four years ago. Apart from her youngest daughter, who is in middle school, the rest of the children are in either high school or college or have graduated from college. She had been to the USA twice before finally joining her husband in the late '80s, who was then still a student in a university in the Deep South of the United States.

Nneamaka did her primary school and tertiary education in Nigeria. She is blessed to have parents who were educators. That influenced the kind of education she received in Nigeria. She is applying some of the things she learned from her parents, as she is involved in the education of her children here. For example, most of her children attended a faith-based private school in their lower levels of schooling. In addition to the good academic program and strong discipline, religious instruction was another reason to choose a faith-based private school for her children. And it isn't simply academics that influenced her choice. If it were just a matter of academics, she noted that as an educator, "[she] can take care of that." This reflects her positive experience with faith-based private schools in Nigeria. However, she added that private schooling "does not come cheap."

Nneamaka, like her parents, is an educator in the Chicago public schools. Although she has a degree from one of Nigeria's first-generation universities— universities established in the early '60s—she had to go through the process of certification before practicing here. She is also an online adjunct professor of a university. She wears multiple hats as a daughter, mother, wife, and educator.

The interview lasted for 104 minutes. At the beginning, we were interrupted by a few phone calls. I imagine the calls concerned something that needed her personal attention, because before the interview she had asked not to be interrupted. She apologized for the interruptions, and the rest of the interview went smoothly.

Nebeolisa

Nebeolisa is the second male I interviewed. He lives in a south suburb with his wife and three children, whose ages range from two to seven. Nebeolisa and his wife are health-care professionals.

The interview did not start as scheduled again because of traffic congestion. Although I had left much earlier due to my previous experience, I was still late, and so I called to let him know I would be late. When I eventually arrived, Nebeolisa was already home, waiting for me. He left work a little earlier than usual because of the interview, saying that he used the opportunity of leaving work early to pick up his children from school. Usually, he or his wife picks them up from their neighbor's house when they come home from work. His wife, Chidimma, had not yet arrived; and in order to have a peaceful atmosphere for the interview, he told the kids to go and do their homework and that he would help them later. Before we began, he expressed his appreciation for my interest and effort in studying what he considers a very important subject for the Igbo community in Chicago. I replied that I was very grateful to him and to other participants, who graciously accepted to grant me interviews for the study. The only time in which the interview was interrupted was when his son came in to ask an important question. The rest of the interview went smoothly.

Nebeolisa first came to the USA twenty-two years ago for postgraduate studies. He went home in the early '90s to marry and then returned three years afterward. His children are in public schools, which he prefers to private schools. Nebeolisa believes that public schools give his children the opportunity to interact with children from different strata of society. He does not like the exclusivity of private schools, because they inadvertently tend to exclude members of society who cannot afford private schooling. Sometimes sending a child to a nonpublic school is not worth the expense, particularly at the elementary level, especially for those who live in exclusive communities. He did not take the decision to send his kids to public schools lightly; he took time to research it before making the decision. Nebeolisa made it clear, however, that security issues can temper his admiration for public schools and that he won't ever be ready to compromise his children's security. Also, he maintains that education is the responsibility of the family. Nebeolisa also acknowledged the influence of his father in selecting schools for his children. His father was one of the few Igbo who received university education in the USA during the '40s.

He sees himself as more than a partner in working with the school in the education of his children. He said, "I see it more as a partnership in the sense that I am actually the one who contracted with the school." He admits that educating children demands tremendous sacrifice on the part of parents, who literally live for their children's education.

The interview ended after about ninety-six minutes of lively exchange. After the interview, we talked generally about the Igbo community in Chicago and the Nigerian situation, expressing hope of a better future.

Nonye

Nonye came to the United States about ten years ago from Europe, where she spent two-thirds of her life. She spent almost a year in a small East Coast state before coming to Chicago. Nonye, who is an educator with the Chicago public school, has a daughter. Having attended schools in Nigeria and Europe, and now as a teacher in Chicago, Nonye has experienced education on three continents—Africa, Europe, and North America.

She attended faith-based private schools in both Nigeria and Europe. She is very grateful to her parents for giving her and her siblings a good education. For Nonye, a good education must be rooted in teaching moral and religious values (such as learning prayers, which are an extremely important part of a child's education, especially in the early stages of development). Rigorous academics and character development are equally important. These qualities influenced her choice of a faith-based private school for her daughter. The education of children is the most important responsibility a parent can have. No sacrifice is too great for the education of your child. That is why Nonye doesn't skimp on anything as she partners with her daughter's school (teacher) and any others, who are involved in the education of her child. What is encouraging to her in this challenging but fulfilling duty is watching her daughter's academic progress. Her daughter is a gifted child, who behaves responsibly, receiving several awards for her excellent schoolwork.

This is one of the interviews that took place outside the home of the participant. Nonye preferred a Thursday for the interview because she is usually free that day after 2:00 PM since she has no classes or lectures. The participant's student-teaching assistant (from a Chicago university) helped to set up a place for the interview in a classroom consisting of two student desks facing each other. She also posted a notice on the door to prevent distractions. Before the interview started at 2:08 PM, Nonye requested more information about the study, which I then provided. She took a few minutes to read the consent form carefully and signed it after asking a few questions. She added that she would have preferred to have the consent form sent a few days ahead of the interview so she could have time to study it. The rest of the interview went smoothly until it ended at 3:09 PM. She was happy to have participated in the study. She requested that I keep her informed of the progress of the study.

Nnaemeka

During the interview with Nnaemeka, his wife, Ijeoma, sat with us, occasionally commenting or shedding light on her husband's responses. The interview took place in their house in a south suburb. Before moving there, they lived in other parts of the Chicago area. Nnaemeka came to the USA almost thirty years ago to attend college. He is married with five children, whose ages range from five to sixteen. His children are at different levels of schooling, from kindergarten and elementary to middle and high school. He is self-employed, while his wife is a health-care professional. He is a big advocate of private faith-based schools. The discipline that these schools impart to their students is one of the main reasons he chose them. He noted his reason for this—that education is not just about getting good grades, even straight A's. Rather, the determiners of a good education are discipline, character, values, morals, responsibility, a sense of fairness, the ability to be rooted in one's culture, and the ability to tolerate and live with others who are different.

After the Igbo welcome rituals—the *Icho Oji* ceremony—the interview began. Ijeoma told her children not to distract us during the interview. She also asked Grandma to take care of the kids to prevent them from interrupting the interview. But as they say, "kids will be kids." Occasionally, one or two of them would come in to demand something that Ijeoma had to provide. She also had to excuse herself to take care of two of her children, who came home from school during the interview, the school bus stopping in front of the house, dropping off each child. Ijeoma would occasionally contribute to the discussion at the invitation of her husband. But there were also times when she would contribute without an invitation. The interview, which lasted for ninety-five minutes, ended at 3:52 PM.

I had a late lunch or early dinner with them, during which we talked generally about Nigeria and of the experiences their two children are having while in Nigeria for secondary school.

Nwakaego

I made all the arrangements for the interview with Nwakaego's husband, Emeka. Actually, on my way to the interview, I took it for granted that I would interview Emeka. However, when I arrived, Nwakaego told me that Emeka had just left. When I asked what time he would be back, I was told that he had asked us to start and then he would join when he got back. I reflected for a moment that the story of the wife might be as good as the husband's, if not better, and so I agreed to that. Before we started, she told her kids to play in another part of the house so they wouldn't distract us during the interview, saying that if they stayed in the room, then they would have to stay quiet. Her last child chose to stay but, after a few moments, went elsewhere to be with her siblings anyway.

More than halfway into the interview, Emeka came back. In order not to interrupt, he just waved hello and then served us some refreshments. Then he quietly sat on the floor and watched us as the interview continued. He didn't contribute very much to the interview, except to confirm some of the stories his wife told me. The interview lasted seventy-three minutes.

Nwakaego came to Chicago almost eleven years ago, six of which was spent on the north side of Chicago. She is married with five children, whose ages range from four to nine. Her parents, especially her father, had a great zeal for education and schooling. They spared nothing in giving Nwakaego and her siblings a very good education in Nigeria. They all attended private school at the elementary level and some federal government colleges[17]—federally funded secondary schools. Federal government schools in the '70s, '80s, and '90s in Nigeria were the *ivy league* of secondary-school education. During the holidays, her father even provided private tutorials for them.

Though Nwakaego earned a bachelor's degree in Nigeria, like most immigrants, she retrained in another field for work in the USA. Currently she combines parenting, work, and schooling to upgrade herself. Even though the public schools in her neighborhood are good, she prefers faith-based private schooling for her children at least at the elementary and middle-school levels. As for discipline, morality, and values, she believes that private schools have an edge over public schools. Discipline for Nwakaego is fundamental to a child's schooling and education. She allows her children to attend public schools from Pre-K to third grade, but then she has decided to send them to a faith-based private school from fourth grade on. She is of the opinion that from fourth to eighth grade, teachers in public schools lose their grip on teaching

---

17   In Nigeria, secondary schools are also referred to as colleges. In the case of federal government colleges, it means federally funded and administered secondary schools by the Federal Ministry of Education (FME).

their students important lessons of discipline, morals, and values. However, the quality of the academic program is the decisive factor—the number one raison d'être—in the choice of schools for her children. She makes an effort to research the quality of the academic programs of prospective schools for her children. She does this online or by visiting the school personally to see the curriculum. Security is another factor that is important to her in choosing a school for her children. She admits that she doesn't have much control over the issue of security, except that she feels compelled to "get down on [her] knees" to pray for kids who are attending public school.

For Nwakaego, she agrees with the idea that good education is more than good grades. Also important are good behavior, character development, and how a child mingles with other members of the community, including elders. It takes the involvement of both parents and teachers to give a child a good education. It is impossible for the teacher or the parents alone to give children the good education they need. Education of a child is both tough and fulfilling. It demands sacrifice, time, patience, vision, lots of prayer, and constant communication with the school. Nwakaego cherishes the support of her husband, whom she regards as the pillar of their home. She said that she often wonders what she would do without him.

Conclusion

All the participants are working parents. Few are self-employed, while others are employees of the government or big- and medium-sized nonprofit organizations. Some combine the duties of parenting, working, and going to school. Two of the participants are single parents. The number of children per family ranges from one to five. The participant who arrived most recently came to Chicago about ten years ago, while the participant who has been here the longest arrived about thirty years ago.

In the next six chapters, I will present the findings of the research, which include how Igbo parents distinguish between education and schooling, their understanding of parental involvement, a description of how they practice it, the challenges they face, and their sources of support. Other aspects of the findings include Igbo parents' relationship with schools their children attend and the influence of their environment as they work with local schools in the education of their children.

CHAPTER 6

Education And Schooling

The participants of this study consisted of ten Igbo parents—six mothers and four fathers. Originally, three principal issues were the focus of this study, namely, (a) Igbo parents' perception of parental involvement, (b) practical ways they exercise their understanding of the concept, and (c) the challenges of parental involvement they face every day as recent immigrants in a new environment. However, other issues were raised during the interviews. After coding and sorting the data, I found it very lengthy; hence, I decided to present the findings in six different chapters (6–11). The six chapters follow the six main themes of the findings: (a) education and schooling, (b) Igbo parents perceptions of parental involvement, (c) parents' parental involvement practices (parents' account of parental involvement practices), (d) relationships between schools and parents, (e) parents' context—environment and parental involvement, and (f) challenges and support in educating children. At the end of each chapter, there is a summary and analysis section, where I will isolate relevant analytical points and discuss them.

My main intention in this chapter is to understand how Igbo parents in this study distinguish between education and schooling and, ultimately, how they understand parental roles within that broader notion of education. I asked them the following questions:

1. How can you distinguish between schooling and education?
2. What would you consider a good education for a child?

Next follows a presentation of their responses to these questions.

Distinguishing Between Education and Schooling

My question—how you can distinguish between schooling and education—came as a surprise to some participants, because most people tend to use the two words interchangeably, or they take it for granted that both mean the same thing. Some participants reacted as Nsobundu did, who had to pause for a moment and then confess, "I haven't thought about it [schooling and education] really." But many Igbo parents in this study pointed out that schooling and education are not the same. Schooling is a part of education. The essence of the question is to help parents identify their roles and that of the school in educating their children. Njideka attempts a definition of both schooling and education:

> So I think I would define "schooling" as what happens at the school and then maybe consider education ... there are so many different parts of training that go into learning. So both what happens at the school, what happens at the church, what we infuse into him at home—you know, even what he gets from his peers. Like education kind of is happening all the time just by living, and maybe schooling would be more specific to what the school imparts to him.

The next level of distinction focuses on the scope of education and schooling. Nonye points out that

> [s]chooling is when you go to school, the lecturing that you get there; that's what schooling means. Education, it's much more than schooling. It's the whole character building, intelligence building, everything. Education is bigger.

It even happens on the way to school (Nnamdi). Nsobundu, after confessing that he had not really thought about it, and pausing for a while, went ahead to distinguish education and schooling. Using labels like formal and informal, he noted that education is life, an infinite process, while schooling is a formal way of teaching and learning that can end with a certificate or diploma. However, you can get an education through schooling.

> But going to school, not everybody that went to school has all the education they are supposed to have. The distinction, there's a difference you know? The distinction is that in terms of ..., schooling has to be formal. And education ... you can pick up education on the street. You can pick up education as we interact and talk. It's [education] not about grades. It's about being able to stimulate those things you learned in academic restrictions within the, you know, the human existence or coexistence. I will say schooling, it's something that's ... it's official, you know? Like your child at kindergarten doesn't know so much. She goes to school to be taught certain things. But I will say education is infinite. You know you can educate yourself 'til you die. But schooling is something else, formal. They go to school to be taught about certain things. But

education, that's life. Every day you learn something. That can also be education. It depends on what you call education. Education can happen at both places. Every day you learn … You teach yourself. Maybe today you are behind a computer; you don't know … maybe how even to send e-mail. A colleague teaches you how to send an e-mail or how to send e-mail. You know that is education. That is informal. At the time, you're not going to be rewarded with any certificate. But I will say schooling ends with a diploma or a degree or a certificate or a grade. Well, education is something that you learn every day. Yeah, 'til you die, 'til you are in a grave. But you can get education through schooling too.

Nnaemeka sees both the similarities and differences between schooling and education. Like other parents, he establishes a link between them:

In some respects they are similar. In other respects they are dissimilar. Take for instance what I call schooling, in a way, for most people—at least for me—is like you have to be kind of … be confined to or go to a special place to have the knowledge or to receive the knowledge through people that know more than you, or at least have some knowledge they can impart to you. Education is happening at all times, at all places. It has no confinement. It has no walls. For me you can be educated in your room or in your house or in the … anywhere else, in the street or in most places. But schooling as I see it is that you have to go to, say for instance, an institution of learning to apply this. And that's the difference between, to me, schooling and education. And what my children are getting from where they are right now is not only that they are being educated but also being schooled. So they get the best of both worlds, and that's what we need in today's society to grow and to be able to, you know, mingle with other people.

Whatever level of distinction one is able to make between them, both education and schooling are essential for one to function in society today.

Education because, as you know, education … no matter where you are, is number one. It's the number one weapon that you use to advance in any society. So again education in school, education at home, education anywhere, everywhere is paramount. (Nsobundu)

Igbo parents in this study agreed that education happens outside of school settings and a wide range of other settings that include the home. Again they understand education as a broader concept than schooling, which implies a formal structure and reward system, such as obtaining a certificate or diploma or grade. In addition, it's not that education occurs just anywhere, but it is ubiquitous to one's life, without limits. This is unlike schooling that takes place within the confines of a building and eventually has a conclusion.

Having distinguished between education and school, noting that schooling is an essential part of education, I then asked Igbo parents what they considered a good education for their children to be.

Characteristics of a Good Education

Nsobundu said that good education is "not just about textbooks." Also, as Nneka notes, "it is not just books," or as Nebeolisa mentions, it is not about "good grades" alone but also about character, values, and being a responsible and informed citizen. Nonye says it best:

> Because education means that ... you know your values, you know your priorities, education is more than just having a good grade but having knowledge of the goodness of man and why you are alive. What is your purpose? What is the purpose of your life? So at the age of twelve, if the child knows that being well-educated will get me to that level to have the love of my fellow human beings, to appreciate life, and to value every ... what is more important than money, that is a good education. Having respect for your elders ... everything that makes you a rounded ... a well-rounded citizen of your country. Responsible citizen. Informed citizen. Be an ...informed citizen good grades. There is character in it. There is value in it. There is also social aspect—how you relate with other people. Yes, informed citizen of the world, having respect for other cultures. You know, cultural intelligence, knowing that culture affects behavior, you know. A lot of things go into it.

In other words, the participants suggested that a good education, among other things, expands one's horizons and grounds the individual in his or her culture. To be truly grounded in one's culture helps the individual to appreciate other cultures, they said, and a well-educated person therefore has the ability and willingness to apply critical thinking to his or her native culture as well as to other cultures of the world. Similarly, participants seem to believe that by expanding one's horizon, an individual can have better footing in order to be a global citizen.

> So a good education will kind of ground you to a culture or to something you cling to. But it can also expand your horizon to other

things all around you so that you have a better understanding of the world, of the universe. If you are well educated … education to me does not necessarily mean that you have achieved by the standards of Western tradition the last stage of, you know, like got your doctorate or … but education encompasses knowledge or some sense of the world in which you live so that you will be able to explain, at least try to understand and be able to move around not freely, but at least with considerable measure of ease in the world so that you will be able to relate to other people. (Nnaemeka)

Other features of a good education are expressed by Nebeolisa:

When I say he's got good education will mean, one, that he understands his environment. That means he understands who he is. He knows what America is all about. He knows what his calling is, because part of being educated is being able to discover your potentials and your skills, for he is equipped to face the challenges of adulthood. Because by the time he starts going to college he's an adult, he should be able to know how to relate … be an active member of the community. And then, two, or more importantly, has a firm understanding of his cultural identity. What does he bring to the table of this cause? Not just knowing the subject matter, but also being able to know … be aware of world events, world affairs, not just local things around his community but being a citizen of the world. That is being broad and understanding in his approach.

Participants see a link between good education, character, and behavior. Nonye said, "If you are educated, you will treat your fellow human beings better." In the same way that the Igbo people say *Anya ma oka kara-aka, ije tupebe ya bu aguo.* (You can recognize a mature or ripe maize when you see one. You do not need to unwrap it to know that it is mature; doing so is a sign that you are hungry). It is simply the appearance of an ear of maize that tells you whether it is ripe for eating or not. Similarly you can tell whether a person has received a good education through his or her character and behavior. But the aim of good education, according to Nneamaka, is to raise a successful citizen.

Summary and Analysis

According to the participants, it is clear that education, whether it occurs at school, at home, or anywhere else is paramount; and it is the number one weapon that both society and individuals need to advance (Nsobundu). Igbo parents' understandings of education and schooling are reflected in comments found in Dodd and Konzal (2002), that schooling in contrast to education is a more limited concept (p.101). They further note that schooling only refers to the responsibilities of teachers and administrators but that education includes the responsibilities of everyone, and that by extension, education includes everything that influences what children learn (Dodd and Konzal, 2002, pp. 100ff). That is, schooling refers to what happens in school settings alone and is primarily dependent on the explicit curriculum and educational policies set forth by the school.

Referring to the cardinal goals of traditional African education, Fafunwa and Aisiku (1982) list the following concepts: (a) to develop the child's latent physical skills, (b) to develop character, (c) to inculcate respect for elders and those in positions of authority, (d) to develop intellectual skills, (e) to acquire specific vocational training and to develop a healthy attitude toward honest labor, (f) to develop a sense of belonging, and (g) to encourage active participation in family and community affairs. In addition to educating a child to be a "citizen of the world" (Nebeolisa), the above list of goals seems a good summary of the notion of good education that the Igbo parents in this study expressed. It targets the integral development of the child. In other words, educating the whole child is the Igbo parents' approach to education, because they believe that a good education has intellectual, social, ethical, spiritual, and emotional traits.

Educating the Whole Child

Igbo parents agree that education occurs equally outside the four walls of school. Schooling is an essential part of education, which is why they work with the school in the education of their children. Such notion of education is geared toward raising a responsible citizen and a fulfilled adult, who will, in turn, contribute to the good of the society and not be a burden to it. For this reason, Igbo parents insist that education is not just grades or textbooks but includes character—the intellectual, social, physical, and psychological development of the child. Flowing from this perspective, Igbo parents believe that neither school nor family can successfully achieve this noble aim of educating the whole child. This idea of educating the whole child is not solely an Igbo idea but a traditional notion of education they have applied over the years, like many other traditional cultures, in their approach to parental involvement.

Educating a World Citizen

In addition, Igbo parents envision education for the global citizenship of their children. To be a citizen of the world is to be able to fit anywhere. It requires the broadening of one's horizons that leads to the respect and acceptance of others. Good education, Igbo parents believe, should be able to provide a platform in which to develop such a global perspective. In effect, educating the whole child to be a global citizen is part of what colors their approach to parental involvement.

This notion of education held by Igbo parents provides a context to understand their perceptions, practices, and the challenges of parental involvement in the education of their children. It is safe to say that they have a fair understanding of the concept of the social institution of education in which they are participating.

In the next chapter, I present the second main theme of the findings: Igbo parents' perception of parental involvement in the education of their children. Bearing in mind that a good education includes schooling and its features, I asked the participants what it takes to educate a child or to give a child a good education in order to have them speak more openly about their perception of parental involvement.

CHAPTER 7

Perceptions of Parental Involvement

Understanding the way in which Igbo parents in Chicago are involved in the education of their children starts with determining how they perceive the concept of parental involvement. Their perceptions are embedded in their narratives, which are responses to the questions I posed to them during the interviews. These questions include the following:

1. What role do you feel parents have in educating children?
2. What role do you feel schools have in educating children?
3. What does it take to educate a child or give a child a good education?

I present the perceptions that emerged from their stories under the following subheadings: (a) "What It Takes to Educate a Child," (b) "The Role of Parents in the Education of Children," (c) "The Role of School in the Education of Children," and (d) "Criticism of Schooling Offered by Parents in This Study."

What It Takes to Educate a Child

"[T]he only thing more important than education for me is the love of God, the respect for God. And after that, it should be the value of education, because if you are educated you will treat your fellow human beings better," says Nonye. And that is why, for the education of her daughter, she gives it all she has got. Nonye represents the view of Igbo parents, who believe that educating children takes a lot. Education of children takes everything (Nkolika). For example, in educating children, there are both physical and psychological demands. Time and energy is required to give love and care and to make the personal sacrifices necessary for the child's success. Additionally, there is the constant struggle to nudge and poke children to do their best, to manage finances, to set performance standards, and so much more. According to Nneamaka, some people these days prefer to have just one or two children, because educating each child takes so much time and energy.

Educating children requires parents to have immense patience as well as the humility to learn from other people:

> It takes patience. It takes love. It takes learning from other people. It also takes from reading and trying to model people, who you think are doing the right thing. When I say "the right thing," in terms of what I've come to know about the culture of the ... American culture that I know is that everybody is in a hurry. (Nneka)

It also takes perseverance, endurance, and patience, for which one has to ask God constantly (Nwakaego). She said, "You need all these virtues to encourage the kids even when they think they are failing." Nwakaego spoke about an incident, where she had to have extreme patience and perseverance in order to persuade her daughter, Ebele, to reenter a spelling bee contest. Ebele had become demoralized in the previous competition, where she came in second.

> In fact ... my daughter doesn't want me to ever mention her name in any of the spelling bees. Of course she's very, very good in a spelling bee, but the last one she went to, she got to the second position instead of the first position, and she missed that one word. So she never got that thing over her. I'm like it's not like that ... so she feels like she has disappointed everybody. I said, "Well, did anybody do anything?" Of course I said ... you did very well. I mean you tried ... but she doesn't want to participate. She doesn't like spelling bee[s] as we are speaking now. But I thought she doesn't have any option. She will be going for it. She will be trying out for it, and that's ... for me that's what I think, you know. It's sometimes ... you know sometimes I can understand their psychology sort of because of the shame. They thought they just brought it upon themselves because they did not pass. I don't want to buttress that shame. I try to tell them that that's the way life is. You win some, you lose some. When you lose, what do you do? You still continue, you know? You don't just go back and say, "Okay, I lost. I'm not gonna do any other thing." Some of the people that are out there, they have lost in so many things, but they still continued and are doing ... (Nwakaego)

Educating children to be successful and well-rounded citizens needs parents who are focused in what they are doing, constantly watching over their children. Nneamaka prefers the term "strong parents" instead of "focused parents" as she explained:

> It takes a strong parent ... in this community with all the distractions from TV and gangs and peer pressure, the parent really has to bring it home with the child down here. This is acceptable in this house, and this is not acceptable in this house. This is what goes on. So whatever they learn from school and they come back home, you have to kind of detox them, okay? Separate them into the ones we want and the ones we don't want. The ones you want, you build on it. The ones you don't want, you drive that out of the child's head. We don't want this in this family. Throw it away. We don't need it. And it's a constant ... you know, it's a constant struggle, constant ... you know, it's a process. It never ends, actually ...

Educating a child is a constant struggle that never ends. On the part of a parent participating in the educational process of a child, virtues like patience, perseverance, love, gentleness, and humility are required in the day-to-day interactions with the child. Besides these attributes, two active parents supporting each other will go a long way to reducing emotional and mental exhaustion that come with the process of educating a child.

Two Active Parents Educating Their Children is the Ideal

In addition to having the virtues of patience, gentleness, and perseverance, the ideal is to have both parents be active in their children's education. It gives a huge advantage to the educational process. Njideka considers herself to be lucky:

> I mean, first of all, I think it really helps to have ... I think it's ideal to have two parents, which I'm very fortunate that my children have the benefit of two parents, two involved parents. I think it also takes certain attributes within those parents, which I don't claim to have mastery of, but I'm working on it all the time—like patience, perseverance, just some ... gentleness just to endure a lot of the things that the kids will throw at you. Perseverance, gentleness, patience, those are the main ones. You also ... you want ... I mean the kids ... to educate kids, I think you have to try to be able to instill in them, you know, discipline. You know I don't think a kid can be really well educated without, you know, moral and spiritual aspects. So you have to be able to impart those things to them.

While sharing her thoughts on what it takes to educate children,

Nneamaka recognizes the value of having a husband, who is active in the education of their children.

> It's not just having the child. You have to make sure that you train the child well. You want to raise the child to be a contributing part of the society too. You don't want to raise somebody who's a burden to the society. So it's a lot of work that has to go in educating the child. Yeah, and that's why a lot of parents have one or two children because it's hard work. And thank God I'm not a single parent so I have help.

So it takes a lot emotionally and physically to educate a child. Parents who have an active spouse consider themselves to be lucky. However, the important role of school (teachers) is still required to effectively educate a child.

It Takes the Involvement of Parents and Teachers Working Together

It is not enough, even when both parents are taking active roles in their children's education. The fact is that children spend many hours per day in class with teachers during the school year. As a result, in spite of parental involvement, the involvement of the school and teachers is absolutely essential to educating children as Nwakaego emphasizes:

> It takes the involvement of parents and teachers working together. It cannot be just teachers. It cannot be just parents. The involvement of both [is required] ... more hands-on parents, more hands-on teachers.

And Nsobundu adds that although a good education requires the constant efforts of both parents and teachers, there is a price to pay if either the parents or school is not actively involved in the education of the children. "If any of you—school or parents—is lacking, it has an effect on the child" (Nsobundu). On the part of both parents and teachers, it also requires time for instructional and non-instructional activities, time for planning and administration, and time for supervising extracurricular activities.

It Takes Time to Educate Children

The way parents manage their time is a major part of what it takes to educate children. Njideka thought that time is the greatest need. "I think probably one of the biggest things is that you need time to be able to dedicate to educating them." Nkolika similarly thinks that discussion about what it takes to educate children should begin with how to manage your time. "It takes everything, a lot, including time … It starts with making out time" (Nkolika) for a lot of things you want to do with your kids and to work with other people involved in their education.

Nonetheless, the reality is that parents have to spend the majority of their time working for a living in order to pay their bills (Nneka). Parents are also obligated to dedicate a large portion of their daily life to the education of their children. For most parents, spreading their time between parenting and family life is a daily struggle. "It is a constant struggle, constant process that never ends" (Nwakaego). "It is a circle. It is continuous … Nonstop" (Nsobundu). The struggle is never ending, and for those unable to achieve the needed balance, Nneka suggests that "at some point you have to choose between having a good family—you know, raising your child well—and making money."

The constant struggle hopefully has a good outcome.

> The joy in it is that, you know, when the child succeeds, you know, the parent is glad, the community rejoices, and everybody is happy. But when the child doesn't succeed, then you know you haven't done a good job. (Nneamaka)

Since learning takes place at home, it requires that parents also take the time to make sure that the home environment is conducive to learning.

It Requires Creating a Good Home Learning Environment for the Children

Also, good education requires creating a good learning environment for the children at home. Otherwise, the goals of education of children will very likely be jeopardized.

> It takes providing the environment—the right learning environment. You know, if the children come home and all they can … there is no quiet environment for them to learn or there is a disinterest or parents are not willing to expose their children to other aspects of learning that they're not receiving in school. (Nebeolisa)

Discipline is another part of creating a good learning environment for children. "It takes the parents being able to bring discipline to the child. You know, because discipline is the key to learning," Nebeolisa added.

In the chapter on "Practical Ways Igbo Parents in Chicago are Involved in the Education of Their Children," I will present more stories on how they create a home environment that is friendly to learning.

Educating Children Requires Money and Others Resources

Educating children is expensive. Though education is expensive, Nonye considers paying tuition more important than everything else. In fact, it is her number one priority.

> Education is more important than anything, I think, also for an Igbo person, and that's why I was willing to pay that. I think I was paying almost $4,000 per year, and it was fine. When I came here newly, I didn't make much money, but that was the priority. I would cancel every other thing, every other thing but to have education and just housing and food—basic things, yes.

Educating a child is simply not "a piece of cake," as Nnaemeka puts it. It requires money and other resources. Parents have to make the money to pay for tuition and provide for the other educational and material needs of the children. These expenses include books, clothing, and nutrition, as well as enrolling them in summer school classes or other "programs that can help shape them into what they want to be" (Nwakaego). It really takes two incomes to fund the education of one's children, especially in the case of families with more than one or two children.

"It takes everything," "it takes a lot," and "it's a struggle" are some of the expressions I heard that echo the reality of the demands parents feel about educating children. To meet the obligation of educating children, both parents have to be active in the educational process, and at the same time, they have to actively cultivate their patience, gentleness, and perseverance with their children and also with teachers. And there are sacrifices that parents have to make that are unanticipated but significant, it turns out.

The Sacrifice Parents Make

Another key element in what it takes to educate children is the personal sacrifice, says Nebeolisa. "More than money ... it is the sacrifice that the parents will have to make, and I see that as the key, you see?" Participants' stories indicated that the sacrifices are enormous. During the interviews, I learned that the sacrifices come in different forms, depending on the circumstances of the parents. Some parents are single; others, though not single, wear multiple hats like being an employee, student, wife/husband, and mother/father. Also, there is the case of those parents who have a large family. It may require giving up one's personal life for the sake of the children. Two working parents may still need more money for educational expenses. Instead of buying things new, they may have to go to thrift shops to save money. They may have to work extra hours or even work extra jobs to pay for tuition and related educational and household expenses. They may have to schedule their work for odd hours at night or on the weekends to be able to spend time with the children while they are awake and finished with their homework and go to bed late and get up early. And in addition to all of that, they may actually have to change the friends that they socialize with, finding better role models for their impressionable kids.

While agreeing that the sacrifices are huge, Nebeolisa noted just why it is so necessary to make these painful sacrifices, especially for parents who really consider the education of children important:

> The sacrifice is enormous. You know, to really, really get the children to where you want them, there are certain things you don't do. The sacrifice in the sense that ... you see, I'm not gonna live in that half-a-million-dollar house or drive that huge luxurious car because if I have to do that, I have to work more hours to be able to maintain that. And then I won't have time to spend with them. So those are the sacrifices that are involved. You know if you want them to go to school in the best place, you have to save money for them to be able to go to school because you don't want them ... if they're really going to go higher than you, they wouldn't have to start with $250,000 debt because they went to medical school or $100,000 because they went to school ... they took a ... student loan to go to school. But it's because you helped pay their way so that they start off with zero instead of minus. (Nebeolisa)

Because the education of her daughter is more important than anything, Nonye invests everything into it, to the extent that she has now literally given up her life for the education of her daughter. Her inspiration is her favorite writer.

> One of my favorite writers is Elfriede Jelinek, an Austrian writer who said that a woman that has a child gives herself up ... in German, *Die frau, die ein kind bekommt, gibt sich auf.* The woman that has a child gives herself up. So for me it was clear that I have to give myself up until she's eighteen. So whatever wishes or goals or anything I had came second to whatever she needs to succeed in life, making sure that she has a place to stay and food and that I pay for her education wherever she wants to go. So it takes everything to educate a child. Yes, and that's my priority. But it's something you want to do. It's a pleasure. (Nonye)

Part of giving up her life includes shopping at a Salvation Army thrift store to save money for her daughter's tuition, enrolling her in summer programs, and to make sure that in the future, her daughter will not have any school loans to pay back after graduation. Not owing any money when she begins her adult life will greatly reduce stress and increase the opportunities for success.

> When I came here, I will take my daughter and we will go to Salvation Army and buy our clothes. And not because we couldn't be ... I was paying for private school. I was paying for... but we will go, and I will buy my furniture from the Salvation Army because I said, well, I kind of like solid wood. They last longer. I might as well go there because at least I know it's wood. And when it comes to food I would like to... I will always try to cook food at home, which is cheaper, than go to McDonald's or go out and, you know, go and sit in a restaurant and pay $35.00. We may do that ... it may be once- or twice-a-year outing. (Nonye)

The other sacrifice that Nonye makes has to do with her private life, namely, that a parent's lifestyle sends a strong message to the children. Children tend to imitate their parents' lifestyle. She goes extra miles to be a role model for her daughter.

> I also wanted to mention on the other part that it takes everything, even my private life ... being a single parent, even if I want to befriend a man, there were times I couldn't do it or let a man stay with me because I am living with a daughter I want to educate. So even your private life, you have to give up for that sometimes. (Nonye)

Nnaemeka and his wife are both employed. This means that they bring two incomes home, but they still have to forego certain comforts in order to set aside a greater percentage of their earnings for educational expenses. They make this sacrifice with the hope that it will yield dividends:

> So it takes, of course, the financial aspect of it with the state of economy as it is here now, of course it will take a fortune now to get a child to go through the school process and of course other process to become finally educated. And for us, we really have to sacrifice to make sure that whatever earnings we have, we use some percentage of it to get our kids staying in school already and continuing with their schooling process. So ... it's not a piece of cake, but we know that it's a kind of investment that will yield some dividends in the future. And with that, we don't mind going through the agony or the pain of sacrificing or doing what it takes to get them educated or trained.

Sacrifice also means that parents sometimes, if not often, have to cut down on their hours of sleep in order to free up more time to deal with educational activities at home or at school. This is not uncommon for parents who themselves attend school, work, and also have to take care of the home front. Nneamaka tells about her enormous sacrifice, which includes sleeping for only four hours a night on weekdays and a little more on weekends:

> I usually go to bed at two in the morning, around 2:30 AM every day. I will wake up at six; the day starts again … Monday through Friday. Weekends we sleep a little more. And then we attend our community stuffs, go to church on Sunday, and then Monday we start again. So you know, sometimes I work far into the night to make sure I get things accomplished, you know? It's not unheard of for me to be awake by four in the morning, and I have to wake up by six. It's not unheard of, yes. So if things have to be done, it has to be done. It is not easy. It is not easy. It's a constant juggle.

She does not give up or get discouraged even when her best efforts do not yield the expected result. She has to keeping going, because as recent immigrants, there is nobody to fall back to.

> You juggle; sometimes you get it right. Sometimes you miss, and you get up in the morning and you start over. And you begin again and you make sure, you know, that it has to work. So we really don't have an option. That's the difference. We don't have an option. That is the difference between us and the people of this country. They might have options. We do not have options, so we don't have parents here who will help you if you are failing. (Nneamaka)

Njideka sometimes stays up late too. At times, she even gives up a whole night's sleep just to do the things that are necessary for her kids' education. She will do anything that will help her kids to be responsible citizens and to have a fulfilled, less stressful, and happy adult lives.

> I mean sometimes I have to say maybe something that I really want to do, I might have to stay up and forego sleep one night. Like maybe there's some cleaning project that I haven't been able to get to. There's no other time. I'll just say, "Okay, tonight I'm not gonna sleep." And this closet that I wanted to arrange, I have to … you know, I'll be up doing that. Or if there's something that … some project … you know, sometimes to encourage the kids you have to make, like, these charts … So there's no time. So sometimes it's like, you know, 2:00 AM. You know, you'll see, oh yeah … the next morning my husband or the kids, when they wake up, will ask

"When did you do that?" Oh yeah, "Last night," you know? So it's hard.

On some occasions, when everything gets overwhelming, she says she is compelled to "outsource" some of these duties. "I try to, you know, outsource. You know like sometimes you get the house cleaner to come and help clean" (Njideka). Outsourcing some of these duties is, of course only for those parents who can afford it. It's certainly not possible for parents who are struggling to make ends meet.

If parents run out of time and resources, sometimes all they have left in their toolboxes is to try to subtly push the kids to get their things done by themselves.

Pushing Children Sometimes

Educating children also requires that parents sometimes have to persuade, encourage, and even push them to do their homework, get enough sleep, and achieve their goals at school however that becomes possible. Nneamaka points out that the pushing should not be seen in a negative sense but rather that it is something that she does out of care and love for her kids because she really wants them to turn out as responsible citizens, who are not a burden on society.

> Our children know that whatever ... everything we are doing is for their own benefit, okay? We are doing that out of love for them to be successful. So you must be successful. Also for our children you tell them, "Hey, if you fail, my house is not an option either." So you must also be successful. So success is a given. They know they must succeed. Everything you have from day one ... once they are born. At birth you throw in everything you have. You expose them to all the opportunities in this country. You tell them, "Hey, the sky is your limit. You go grab it because it's out there for you. You do whatever you have to do that is legal, okay, to do your work." It doesn't happen, but you keep pushing. It's gonna work. Okay, sometimes it does work. Sometimes they deviate ... Don't let them fall. Okay, keep working. Keep pushing, yeah. It's a continuous process ...

> Nobody ever said that parenting is easy. Parenting has never been easy. It's a hard work to be a parent and a good one too. You know? It's not just having the child. You have to make sure that you train the child well to be a successful citizen and ... useful to the society. You want to raise the child to be a contributing part of the society

too. You don't want to raise somebody who's a burden to the society. So it's a lot of work that has to go in educating the child. Yeah, and that's why a lot of parents have one or two children because it's hard work. And thank God I'm not a single parent so I have help.

Most parents who "talk the talk and walk the walk of educating children" (Nwakaego), even as they make enormous sacrifices, are still energized and motivated in anticipation of the positive outcome of their efforts. This idea is developed by Nneamaka, who says that even though sometimes a parent's best efforts do not yield the expected result, you have to continue, trying yet a different approach:

> At the end of the day, you are happy with the progress. You see your children making a difference. You are happy. It gives you the energy and the strength and the determination to continue what you are doing. Because you pat yourself on the back and you say, "Hey, okay, I am doing a good job. Okay, I'll keep working on that." Yeah, and the one [approach] that is not working, you tweak it. You change it. You turn it around. If it doesn't work, you drop it. You pick up another version of it that you hope will be, you know, successful and will work for the children. It's a continuous process.

And most of the participants agree that it takes both teachers and parents working together to be successful on the common mission of a child's education. It requires a huge sacrifice on the part of parents to educate children. Igbo parents (and teachers who themselves are parents in many cases) know very well why they undertake such painful sacrifices to make sure that their children receive a good education: it is their main goal to eventually see these children become responsible citizens and fulfilled adults.

But how do Igbo parents in Chicago understand their role in the education of children? In the previous section, we learned that it takes active parents to educate a child. Next, I present how Igbo parents perceive their roles in the educational process.

The Role of Parents

"Impossible! Impossible! Parents must be involved!" declares Nwakaego. What she meant is that it is simply impossible for the school or the parents alone to educate children. Children spend time learning both at school and at home, so merely supporting what happens at school is not enough. "Parents must be involved" (Nwakaego). Nneka agrees that it is "not just about a child going to school. The parents also have to be active ... it takes not just the school to work ... the parent has to be number one, active." She gives a hypothetical example of how parents and teachers could work together to resolve an issue that might arise in the educational process of a child.

> Parents have to work with the teachers. So both listen to each other to see if ... where they are meeting, if they are meeting in the middle at all. Because you can have a child display a different character at school and a different character at home, and it becomes a problem. So if the parents and the teachers are meeting on a regular basis, they'll be able to handle the conflict well. They can resolve it with one or two strategies or solutions they have. So that's the good thing. That's a very ... that's a plus when you participate in all this. (Nneka)

In working with the school, the initial education starts at home and continues in the school and in the community, "which means that they do not start from zero, but they start from a higher platform so that they can leap off to a higher height" (Nebeolisa).

Nebeolisa goes on to say how the school and other educational agents build on the foundation that he and his wife have laid:

> To me education starts at home. Who they are is not going to be based squarely on what they are taught in school. Maybe I need to back strike a little bit. My idea of education is that it is the responsibility of the family to educate their child, to train and educate the child. Now because I am not at home 24/7, I am now contracting with the school to provide part of it. A good chunk of what they will know will have to come from myself and my wife, and what they also pick up from people around them. You know because that's what I believe makes for the socialization of the child. Schooling ... formal education is one part of it, but a good chunk of it is both cultural education and also societal education. How do you communicate within ... how do you navigate your way through the community? Who I am today is not just what I learned in school. A lot of it is what I also picked up from around the house. I am responsible, but the school happens to be an active partner in the sense that if I had my way I will home school them. But since I cannot homeschool them, then I'm asking the school to be part of it ... And if I don't like the curriculum I will protest because the school is there to serve my needs, and I will support the school to do that. You know like I've always told the principal, I said if there is anything that you know that you need that the children ... for you to be effective in training the children, do not

hesitate to let the parents know because we can all work with you to accomplish that.

Laying the foundation for education includes providing for the children's basic needs and teaching them reading even before they step into a formal education structure.

> Initially at very young ages, we start reading. One, two, three years—they start reading before they even start going to school and preschools and then day cares and all those steps before they even start kindergarten. Of needs, you have to take care of the basic needs first—the clothing, the housing, and then the character part before the child can even learn. The cognitive part comes like in the middle. So the child has to develop first, you know? And all this education actually comes in the house before the school comes in. So if the child didn't get that basic [education] from the middle down, the child is not going to be well educated. (Nneamaka)

Parents' work is not finished, even when they have laid the foundations of education at home. Parents actually have much more work to do when the child begins his or her education in the school.

During the interviews, most parents stressed the importance of working with the school in the education of their children. Based on this revelation, I wanted to know next just how they described their relationship with the school, which introduces the discussion about whether a parent is a supporter or a partner. Most of the participants regarded themselves as partners with the school in their children's education and schooling. This is the way Nneka understood her partnership with the school:

> You have to keep an eye on your child no matter what happens, and that's why they come back with homework. You have to follow it up and see what they're doing. And you can go back to the teacher and say, "Well, I thought my child is doing this way. What do you think?" So you can put things on the table and ask the teacher and say, "This is what I noticed how my child is doing at home. Do you see her that way in class?" Are there ways that we can use to strengthen ... are there things that can be done to strengthen this child's ability?

While Nneamaka saw herself as a more invested partner in education, Nebeolisa considered himself as the senior partner in his child's education. But Nsobundu saw his role as an active partner.

> As an active [partner] ... you are helping the child learn whatever he or she did not pick up at school. And that helps the teacher to move

faster. Otherwise, they might slow down in getting the child ... [unless] it's a conscientious teacher, not letting the child get behind. It will take time to bring the child up to date with the rest of the class. But if you do that at home, you partner with the teacher to, you know ... for the child to succeed. I think it's more of a partner than a supporter.

Nsobundu believed that parents are more partners than they are supporters. "You partner with the teacher to, you know... for the child to succeed. I think it's more of a partner than a supporter ..." Nonye agrees that the parents' role has to go beyond merely supporting what the school does.

I think support ... parents supporting the school is not enough, especially ... in this era of television ... and there is so much going around. There is so much going around in the world that children are confronted with. They have so many things fighting for their attention. So as a parent, you have to be a partner. You cannot just be in a support position. No you have to be an equal partner ... to the education of your child, yeah.

Nkolika sees her role as both partner and supporter, leaning more toward a partner because, after all, it is her child, not the school's student alone.

Because whatever is good for my child at the end of the day will benefit me and my husband. I mean the school is just teaching her. At the end of the day, she will come back home. At the end of the day, she is my daughter. So I have to be a partner in whatever she does with the school. And then also, I support what the school does by teaching her.

With regard to the parents' role as partners, Nnamdi sees his role differently. Although he does not disagree with those who see their role as partners or supporters or as both supporter and partner, he considers himself a cheerleader.

I am ... there for the process to take place. That's my job. That's why I define myself as a cheerleader. My job is to cheer them on. Part of cheering them on is to catch them when they're doing something right. Yeah, because when you catch them at the right moment and give the right praise, that will embolden them to do more.

Once the foundation is laid and the child continues his/her education in school, it is expected that parents guide and oversee the child's education in school and also monitor the influence of other agents in the education of children. Njideka shares her experience on how she plays this role.

So I mean [part of my role] it's to guide them and to teach them and to put them in the right situations to be taught so overseeing their work. I know talking and communicating with them on a very regular and consistent basis just so I am aware of what they're doing and not doing, both what they're doing in school and not in school, even what's going on with them and their friends, what's going on with their outside lessons, sports activities, understanding … learning to understand them, to understand which things that they maybe have difficulty with in their educational process, or just overall, you know, oversight over kind of everything.

For Igbo parents who participated in this study, there is no debate whether they should be involved in their children's education or not. Rather, the discussion is about the nature of the involvement—that is, what constitutes parental involvement and how it is carried out. They conceptualize their role in terms of (a) laying the foundations of education at home and in the school, (b) partnering with the school, (c) getting the children ready to go to school every day, (d) creating a home environment conducive to learning, (e) following up on schoolwork and complementing it, (f) providing good meals and other nutrition good for learning, and (g) acting as a cheerleader. Next, I will present what participants said about setting educational standards and expectations, giving emphasis to the particular perceptions that Igbo parents have about parental involvement.

Setting Standards and Expectations in the Education of Children

Igbo parents also believe that it is one of their duties to set educational standards and expectations for their children's learning. In playing this role, they draw inspiration from their own parents, what they had learned from other parents, or the negative educational decisions of other parents that they observed.

Njideka suggests why it is necessary to set not just any expectation, but a sufficiently high one. Indeed, she does not agree with the people who believe that children should be allowed to "be who they will be." Her father is her inspiration:

I know every … I mean all the women that I know and associate with, like everybody is invested in their children and their children's future. And you know everybody thinks they're doing the best for them. People have different ways of going about it. I think because … you know, some people think too much pressure regarding schooling and education is bad and that they don't want to force their kid to say, "Oh, you must get all A's and you must get everything right." And I find myself a little bit on a different ... I didn't grow up that way, and because I feel that my educational background and everything with my schooling has gone well, I want to do things the way it was done to me. So I've set the standard very, very high, and I think ... my daddy used to say if you want to reach for the tree, you aim for the sky. So if you miss the sky, at least you'll get the tree. So I don' tell them that "Oh, just do what you can and any score you get is good." I'm saying you should get every one right. And I know some people say, "Oh, that puts too much pressure." I've met a lot of people who thought that that was too much pressure for kids and you should just let them be who they will be. So there are different styles, and I think all work. Going to Harvard ... I tell them ... I ask them where they want ... where does Mommy want you to go? They know. But they don't know that that means that the bar is high. They just know that's where my mommy went, and she says it's a good school. She says it's one of the best, and that's where she says I should go.

Njideka goes further to relate some incidents that show the kind of standard and expectation her family set during her school day, pointing out how her father was never satisfied with her performance. She believes that the high standard her father set for her and her siblings had truly paid off:

He [my dad] knew exactly like, "Okay, you had this test on Friday. It's now Monday. What was the results?" And I'd say, "Oh yeah I got 96 percent." He says, "Okay what about ..." like he knew the people who were the top people in the class. He knew like the top five of us, so he would say, "Okay, what did Mimi get?" I said, "I think she got 97." [Then my father would say] "How come you didn't get 98? How about Jeremy? What did he get? Okay, good." Like you have to be at the top every time, and you know, at the end of the year, they wanted to give the award to the best in the class, and so there was one girl and me, we kept getting it. He was like, "You need to get it every year," you know. So ... a lot of pressure, setting the goal very high, always wanting the best. I remember that was definitely established very early on for all the children.

Like Njideka, Nwakaego's father had high standards for her too. What is interesting is that he did not get far in school, yet he had set a very high standard for Nwakaego and her siblings. He expected that each of them be at the top of the class at the end of every school year. Nwakaego tells about a familiar conversation she would have with her father at the end of every school year, where she knew she had to be ready to explain why she wasn't first in the class:

> When you are second in the class, my father will ask me, "Why are you not the first?" Even when you take the first place, he will still find some time to say. You know that kind of thing ... it's like everybody must be first. Yeah, that was the target. That was always the target—to be first. That is always the target, so you know, to be first every year, in every year, to be first.

Nnaemeka and his wife set the same type of high standard for their children and described how they reinforced it with rewards. Their children are A and B students. However, if any of them ever brings home a C, they have no alternative but to accept it:

> We will always want A or B. We don't encourage C. They are all on the level of A or B. Not that we will care if the grade is C. Yeah, not that we will do anything, but we want to put them to that standard so that they keep going ... sometimes we give them, I will say, compensation. If they do well, get good grades ...Yes, we set the expectation. We set it high so that they will ... and plus, we reinforce this by providing them some kind of ... To go to convention once in a year. We take them out of Chicago or Illinois and go to convention. They've been to Dallas. They've been to New York. They've been to some other places. So every year, depending on how your result is, we buy tickets ... They look forward to it, yeah. They know that we're serious about it. We're not just saying it for the sake of saying it. We tell them if you do this, this is what we're gonna do for you. We try to ... They work hard and they will get it ... you know, make sure that they get that done.

For Nneamaka's family, it is not just for academic performance that they set standards and expectations. In addition, there are yearly family-related and individual goals that they expect from their children:

> [I] tell them, "Hey, this is my goals for you." Like, you know, the beginning of every year we have family goals for the year ... so the children, you know, they know going into that [new] year ... like you know every Christmas holiday going into the New Year, this is what we want you to accomplish. So we have family goals and stuffs, you know ... and then we also have expectations for every child at each age.

It is also the duty of parents to work with the child to accomplish goals. In situations where a child is not measuring up, parents have to provide a morale booster. Nneamaka talked about how she encourages her child to move on when that happens:

> Sometimes, they fall short, don't get me wrong. But if they fall short, spank them on the back—"Hey, come on. We're still in this race. We are still... you know we still got to make it happen. We still have to make it happen." Sometimes they deviate, you know, one or two years, but you got to ... still have to push them—"Hey come on, come on. Don't slack." So if there's constant push, you know, you don't let them fall. If they are falling, you catch them. You embrace them. You give them a big hug, encouragement, chastisement—whatever it takes to move on—to accomplish that goal. We have this goal. We have these big dreams, and I thank God some of them are getting there. Some of them are getting there.

According to the participants, setting standards and expectations is a part of Igbo parenting in Chicago. It is a natural human characteristic to want to work toward a goal. What makes the difference is whether those standards and expectations are too low or high or simply unrealistic. Parents in this study believe that with hard work, such standards and expectations can be realized. Attaining these standards includes things that are sometimes taken for granted, such as getting children ready for school every morning.

Making Children Ready for School

Another important role of parents that "people don't think about" (Nebeolisa) very often is getting children ready for school. "If they don't show up, they're not gonna learn. So at least I have to make them show up healthy, well fed, well rested ... and disciplined" (Nebeolisa). In the same way, Nneamaka thinks that school might not be able to fulfill its role if she doesn't get her children ready for school properly every morning.

> If I don't give the child that opportunity, the school is not going to help that child ... to impart that knowledge. So I have to do my part in the home to make sure the child goes to school daily and the child is ready, nutritionally well-nourished, ready to receive the knowledge from the school.

When the child comes back, the parent has to continue from where the school left off. "So I have to make sure in the home that whatever the school is doing that I'm reinforcing at home also" (Nneamaka).

Providing adequate clothing, encouraging a healthy lifestyle, good nutrition, and shelter are basic ways of making sure that the child is ready for school every day, which generally ensures regular attendance. These kinds of things ultimately engender a better teaching and learning atmosphere for the child.

Creating Learning-Friendly Environment at Home

"[For me], education of children is nonstop" (Nsobundu). It is like a circle, from home to school and community back to home again. In school, professional educators are seen by participants as the ones responsible for taking care of teaching and guiding the children and administering the school. However, as partners, Igbo parents in Chicago see creating learning-friendly environments at home as one of their chief roles in their children's education.

This is how Nneamaka understood her role with regard to creating an educational learning environment at home.

> When the child comes home, I have to take it to the next level and make sure that the child is learning all those things—doing homework, doing projects, studying at home ... making sure they have a comfortable reading environment, remove all the distractions—the cell phones, the TVs, the radios away—for the child to concentrate and do what the child has to do. So I have to make sure in the home that whatever the school is doing, that I'm reinforcing at home also.

Though each family is unique, participants agreed that setting rules and regulations for the use of TVs, cell phones, and computers is a constant task. They generally said that a parent has to monitor the friends their children hang out with. Also, they have to be cognizant about exposing their children to the right learning opportunities in the community. Finally, it was clear that providing material for study and homework are part of the parents' responsibilities. These are some of the ways Igbo families in Chicago try to create a learning-friendly environment at home.

Igbo parents consider their role in the education of their children as very important. For one, family or home is one of the three environments in which children learn and grow. "Children learn and grow at home, at school, and in the community. Their experiences may be positive or negative, but it is clear that the people in these three contexts influence student learning and development from infancy on" (Epstein, 2005, p. vii). Even in modern society, the home continues to be an important milieu for educating children (Barbour and Barbour, 1997). Lightfoot (1978) further suggests that the family's role is critical to both the child's development and his or her successful schooling. In the case of Igbo parents, this crucial role includes laying the foundation for their children's education, setting standards and expectations, creating a learning-friendly environment at home, making children ready for school, and working with the school.

The Role of the School

Some people mistakenly equate schooling to education. But as we have seen, Igbo parents in Chicago are indeed able to distinguish between the two; and they affirm that education, being a broader concept, includes both schooling as well as other teaching and learning activities outside of school that are under the supervision of the parents and other agents of children's education.

Nneka uses the eye as a metaphor to describe another role of school in her daughter's education. She sees the school as an important partner in identifying a child's strengths, talents, or even weaknesses, which they try to resolve together.

> Well, school is very important … they are *the second eyes* that you have beside you the parent. So the school also helps to identify the child's strengths. And then you can … when they identify such things, you can also follow it up and see if it's true or not. So … because I remember the school calling me at some point and saying, "Oh, she is good. She holds her … in art she can hold her pencil well. See if you want to enroll her in an art class." And so that's a plus for them to notice that. Or when they notice that your child did something and report to you, you can follow up and see. Or if your child is throwing a tantrum … you can follow up and see where the anger is coming from, why the child is upset and work that way. That way you prevent what is going to be in the future. So school is also the second … I see them as the second eye, not the first eye.

Another important role of the school is that it keeps parents informed of their children's learning activities at school. Njideka recalled an incident when her son was in kindergarten. She feels that schools keep parents abreast of the goings on, because they too are invested in the children. And often, if not always, they work with the parents to resolve any issues that might arise.

> I mean the school is excellent and … at least with my son for the kindergarten … you know, official schooling class—kindergarten, first, and second—I feel like the school has been very helpful and has been very invested in him and kept me abreast of things that are always going on. And you know if … for example, for Chijioke Jr.,

sometimes I think he was a little bit ... he's the youngest in his class and so that has posed some issues in terms of his maturity level and not being as mature as his peers. And so in different ways that may manifest itself, you know, the school always is sure to bring that to my attention. And then we always sit together if there's anything that we have to, you know, discuss or any strategies that we want to try to employ. And I've always felt that the school has been on the right page. I've found them very supportive and working with me and Chijioke Jr., and it's been good.

School plays an important role in filling in where parents are unable to. This creates a more equal playing field for children of different backgrounds. Nebeolisa suggests reasons why formalization of schooling is necessary for his children's education:

One ... I think one is to first of all formalizes it. In the sense that, I mean if it's left to every parent, then at some point there is no standard because what is important to one parent is not important to another parent. But at least one is to bring some kind of formalization, say, "Hey, this is the body of knowledge that every child needs to know by the time they are at this stage of life." That is one. Two, it provides a stop gap because not every parent is at the level where they can ... truly educate their children. You know because then what that means is if I dropped out at sixth grade, then my child cannot go beyond sixth grade. So their parents who might not have all the skills and aptitude and ability to help, to be involved, then the school can ... comes in as a stop gap. And then, three, it's just the way the society has evolved. You know it's just the way the society has evolved, that there should be some kind of accountability. That is okay, if you think your child has learned enough, then let's test the child to see where the child is.

Because the school develops the curriculum, Nsobundu believes that they set the tone for the education of children:

Well, they [schools] play an important role. They play a central ... they play an important role because they set the tone. They give the curriculum, age-appropriate curriculum. And most of the times that's what we follow when they come home. When they bring home homework, we go with them and we go through the curriculum with them, whatever they have learned or whatever they are struggling with. And so that's ... the school, you know, plays a very important role. They set the tone.

According to Nebeolisa, "discipline is key to learning." School plays an important role in teaching this important virtue that is crucial for effective teaching and learning. And Nkolika narrates a delightful experience of how school plays this essential role in relation to her daughter:

> There are certain things school does that I really like. Like getting the child to be responsible and getting them to be disciplined. School plays a very good role in that. Like one time I dropped my child in school and they had something ... a play pen. And I told her to go in. So when I dropped her, she washed her hands. I told her to go up and play in the play pen, and she looked at the teacher for permission even though I told her, "Yeah you can go right away and play." But when she looked at the teacher, the teacher said, "Oh, you know how many people are supposed to be there, so wait for one person to come down before you could go." So I really felt ... I felt good, I mean knowing that my daughter is disciplined. I mean she knows that she has to ask before she goes into that. Yeah, they teach them how to talk. Like they teach them not to scream. They teach them how to be disciplined. They teach them, like, to be on the line and all those things when they're going to the bathroom, you know, to be on the single file line. They teach them those things.

School Is There to Serve My Needs in the Education of My Children

Some Igbo parents believe that the responsibility for educating their children falls on their shoulders. While acknowledging that the school plays a vital role, they believe that school, even in the role as a partner in the education of Igbo children, is there to serve the needs of the parents, who have the ultimate responsibility to educate their children. This is the opinion of Nebeolisa, even as he enumerates other educational roles of the school:

> I am responsible, but the school happens to be an active partner in the sense that if I had my way I will homeschool them. But since I cannot homeschool them, then I'm asking the school to be part of it. So my involvement with my ... they're going to the school system ... to get some of that education requires that I know who their teachers are; I'm involved with their extracurricular activity, you know, if they ask for ... PTA ... Parent-Teacher Association meetings, I will be there. And also, you know, go for the teacher conferences now. And if I don't like the curriculum, I will protest because the school is there to serve my needs, and I will support the school to do that. You

know, like I've always told the principal, I said if there is anything that you know that you need … for you to be effective in training the children, do not hesitate to let the parents know because we can all work with you to accomplish that.

Nebeolisa added that the school's role is to activate and sustain interest in learning among the children:

You see, I believe that what the school ought to do is to activate that interest in children to learn. If that child has an appetite and desire to learn they will always excel, unless that child does not understand. But if the child has all their faculties intact, that child that has the desire to learn and is challenged to learn, not just being taught to perform … that child will be more useful to the community. Some of … in my experience I know some of the kids that we all went to school with, they weren't performing at the top level, but they ended up doing better than many of us are doing … performing at the top level in life because of the way … you know they educated themselves, the way they learned. But I think it follows that once a child has an interest in learning and has applied themselves and has a broad approach to the whole concept of education, that they will perform at a good level. Grades to me will not … is not the goal, but character and the ability to be an integral member of the community is more important.

School Continues the Education Process Initiated by the Parents

Nnaemeka, like other parents in this study, sees school "as basically continuing the path that parents have already set at home" (Nonye). Besides, he construes such a role as providing another stage in the educational development of children that runs concurrently with the continuous role of parents.

Apart from that, outside the confines of the home, the school is another medium that is provided by the society for children to, again, pass through another stage of development in their education. So the school provides some level of discipline and extends that initial education that happens within the family. So the school has a very important role because between their initial education and going further, you know, being out there in the world, if the school is not an intermediary then the children or the child might have difficulty knowing what to do after initial training. And also the school provides some kind of social resource medium. Then you get to meet other kids or other children like you. You interact. It's, in a way, kind of a miniature world you have to experience before you go into the bigger world of work. (Nnaemeka)

Criticism of the Role of Schools in the Education of Children

The fact that school plays an essential role in the education of children does not lead Igbo parents to forget that some aspects of schooling still need improvement. For example, Nnamdi, while criticizing the educational system, points out that the school is failing in what it is supposed to ultimately teach children.

> School is supposed to be teaching you two things and two things alone—how to think and how to be happy. School don't teach that, okay? But this is an entirely different situation because if you know how to think and you know how to be happy, no one can control you. I think if I am to suggest anything regarding the educational system, I think schools should get back to teaching children about thinking. I don't know how they can do that, but right now it's nothing but a test taking and test-passing situation, instrument. You know and then children ... people graduate from ... and this is what we use to have in Igboland. When you became eighteen years old, you have a keen idea. In other words, nobody is directing you, "Go here, go there." But you know children graduate ... some even graduate from college, and they still have to be directed. And I think that stems from the system not teaching ... I don't know if it's ... to be that way because you never know. But ... if schools should get into teaching children how to think at a very early age and then how to manage their thinking so that you're in a place that you're feeling good and happy ... if you can teach people how to think and how to be happy, they can become anything they want to be. And maybe I have to open up a school myself. Maybe I have to do that.

Nnamdi continues his criticism of the educational system in more unsympathetic words:

> I'm not a big fan of the educational system here. I'm not a big fan of it, but what I will say apparently is that outside of what they do in school; they're just babysitting. They're housing their bodies in school for eight hours. You know because ...There's a difference. There's a slight difference. In an educational system whereby you are just giving a kid enough to meet the mark ... "testing culture" ... That's the thing. If that's all you learn for the fifteen or twelve years

you go to school, whatever, then when you come out, that's what you know how to do. In other words, you won't have the ability to lead or take charge or be a trailblazer.

Nwakaego's criticism identifies one of the challenges schools face, namely, that they have to deal with so many children at the same time as they play their crucial roles in the education of these children.

For me ... it is a hard one ... because they are dealing with so many children that they don't really know their method of learning. So ... and that's why ... they sort of generalize teaching ... that's what it should be because of, you know, the setting of the school. So it's more generalized teaching. And the teacher can only do what he or she can do best, you know? So just giving them the fundamentals, you know? Sort of the fundamentals for them to know the basics, you know? Just the basics!

Schooling, as Igbo parents in this study acknowledged, is an essential part of education. School is the second eye of the parents. It sets the tone of education, it keeps the parents informed of their children's education, and it continues the process of children's education initiated by parents. In this age, society has embraced a market philosophy of life. With regard to education, the market approach emphasizes skill acquisition over any other aim of education, where school's major role is to prepare the workforce needed by society for the march of civilization.

Summary and Analysis

Igbo parents' perceptions of parental involvement revolve around three themes: what it takes to educate a child, the role of parents and the role of school in children's education. Participants agree that it takes both teachers and parents working together to successfully achieve the common mission of educating children. Such an important mission calls for a huge sacrifice on the part of Igbo parents. They gladly undertake such painful sacrifices to make sure that their children receive a good education and eventually become responsible citizens and fulfilled adults.

As for their role, there is no debate for the Igbo parents, who participated in this study, that they should be involved in their children's education. Rather, the discussion is what constitutes parental involvement and how it should be carried out. They conceptualize their role in terms of laying the foundation of education at home and in the school, collaborating with the school, getting the children ready to go to school every day, and creating a home environment conducive to learning. Other ways they conceptualize their role include following up on schoolwork and complementing it, providing meals and nutrition good for learning, acting as a cheerleader, and setting educational standards and goals.

Schooling is an essential part of education. According to Igbo parents, school plays many roles in children's education, such as building on the foundation parents laid, developing the curriculum, and keeping the parents informed about their children's progress. As the second set of eyes for parents, the school helps to identify both the strengths and weaknesses of their children. Since the broader responsibility of educating their children falls on them, Igbo parents believe that school is there to serve their needs, rather than simply the needs of the school system. This contradicts much of the language of parent involvement, which tends to situate the school at the center and think of parent involvement as a support for the school to achieve its priorities. There are three main points that support this repositioning of the school and parents in the broader education of children.

Igbo Parents Filter What Their Children Learn

Igbo parents raising and educating their children here in America find themselves picking and choosing what they themselves teach or what they allow their children to learn. The fundamental question at the back of their minds as they filter what their children learn is which values and lessons will help parents achieve the goal of educating their children to be responsible adult Igbo American citizens? In effect, part of parental involvement for Igbo parents is not only being gatekeepers of knowledge but also helping their children to evaluate their learning and experiences.

Role Models

Igbo parents are role models. The Igbo saying, *Nne ewu n'ata igu, nwa ya ana ele ya anya n'onu,* depicts the power of teaching by example—in English, "As the she-goat chews palm leaves the baby goat watches her mouth." The lesson is that the baby goat learns how to chew palm leaves by observing how her mother eats. Igbo parents know that teaching their children responsibility, hard work, respect for others, discipline, kindness, honesty, trust, and so on requires that they themselves live out these virtues and values.

"The School Is There to Serve My Needs"

One of the interesting findings is that some Igbo parents do not see school as the dominant partner in the education of children; some parents see themselves as a higher or even as a senior partner in collaborating with schools in the education of children. This view of school is not surprising because Igbo parents in this study believe that the responsibility of educating their children ultimately falls on their shoulders.

The perception of parental involvement of these Igbo parents is a combination of their understanding of the concept of what it takes to educate a child, including setting educational standards and expectations and what it takes to attain them. It also includes the understanding of their roles and that of the school in the education of children.

Practice, on the other hand, is the concrete manner through which Igbo parents express their beliefs, attitudes, and understanding. Perception informs practice. Since there is a link between perception and practice, in the next chapter, we will hear the account given by the participants of how they live out their perceptions of the concept in practical terms.

CHAPTER 8

Parental Involvement Practices

In the previous chapter, I pointed out that practice is the concrete way of expressing beliefs, attitudes, and the understanding of parental involvement in education. This chapter presents the various practical ways Igbo parents told me they act on their beliefs, attitudes, and understanding with regard to their involvement in the education of their children. In other words, this chapter is the articulation of how Igbo parents I interviewed perceive their own actions or practices[18].

To help appreciate the different ways in which participants said they were involved in the education of their children, I begin with the questions that I posed to the parents that helped to provoke their stories. These questions included the following:

1. Can you walk me through a typical day in your family?
2. What else does your child do besides going school that you'd consider "learning" or education?
   a. What other activities does he/she engage in?
   b. What other places does he/she spend time in?
3. What influenced your choice of the school your children are attending?
4. What is your child's home learning environment like?
5. What are you doing to realize the dreams—*ekpere nne na nna obula bu onye Igbo bu ka umu ha karia ha*—you have for your child?

A variety of themes arose from the interviews that relate to how parents

---

18   Although I am talking about practices, the data point to the interviewees' *perceptions* of their own practices. The study did not include observations of their actual practices. Nevertheless, their perceptions of their practice are important because this study is about how Igbo parents make sense of the family-school relations.

say they are involved, including schools, laying the foundation for education, setting standards and expectations, teaching and learning at home, homework, volunteering, extracurricular activities, teaching Igbo language and culture, ensuring regular attendance and making children ready to learn, creating a learning-friendly home environment, and dealing with culture clash and conflicts.

School Choice

Igbo parents and indeed all parents in the USA have the option of sending their children to a public, private, or special school. I found out that among the Igbo parents in Chicago, school choice is an essential part of parents' involvement in the education of their children. Njideka said that "it [is] a big decision" that she makes with her husband. Nneka, though not expecting the question, was very delighted that I brought up the issue: "That's a very good question. Oh my God. I wasn't expecting it. But that's a good question."

A combination of factors was responsible for Nneka choosing a faith-based private school for her six-year-old daughter, Ogechi. She acknowledged that the public schools in her neighborhood are good, but nonetheless, she decided on a faith-based private school. Factors that affected her choice included the need to acquaint Ogechi, her daughter, with religion and religious issues as early as possible, to let her daughter know about her peculiar situation as a single parent, her faith community, and the network of mothers she has in the community.

> Well, we live in a community that is good ... Most of the taxes go into the schools. But I worship at a parish that has supported me so well. And I like the school ... public schools in [the community] they are really good, but then it takes two to make it so ... but I have good support at my parish, and they have very good program, not just the support. And it's also where I worship, and I would also like my child to be exposed to religion as early as possible. Most public schools don't talk about religion or your faith, so ... and I think faith is very important, and I grew up in a very strong faith-based family; I think that it has helped me up to this ... And so I'm able to expose Ogechi to religion so it's not foreign to her when she goes through public school and comes out and people are discussing faith. She's out there like, "Oh my God, what is going on here? Who is God?" and all that. So at an early stage, she's taught about God. It's not foreign. She doesn't hear it for the first time in the media, so she has her own ... she forms her own opinion early.

It's not forced on the kids, but they introduce it. And if you like it, that's fine. If you don't like it, that's fine. You also have the option of opting out if you don't want your child to be in a religious class. That's one good thing about our parish school. But she is exposed … that's an edge for her to know about faith in general. You're not asked to be Catholic or Protestant or Methodist. It's just having an idea that there's some kind of existence of God. There's some kind of … there is something that is bigger than you. Because even now that I'm in health care, we do all that we can for the patient. But by the end of the day, there is something bigger than us. And while we're at church on Sundays, she participates in carrying the basket. So that's … that's why I like our parish.

Other reasons that influenced Nneka to choose a parish school for her daughter are as follows:

I have a good network with them, the mothers especially. They have good teachers. Everything is online. You have access to what your child is doing online, and you have access to the teachers—their qualifications and all that. Nothing is hidden. It's put out there, so you have twenty-four-hour access to what is going on in the school and what they're doing at the time. They also encourage you to prepare meals from home so you're not dependent on them … like the public school, where you have meals prepared at school, then kids are feeding from vending machines. It's not like that … those are the things I like [about] the school. Attention is given to nutrition … parents are encouraged to be active in their child's education at our parish school.

They have good security because I'm working with mothers that I know. I'm working with characters that I know. They are not just people that I met in class and I met their parents. These are people that I worship with, that I can see, okay … I can talk to the principal. I can go to the parish priest if I have [to] … if my concern is not taken care of at the principal level. I can go back to the parish office and leave my complaint, and that will be taken care of.

Although Njideka attended faith-based private schools throughout her elementary and secondary school years, she prefers the local public school in her community to a private faith-based school because of the former's academic superiority. Njideka and Chijioke sought the opinions of older residents in their neighborhood before finally making their decision to send their son to the public school.

It was a big decision. I grew up and only attended religious schools from nursery throughout secondary school. So … and Chijioke [my husband] … so both of us were considering the Catholic school versus the public school and then also looking at some gifted schools. So in measuring all the factors, we thought that we could get the best of all worlds, like still taking advantage of the public school because the public schools academically were stronger than the local Catholic schools. Although the local Catholic schools aren't bad, but everyone … I had interviewed many different parents—some who had gone to the Catholic schools, some who had gone to the public schools, and some who had gone to both and switched. And so from all my, you know, investigations, it seemed like the public schools actually had more resources and more things to offer. And I would still be able to get some of that Catholic education through the youth catechesis program. And also we would be able to do our home fellowship at home. So we thought that he [Chijioke Jr.] would still get the best of the spiritual and the academic foundations, even attending the public school.

Nnamdi's three children have gone to or are attending public, nonsectarian private schools, and a special school. He took time to research his options. Security and the child's talents did influence his choice of the three types of school his children attend at any given time. However, while academics has remained a constant factor, financial considerations have also been a big issue in his choice:

My daughter goes to private school—the middle child, the nine-year-old. She goes to a school called Jackson. It's alternative … it's alternative education outside of the regular reading, writing, and arithmetic. She's art inclined. She's gonna be a painter and an actress. My son is a musician so … he went to a mixture of private and public schools. But you know, the public schools he went to were two types of public schools here: top ones and the regular ones. He always went to the top one because I researched into it. Well, there are financial considerations. That's a big issue because the school he was gonna go to at the time was $18,000 a year. My son, the private school he was going to be going to is in Evanston. And he was gonna be there for four years. And then we were in between that. Actually … he was actually gonna be registered down there, but in between that, he took the placement test to get into the top-notch high schools. Fortunately for us, he did not pass at first tier to go to the higher school. But there are four schools; he was successful enough to go to one of the four. So my thinking was instead of paying this $18,000 a year ... and then the academic credentials is equal, or even the school he went to is better! I'm like, you know, the credentials is better. So we opted for that. So it was economic consideration and the academic credentials of the school. The reason is twofold.

Security is an important consideration:

Safety! Safety is a big consideration because, well, it is a consideration but not so much of a consideration because only a particular kind of kid ... there's definitely the particular kind of people that go to the type of public high schools he went to.

Even the grade school he went to is public school. I don't know ... he was at the particular school from grade one to grade four. And then he has to move to a middle school. He went to Boyle ... It's a private school, Montessori school for middle school. And after the middle school then he went to high school. Yeah, but you know, one of the considerations was ... well, the quality of education was very important, to get good quality education. So all in all, just the schools he went to were really, like, the top two percentile ... whether private or public.

In addition to academic quality, Nkolika chose a non–faith-based private school for her daughters because that's what suited her work schedule.

Because the public schools don't have the hours that will suit my work ... my hours at work, I chose the private school. The public school closes by 2:00 PM, and by 2:00 PM I'm still at work, while the private schools have a provision for you to come by six to pick up the kids, yeah. Well finance is ... Finance is a little bit high, you know, but for academics they do well. Also the public schools do well, but I just prefer the private schools academically. But the public schools in suburbs are better than the public schools ... in the city. Maybe if I eventually move to the suburbs, I will put my kids in the public school.

For the family of Nwakaego, the level of her children's schooling is one of the determinants of school choice. This means that all of her children go through both public and private faith-based schools during their elementary schooling period. From Pre-K to third grade, her kids attend public school. But from fourth to eighth grade, they go to Catholic schools. Her reason is that teachers in the public schools tended to lose their grip on the children once they were in the fourth to eighth grade. An unintended consequence of this is that her children have the experience of both the private and public school worlds. However, morals, values, and academics were the constant factors that influence their decision.

> For me, with private school … not just private school … I chose Catholic school … because, you know, being a Catholic and liking the knowledge that you get from the Catholic school. You know, everything, like with discipline and everything. I mean education for me … the grade is still a priority, you know; but at the same time, the morals and the values that are most important, you know … for me they are the topmost on the list. So that is why … for me when they get to the fourth grade, because I know that from the Pre-K to the third grade in the public school where they are is good. But then when they get to fourth grade, I change them to the Catholic school, you see? So … because the public school from fourth grade to the rest, you know, to eighth grade, the teachers don't have that much hold on the students. But from Pre-K to third … I mean I go there to volunteer. I stay there with them. The teachers have … I mean they still got a grip on the kids because, you know, children … that is the time you mold them … they are easier to mold at that time. But from fourth grade, fifth grade, I send them over to another school. So once they get to fourth grade … it's a whole lot different. So that's why.

> Public school … I don't have anything against public school. Public school except for the ones that I know that are … you know most of them … most of them are good. Some are good, but you just have to do your research and, you know, follow whatever … your research … whatever you come up with. But for this one that I know … it's not … just like … I mean when the teachers … when the students can no more be controlled by the teachers … that is a red flag for me. Like from first … kindergarten to third grade of this school … of this public school they are excellent. They are excellent, you know? But after that, I am not sure of the rest, you know.

When I reminded Nwakaego that Catholic Schools are very expensive, she responded:

> Yes, I mean of what use will it be if I make the money and lose them, you know, in something that is not worth it or something that I could have rectified. Not … that the other [public] school cannot influence them. But at least most of the time … you know at least

you can see the discipline and, you know, you can see their code of conduct, which is very good. The teachers, they still got control of the students, you know.

The driving force in the choice of schools for her children, according to Nneamaka is faith—religion. Academics equally played a part in her choice:

> Actually for me, it was the faith because they don't teach religion in public school. I needed them to get some Catholic education as I did when I was growing up. Actually that was the major thing that influenced me. I wanted them to, you know, get the Catholic faith growing up at least until … Definitely the public schools in our community are good in academics. But like I said, it's not just academics for me; it is the religion part. It is the knowledge of God in their life that really influenced me. It wasn't the academics because I can take care of their academics, me as a teacher. Okay. But the religious part I couldn't quite impart effectively, so I needed that part to be filled. It's like a void that I couldn't fill because they might not listen to me. I am not a professional in that area. So the academics part plus the religious part, you know, combined. That was the major thing that influenced me to send them to Catholic schools, not just private school. I had to send them to Catholic school to at least get the initial molding, you know, their initial years to get that going.

According to Nebeolisa, whether the children attend public or private school is a common topic of discussion among Igbo parents. I found the reason that influenced his school choice for his children interesting. He prefers public to private school because it allows his children to interact with children from every strata of society.

> That always comes up, I think … it's in my view, maybe shaped by my father … back home. I've always … I would like my children to go to public schools so that they will interact with children from every strata of the society. I can send them to special schools, but sometimes the expense is really not worth the need. From my investigation, you know, the school at this level is good. And that's where their friends go to … and to me they are learning at the level they are supposed to learn. I hope that it will continue to be the same, but what I have always said is that I would rather have them go to public school—have that experience of meeting real people and not just people maybe at a certain social class. But then I can

always get them arranged for private tutoring to make up for what is deficient. That was the way my dad raised us. We went to the public schools in Nigeria, but he had private lessons for us. I think that helped shape who I am … you know, in terms of … the way I look at life. (Nebeolisa)

He also thought that some parents who send their kids to private school, especially those who live in expensive neighborhoods, might be doing so just to show off or to have something to brag about. On the other hand, Nebeolisa acknowledges that there may be a pressing need to choose a private school, especially for those who live in places where going to a public school might be a challenge, if not a risk or a threat to the life of the child.

For some parents, they want to go about … go to parties and tell how they are paying so much to keep their child at a certain level. But when you look at the progress of the child, it's no difference for the child who goes to the other school. A lot of it, I guess … there might be legitimate reasons if, at some point, he says he's going to a public school and there's a lot of gang activity there, I may not want to expose him to that. But for now where he's going, you know, he's relatively safe, and he can get the kind of education he needs. It's not a status thing for me. Like for some parents, I guess … it's a status thing to tell the story that my child goes to private school. I have friends who pay quite a bit of money to have their [children go to a private school] … they live in good neighborhoods. They bought their houses in expensive communities. Yet they also pay heavily for their children to go to private schools. No, especially at the elementary level, I don't think that's important. If they are in Chicago, maybe a place where even going to school is a challenge, then I can think about going to a private school, where I know that a lot of the kids there want to learn.

Nsobundu did not regret forgoing private school and sending his children to public schools, not only because of the expense of private education, but also because some of the most successful Americans went to public schools. For him, his children can become successful and responsible citizens by going to public schools. Nevertheless, he admits that there might be a situation where a child would need private school:

Well, I'm sure everybody would like their child to go to private school, but private school is also very expensive. And even if I had the money, I wouldn't be so quick in sending my children to private school because if you look at people who are successful in this country, they are not all ones that went through private school. But it is also good that you go to private school and again it depends on the child. Like my fourteen-year-old is also in a gifted school, and she has done extremely well. So we're not ... I don't think we're missing it. You know the private school thing is not something that we cry over. But there might be a point where a child might need that kind of private polishing, yeah. So we didn't miss it.

Nnaemeka and his wife, Ijeoma, considered student performance, a harmonious environment, the level of discipline, and the type of neighborhood before choosing the school their children would attend.

In conclusion, listening to the reasons these Igbo parents have for choosing a particular school for their children, we can say that though there are various factors that influence their decision, academics is the driving force.

Typical Days Revolve Around Education

Here, I present how parents said they spend a typical day, whether weekdays or weekends or holidays, involving themselves in the education of their children. For most parents, it is usually a long day, especially for those who combine parental involvement with working or going to school. Activities in a typical day include waking up, showering, dressing, making breakfast, taking their children to and from school, making dinner, doing homework, reading, performing extracurricular activities and projects, and finally getting ready for bed, saying prayers, and ending the day.

Nneka talked about a typical day with her six-year-old daughter, starting with waking up, dropping and picking her up from school, and ending with bedtime.

> Well, a typical day starts with us waking up in the morning. Like I said, we share brushing of the teeth. So I do it in the morning; she does it at night. And then she knows we're going to school today. And at school they tell them what to expect the next day, so she has an idea what is coming up. And then I take her ... drop her off at school, and then I pick her [up], say, about four or five. And then we ... when I pick her up ... coming back in the car, she tells me ... I ask her questions about her day. She relates that to me, and that way we are not just heading home. We are also like looking back—what did we do today? And she gets to ask me questions too. "Mommy, what happened today?" She will ask me, "Mommy, do you have homework like me too?" Isn't that funny? And she thinks that myself and her are competing because I'm at the same school

at the same time with her. And it's funny when she asks questions like that. And she tends to find out when I'm driving fast and when there's a stop sign. And so she pays attention to all that.

And then coming back home, depending on the traffic, we get to wash our hands. Sometimes I don't remember. I forget, and she will remind me that washing hands is good because you wash out all the germs. That's a typical preschooler because they sing along how to cut down bacteria at school, and she'll remind me, "Mommy, no, we have to wash our hands first." And we do that. I fix dinner. Depending, I will ask her what she wants; she might say pizza or pasta, but then I will ask her, "How about the green?" And she will say, "I don't like it." And I say, "How about the flower?" We call broccoli "flower." So that way she sees it as a flower, and she likes it, and she will like to eat broccoli. So we put broccoli with pasta. So we are not dismissing what she wants to eat, but we try to make it healthy by adding broccoli. Have flowers with the green flower. And then after … we don't usually … I don't usually like to have the TV on when we're eating, but sometimes I break the rule. I'll want to watch the news, and she'll say, "Mommy, no TV. Remember you said this." And so we eat without TV, and we progress from there. We take a little break, and then we do PBS.org depending on what … or we play with puzzle. Or probably they did some painting at school, and she will show me what they did. And I am proud of her. We put it on … I have a billboard for her at home, where I put all the work that she brings that day, and you know, I tell her it's a beautiful work, and I display that for the day. So by the end of the week, she picks out the one that we're going to put down because next week is coming. And so that way she's encouraged to bring more back home. And when she's at school she's doing all this, she knows that mommy appreciates it. You know, she's doing a good job.

For Ogechi and Nneka, a typical day ends with bedtime:

We try to go to bed as early as we can because we are early birds. I try to get her to bed at eight. I tried seven thirty, but it was not feasible … it doesn't work most of the time because depending on the traffic when we come back, we have dinner and do other things. But we … I was tracking on eight because then if she sleeps early, she will get enough sleep, enough rest. And so before going to bed I try to read her a story or let her sing, do what is fun. That way she winds down and that's it. So that's what our typical day looks like.

Then I wanted to know from Nneka's perspective what the weekend looks like:

> [The] weekend is different. I try not to do it all by myself. I try to call up one or two parents and see what they're doing over the weekend, see if we can do things together with other families. Otherwise, we can also choose … I can also ask her [my daughter] what she wants to do. At this point she has an idea. You know, "I want to play with my dolls." I want to do this, I want to do that. And we work it out. And some weekends I'm not there. We have a nun that comes in to help us and sit with her. Sometimes they take a shuttle bus and go around the city, or they go to the library, depending on what they are doing. Or they take a walk to the park if it's a beautiful day and the weather is good.

Njideka works four days a week, and that defines her typical day as she tries to involve herself in the education of her children.

> So a weekday would be … mostly, it's waking up and getting ready for school. They wake up around six thirty, seven. And then school starts at eight thirty. If there's a lot of time between when they finish eating their breakfast and getting ready and going to school, you know, they can read. They try to read a little bit every day, so they might try to read a few minutes. If they have a test, usually in the morning we'll be reviewing the final last minute to make sure that they still remember everything for their exam. We'll review the questions that might be on the test. Then go to school. They'll be at school all day. School ends at three fifteen. And then after school, if it's a Tuesday or a Thursday, that's when a babysitter will take them to the educational center, where they'll get their additional instruction and the additional assignments. And then they'll come home and do their homework, dinner, and then hopefully around then, I'm coming home to meet them, can review their homework, you know, review anything else. Maybe they have another test or more projects. We'll work on any projects that might have to be done. You have to sign their homework and then prepare for bed, bath, and then prayer time, and then sleep. Bedtime is … we say eight, but it doesn't usually happen until almost nine. Eight thirty, nine.

The weekend is equally busy for Njideka and her children:

> So weekend, it depends. Like usually they have all their birthday parties with their friends, but Saturday morning without fail …

every other Saturday morning from ten to one, they go to the Igbo class. Then after that, it's usually more … I mean they have to do their enrichment packet, their enrichment packet which should take them less than an hour. There's no TV on Saturdays. No TV or computer on Saturdays, so they have to find other ways to, you know, to occupy themselves. Maybe after Igbo class, after the chores of cleaning the house and putting away their papers and cleaning their toy area, then maybe we will have an activity. We try to either … maybe we go bowling or go to Chuck E. Cheese. Or they might have a birthday party or something. Then yeah, it's kind of unstructured after the Igbo class and their academic lesson. It's at Dominican university. They try to stop in the summer, and then in the summertime, they organize the Igbo soccer camp.

Nnamdi is self-employed, so his time is a bit more flexible. He does most of the routine daily work because his wife works while also going to school. However, she takes over and does her part when she comes back from work and school:

A typical day starts, you know, like around … for them 6:00 AM. I wake up anyway before that to prepare what they eat and what they will take to school. You know, I wake up before my wife, and then my wife comes to the kitchen. By that time, I've prepared the food they're gonna eat. And then next step is dressing them up for school. That is the busiest hour of the day in the morning. And then I have to take my daughter first, and I come back [and] take my son. They are at opposite ends of the city. You know, so he's off at two fifteen, and I pick him up, I put him in the car, and I go get her. And then we get home, and then we eat lunch, and they get in their play. You know, that's about it. And then my wife comes … my wife is like you. You know, she's in school. And then she comes home in the evening. And when she comes home, I retire. Yes … but in between that, you know … the older girl she practices cello. And then sometimes she does a concert. She plays, you know. And at night we have dinner, and there are stories before bed and reading before bed. Sometimes she reads … sometimes, you know, there's a series of books she reads. There are two stories, two books. You know she's at tenth now, so sometimes she comes home and goes away and then reads that for two to four hours, depending on …

The weekend is primarily for extracurricular activities:

Weekend is different because that's where their extracurricular activities and playing a whole lot with [other] kids. Sometimes we go to the museum. She used to go to ballet class and stuff like that. You know, do this, that, or the other. We go to the park, go downtown, you know … (Nnamdi)

Nwakaego describes a typical day by pointing some of the duties she shares with her husband. She also talked about how she balances a typical day's duties with her own schooling.

Okay, from the time they wake up. Okay, they shower, and breakfast will be provided for them. I'll dress up the ones that need help with dressing up, okay? And … then serve breakfast. Then after eating breakfast, I'll go to drop them off. We divide it. My husband will carry the one that goes to the private school. Then I'll drop off the rest that go to the other school. And when I drop them off, I go to my own school, and he goes to his business. And when it's time for pickup, I go back for the pickup. By then I must have been done with my classes or some of my classes for the day. Some days I won't be done, and then he will go and pick them up. Other days, if I'm done, I will pick them up.

And when we come back, just like I said, you continue from where you stopped with them. You start with the assignments, you know, the homework that they got. So what I do is I start from the ones that need help. So the ones that don't need help, they will do it on their own. Then after they will come and assist the ones that need help while I'm still getting to meet up with them. Then when I get there, I will now finish up whatever that they left unfinished. Then at the end of the day, by the time we are done with this, it's time for dinner. And I prepare the dinner, and dinner will be served. Then they will eat and play a little bit.

Then it's time to go to bed. Then we pray. If I'm now too exhausted, they will pray with their daddy, and then they will go to bed. I will want them to go to bed around nine so I will get some time and do my own stuff because I still got some homework to do. So at the end of the day, you know, it's the bed. (Nwakaego)

The weekend, according to Nwakaego, is still the same "running around" but perhaps in a different direction—attending to the children's extracurricular activities.

On weekends … Saturdays are … sometimes they are enrolled in some activities like basketball or football. They go to Igbo school too, where we teach them the language. Yeah, so some days are like that. Then within the same weekend, we go for, you know, any celebration that we have in the community, like birthday parties, graduation parties, or wake keepings. Yeah, then they go and … they go for a choir practice in the church too, so it's still the same running around sort of, because you run from one end 'til, you know, it's time to bring them back … and you stay there most of the time though …

Nneamaka has five children, but in a typical day, her fourteen-year-old middle-school student gets most of the attention, while the others can take care of themselves in the daily routine: waking up, getting breakfast, going to school, etc. Though weekends are for extracurricular activities, they also provide the opportunity to get some extra sleep:

A typical day looks like we wake up. I have somebody who leaves here by 6:15 AM in the morning; my last child … the bus picks her up like six twenty. So in a typical day, my husband wakes her up personally five forty-five. So she takes a shower [and] dresses herself because she can do that now. And then we prepare a light breakfast for her to eat. By six twenty, she is picked up by the bus. And then I go get ready myself to go to work. While the big ones who are in college, they usually get up around seven thirty, eight. They are ready … they leave the house around nine, depending on their … you know the time they have their lectures. They usually start their lectures, some people, at ten most of them. So I'll leave the house approximately seven twenty, seven thirty every day, and then I can return around three thirty, four. So my child comes home. The last child comes home … she is fourteen now. She comes home around two thirty, and she's received by my mother, who is home. Okay, so they stay until I get back home in an hour's time. I usually come home at three thirty, four … and then we will have homework, and then I start my second job, you know, on the Internet after I have taken care of her homework.

And then my big children, they return late in the night—11:30 PM, 12:00. One of them works in the schools, you know. So it's like after classes, he does some work in the lab. He's employed in the lab, so he works in the lab 'til like nine. And then they study from nine … and then the other one … you know, usually their classes end at nine, so from nine to eleven, eleven thirty, twelve, they are studying. And then they come home around twelve thirty. And when they're home,

I'm still awake, so we go to the next phase of studying. So twelve thirty for them 'til like two, they will study in the house … 12:30 AM to 2:00 AM they are studying while I am doing my work. So they study for at least another one and a half to two hours, and then they go to bed. And then I usually go to bed around two thirty myself. I will wake up at six; the day starts again, Monday through Friday. Weekends we wake up late. And then we attend our community stuff, go to church on Sunday, and then Monday we start again.

For Nebeolisa, a typical day includes preparing his son's mind for classes on their way to school:

[The day begins] usually in the morning, just trying to get everybody up. I take them to school. My wife used to do that, but then because, you know, she will not take everybody with her to go. So now I do that on my way to work. And that ten minutes I find quite instructive because I'm preparing his mind for school, you know. "So what are you guys gonna learn today?" or "What did you guys learn yesterday?" And then before he leaves the car, I pray with him and say, "When you go, pay attention and listen to your teacher. And don't play rough play. Make sure you stay away from trouble." And then he runs off … goes for breakfast … then I don't pick them up from school because the time … they finish by two thirty, I am still at work.

Picking them up reveals something interesting about one of the strengths of their community:

But the interesting thing that happens here … because my wife is available, let's say Mondays and Fridays, to pick them up in the evening. And days that she cannot pick them up, the women from our community here, any of them that goes to the school will pick them up. You see that's the beauty of community. You know, I was really impressed … on one of my off days, so I had to go to the school to pick them up. By the time I got to the school, I didn't see my children. But one of the ladies from my community—one of the Igbo women—had already picked up all the kids. Because what they do is if anybody arrives by three, all the kids will follow them. They know everybody goes with whoever comes … like if it's winter they [children] will go to their [women] cars and wait. So as other parents pull up, you then pick up your own children. So by, say, three … or fifteen minutes after there is … none of us is coming, the woman will take the children to her house or call on the cell phone and say, "What's holding you up?"

In a typical day, waking up is still a problem for some of Nnaemeka's children:

> Getting up ... in a typical day, I would say getting up, we wake the kids up. So actually it's interesting because that is one part that my kids have not yet [learned], the ones that are here, like Ekene and Tobi, I seem to wake them up every morning. I guess they figured Dad will always wake them up. So I have told them to listen to the alarm. If the alarm can't wake you up, I don't see how I can. Because there may be days I may not be around here to wake you [them] up at the same time every morning. And once I call them, they get up and go take their shower, take their bath, and get everything ready ... Eat and then they are ready for school and walk to the bus. So they go to the school, and we haven't had any problems at school or anything of the sort.

> But when they get out from school, they normally come home, and they will always have our permission before they go outside to play or even join their friends or ride their bike anywhere. Or one of us must be there because we don't let them ride their bike with only friends. You know, these days it's scary over here. It's not that we have already experienced any of such. No, but we're just trying to prevent any incident. But from knowing what's ... from the news and from all the things you hear about, it's just that we want to make sure they are safe wherever they are. You know, so if they decide to go to the park or to do whatever, we just join them and spend a few hours with them. So every school day, they get busy. They prepare. They go to their bus stop and just ride with other kids and come home, start their homework as soon as they get home from school. And they finish their homework, and then the rest of the evening they have to themselves. Either they go play basketball in the backyard or decide to ride their bike around the house.

He sets the alarm to remind his kids that it is time to go to bed, but that has not really worked.

> Normally, I set alarm at eight, but sometimes it's hard. We've always instilled in them that it's good to go to bed like between nine and nine thirty every evening. Some days they just take extra minutes and go to bed like 10:00 PM, and they wake up like six. (Nnaemeka)

The weekend is used for house chores and other extracurricular activities.

> Weekend, I would say it is different. It's not all that different. It's different in the sense that they get to stay in bed for extra two or three hours. When they get up, of course, they participate in helping to keep the house clean ... clean the house, help with any cleaning, clean the bathroom. We divide it. We divide the work. So somebody will be cleaning the bathroom. Somebody have the kitchen, somebody the parlor, so it's like everybody has a share of things to do.

In these families, a typical day revolves around education—schooling, dropping and picking children up, homework, extracurricular activities, etc. For some parents, it is the typical day that dictates their daily schedule. The weekend is different. Basically, it is the same running around but in a different direction to engage the children in educational activities.

Homework

Homework is a regular menu item in the typical day of the children, whose parents participated in this study. Nneka says it is the parents' duty to assist the kids with their homework. "We have to participate in their homework, whatever it takes to get them ... get it done." As we shall hear, these roles include retrieving the homework and instructions from the child's backpack, reviewing the homework, assisting, supervising, reading the teacher's comments on the previous homework, and correcting and signing the homework sheet.

Nsobundu says that assisting in homework begins with retrieving the homework and instruction from his son's backpack and checking the teacher's comment on the previous work and then taking it from there.

> He [my son] comes home. We look at his backpack, you know. They come in from school, what homework needs to be done? And then we talk about it, you know? Like when I come home I say ... or like I call on the phone and say, "How was school?" You know they always say, "Good." [Laughter] And then when I talk to my wife, I say, "Who brought him home? Did you check his backpack?" You know, "How did he do? Any comment?" and all those things. So we do his homework, and he does his studies, but we look at the comments from the teacher; making sure ... and look at his homework that

he did the previous day to see what kind of grade that he has in all those ... and we take it from there.

Nnaemeka and his wife are strict with homework and expect the teachers to be firm and report to them if any of their children fail to turn in homework. They mentioned one occasion where they had to ask for more homework for one of their sons, who seemed to be bored with the regular homework and school activities:

> And regarding the homework ... if they don't turn it in, we don't let them come in. So we are strict in the house, and we want the teachers to be firm over there so that if they don't bring their homework back, please call back here and let me know. I have to know why that homework wasn't turned in. And ... one time we were at a parent-teacher conference even though they didn't want us to be there because we don't just take anything. So at the conference, we were telling them that the class seems to be boring for Ekene; we need you to give him more homework so that he will get busy when he comes home. If you don't give him enough things to work on, then he's not using his brain. Then he will just channel it to the TV ... but if he has enough homework, then his attention ... everything will be focused on the homework. Of which that teacher, since then, has been giving him enough homework.

Nwakaego knows that she can't help all five of her children with their homework at the same time. That is why her first step in managing her children's homework is to find out which of her children need help the most:

> And when we come back, just like I said, you continue from where you stopped with them. You start with the assignments, you know, the homework that they got. So what I do is I start with the ones that need help. So the ones that don't need help, they will do on their own. Then after they will come and assist the ones that need help while I'm still getting to meet up with them. Then when I get there, I will now finish up whatever that they got unfinished. Then at the end of the day, by the time we are done with this, it's time for dinner.

Nkolika gives priority to her children's homework once they come home from school. Her oldest daughter sometimes takes the initiative to ask for assistance:

> So when they come back, I feed them. I allow them to rest. Then I turn off the TV or anything that is on. And then I put them

in a chair, then we start to do some schoolwork. At least we take like one hour, one and a half hours, we're done with schoolwork. Then I allow them to ride their bikes ... play with their toys, you know? That's what I do. Yeah, my daughter, my first one who is in kindergarten—if she has work that is very hard for her, once she comes back home, she will tell me, "Mommy, this work is very hard. Can you help me out?" If she has homework, she calls me right away. "Mommy, can we do our homework together?" Like ... they are reading books now in school, and ... she's in book twelve. Once I come to pick her up, she's happy to tell me she's on book twelve.

Despite her tight work schedule, Njideka still plays a role in helping with homework:

There are only so many hours in the day. And because I do work at least four days a week, I do have to get help for transporting people to the different activities. And then when they come back and they finish the homework, the work will be waiting for me to correct it after they finish.

Nonye makes the effort to be present while her daughter does her homework:

My staying with her when she does her homework is to show her, "This is what is important for me. It must be done." But I trust her that whenever she says she can do something, she will do it.

Igbo parents see homework as an important aspect of their children's schooling and education. That is the reason they make the best effort in assisting them. The multiple ways in which they assist their children (even just being present while the child does the homework) is indicative of their dedicated parental involvement.

Teaching and Learning at Home

As we have seen, education includes the teaching and learning that occur outside the school. Moreover, "every moment is a teachable moment," says Nnamdi. In this section, I will present the various ways of teaching and learning that Igbo parents are involved in that go a long way to enhance a child's education. This includes discipline, personal hygiene, values, morals, integrity, perseverance, punctuality, and time management.

Njideka considers teaching her children discipline and how to make the best use of time—two of her important educational duties toward them. She regards this teaching as planting seeds and does it by making house rules and regulations.

> The playroom … but also we have a clock and a desk in the corner where the idea was that … for some of their things I want them to know that, you know, you can't just sit and be fooling around and take two hours to do something that should take ten minutes. So the clock is there so that you have an idea of when you started. Some of the assignments he brings home, they ask you the start time and finish time so they can see how focused and how quickly you're able to do it. So you know, we're supposed to have a quiet area. But when people are doing homework then the play doesn't happen. So you have playtime, and if you're playing … like if the younger kids are playing then they should play upstairs while the kids are doing their homework downstairs. And then when everybody is finished with their homework then everybody can play. So you know, trying to have a separate area for study, making sure that everybody knows no TV is on until all homework is complete … so even if you finish your homework, okay, find a book to read.

In addition, she teaches them to work hard to earn things and not to take things for granted, but rather to appreciate what they have. She uses every opportunity that presents itself, including family prayer time, to teach them these important lessons about life.

> But I think it's good to be cautious. I think it's good to not give kids everything and say yes to … everything they ask you. I like them to earn things. Like if they say, "Oh, I would like to play with Kelvin. You know him. You met his mom." I said, "Oh yeah, I did, but let's see how you behave this week. Then we'll decide." Then every time he misbehaves, I say, "Oh, I guess you don't want to play on Saturday with him." [Her son says] "Oh okay, okay. I'll go clean it. I'll go clean it. Okay, I'm cleaning," you know? So make them work for something, because I mean, my kids are so privileged, and I don't think that they fully understand that. But I need to be able to teach them some responsibility and not just to have them think that oh, everything is so easy. You know, we always talk about how … like one prayer that we have is, you know, God … we start talking about the things that we're thankful for and things that, you know, not everybody has. So they have some appreciation that, you know, everybody doesn't have like, this kind of house. And everybody doesn't have like two parents, even. Everybody doesn't have brothers and sisters that they get to play with. Everybody doesn't have a

wardrobe full of clothes. You know, so they say that sometimes to their parents. You know, "Thank you that we have a nice house." I say … okay … somebody taught me this prayer, and I thought it was so beautiful, so the kids use that format. They say, "God, it would have been enough if I had one loving parent, but you gave me two loving parents. It would have been enough if I just had a roof over my head, but you gave me a beautiful large house …" And so they just keep going on about … how they have more than the minimum. (Njideka)

Njideka is optimistic that these seeds will germinate and yield a plentiful harvest, and that is the reason she does not give up.

So hopefully they … you know, you just keep planting all the seeds. You hope it germinates, you know? But you just have to … you still have to plant it, so we're just laying down all the seeds.

America is a competitive society, say many of the participants, and so children have to be taught right from the beginning how to deal with failures and successes. A failure can be an opportunity for growth, if one is willing to learn from it. Nwakaego uses the occasion of her daughter being demoralized about her coming in second place in a spelling bee contest to teach her an important lesson about perseverance, the necessity to learn from one's failures, and the need to improve on one's performance.

In this particular case, she disagreed with the teacher, who thought that Ebele should be left alone because she didn't want to compete again:

I brought it up with their teacher, you know? That is one of the parent-teacher meetings that I went to. Of course you'd think that the teacher would say, "Oh come on, you can do it." No. My daughter said, you know, "I don't think I can do well in spelling bee." The teacher responded, "I don't like the spelling bee competition either …" I was like, "Okay, cut it out, teacher. Cut it out." That's not what I want. She feels that's not the true test for children. I understand that's not the true test, but then that is part of, you know, just being competitive in that aspect, you know? It's academically challenging oneself, you know? (Nwakaego)

Hygiene is one of the things that Nneka teaches her daughter Ogechi:

I also try to let her know things about playing with other kids, that sharing is a good thing but not sharing things … maybe toothbrush or something because she will get bacteria. I always give her the feedback why she should not share her toothbrush or whatever she is eating with somebody. I also make her participate in brushing her teeth. So we have a schedule where she will brush her teeth at night; mommy will brush for her in the morning. And that worked out well … and so she knows … her turn is at night, and mine is in the morning. That way she keeps [a regular schedule] … it's good to work with a child on a routine, so that keeps her on a routine. And she also … I try to let her know that she can fold her clothes. She can help mommy. And so she's not waiting for me to do it for her … do things for her all the time. So she folds her clothes. So it doesn't matter how well she does it, but that's a step, a beginning. When I'm in the kitchen, I can always call her for help. She can help hand me plates or spoons. Or she can sit down there and watch mommy. So … it's partnering with her and also the school at the same time.

"Discipline is key to learning," said Nebeolisa. In fact, that is one of the reasons he uses every opportunity to teach his children discipline, even if it means taking away some of their privileges. He has found out that sometimes a parent has to teach a particular lesson several times "for kids to get it." For example, Nebeolisa's son turned on the TV while doing his homework during the time that he knew his father was busy doing an interview with me and that his mother would not be back yet. He knew this was against the house rules and that he should do no such thing. Nebeolisa explained:

I've made it clear to them. "You have to learn." And so for you to learn, this is the way, the kind of discipline that you bring to it. You know, because discipline is the key to learning. You can't watch TV while you are doing your homework. Otherwise, I will take away those privileges. You know but kids … I hear the television because he knows I'm busy. He will put on the television and try to do his homework.

Nkolika says that it is also her duty to teach her children politeness and discipline even though the school also teaches that.

You know … [I] teach them not to fight, not to cry when they want something, to use words when they want something, not to scream or cry in order to get what they want. So … my role is to teach them things too, like I teach them how to be polite. You teach them to be disciplined. Even though the school does the same thing, I still do it.

Children should be taught to "own their own lives" as early as possible. Nnamdi feels that he actually taught his son, Dozie, how to own his life at the age of fifteen, when he gave him a book to read:

The Secret is a book about … *The Secret* taught people about owning their affairs and becoming what they wanna be. I put that book in my son's hand when he was fifteen, sixteen. After he read that book, he was clear as to what it is he wants to become. All this time, we are planning on going to the University of Chicago and studying economics or going to Harvard Law School. That was the plan. By the time he was seventeen, everything changed.

Nnaemeka said that "from time to time [they] would pick a topic and start to discuss it" in order to teach his children the importance of dialogue and how to engage in a discussion.

Teaching children enduring life lessons also occurs at home, outside of the school. It occurs through the child's personal experience, which parents help them to process and digest. It can take place through the direct teaching given by parents or through the exposure to educational environments, which the parents provide.

Volunteering

Volunteering is one of the ways that parents are involved in the education of their children. Whether it is mandatory or optional depends on the school. Areas where parents are asked to volunteer include playing with the kids, reading to them, helping in the lunchroom, assisting a teacher in the classroom, chaperoning kids during field trips, helping to organize social functions, and helping the school secretary and receptionist.

For example, parents are encouraged to volunteer at Assumpta, a suburban faith-based private school, which Ogechi (Nneka's daughter) attends. Parents who wish to volunteer have to sign up for it at the beginning of the semester. Ogechi is always happy to see her mother volunteer.

And another thing that I didn't mention about *Assumpta* [parish school] is that they encourage parents to come in and read a story to the kids. You know, maybe [at] story time, the parents can bring in a book from home and spend ... maybe two hours, an hour, or half an hour, depending on what time ... what the parents want to offer in an hour, or play with the kids or teach them a play. It's on a volunteer basis. Well, it's if you can do it. They put it out early at the beginning of the semester of a school year and ask each parent what date on the calendar they would like to come in and help with the kids. And that's a beautiful way, you know, of having to participate at the school. You know, reading to the kids, playing with them, or even helping serve probably their lunch or their breakfast that they have in the morning. That is really helpful. The school appreciates it. And they take pictures of the day that you're there, and they put it on the board, you know, put it all over what you did with the kids that day. Probably it's an artwork that you did with them. They put it all over. And the kids, they get to remember that … Some parents were here the other day … My mother came to teach us. I remember that very well. I know I've participated. I've read … I've gone to read a story … a book to the kids. And that was really nice, and Ogechi was very proud that her mommy came … to help at school. So that's another way of participating. (Nneka)

Some parents volunteer on their day off. Though it is not a requirement, Njideka sometimes volunteers on Wednesdays if she is invited. She recalled one such day:

You know sometimes I'll volunteer in the school … it's not a requirement, but like the teachers sometimes need help in the classroom. Sometimes they just want people to help them organize the lessons for the next day; just … maybe just … collating papers or even just Xeroxing. So like, I have just done that. I can do that sometimes on Wednesdays. They've called me … once for … that was for the preschool, they asked me, you know … to read. And then one time they said, "Oh, since you're a doctor, could you come and do a medical presentation to the kids?" So you know I came with my coat and my stethoscope and my reflex hammer and was doing a few things for the kids. They thought that was fun.

Nwakaego has volunteered on several occasions. But she recently started going to school, and that has considerably reduced the number of hours she can volunteer:

Before I used to volunteer, but since … I started school, I don't volunteer anymore as I used to. Yeah, before I used to volunteer. But now I just go to probably … sometimes on field trips. I make sure that I attend each and every one of their field trips. The one that's accessible for parents to come, I make sure that I attend those ones. Then when they have functions in school, you know, like participation at midday … the ones at midday I try to come if they are doing something special, you know. Participation … of course has gone down since I started school because of time. Or I go sometimes … when they need somebody to … talk about maybe Africa or something that we do. Maybe the way we dress or the way we cook. Then other times I will just go and assist the teachers, with the reading, you know, then preparing for some celebrations. We try to set up and play games with the kids ... and just from academics to everything. Oh they have gone to apple orchard. That is where they grow apples, so they pluck apples. They see how they are grown. Then they see how a bee makes honey. Then they have gone to a play, you know, shows, drama. Then they've gone to Governors State University, where they were shown how the body works. And they have gone to see the astronauts, you know ... what's in the sky and everything. Then they have gone to children's museum and a museum of arts and technology, you know, for all those dinosaurs and things. So they have been to different places. And they have gone to a farm, you know, to see ... where they rear goats, pigs, donkeys, all those [animals], chickens, and ... stuff like that.

In some schools, "volunteering" is not an option. Nneamaka says that in the school her youngest daughter attends, parents must volunteer some time on behalf of the child. Every year each parent must sign up for a certain number of hours.

You sign up every year. You must have hours you have to volunteer for every school year. It's mandatory. You have certain hours you have to volunteer. We do market days. We do baseball. We sell all these things. They do baseball. They sell candies, pop, and all those things. You have to monitor the game, take care of ... you know, whatever, clean up, sell items, clean up after the children's games, basketball, volleyball, baseball, market day, school activities, school dance, Grandparents Days. Volunteering is the name of the game, definitely. Yes you have to volunteer. You have to volunteer so many hours each school year on behalf of each child. Now it's ... for each child because each of the classroom teachers expects you to do this for your own child in his or her class, so you have to do that. And then you have general expectations from the school also.

While Nebeolisa rarely volunteers, his wife often does, because her time is more flexible. Usually, the school takes the initiative of inviting them to volunteer:

You know, they have special trips. I've been on one of the trips. It was a museum trip. But my wife often volunteers ... anytime they have a trip ... and she's available ... they do ask, but I have volunteered. But usually my wife is more ... because her schedule is more flexible. So we worked it out in such a way that ... I mean she can be with and attend to their needs ... her schedule is more flexible than my schedule, you know.

Nnaemeka sees volunteering as an important aspect of parental involvement. First, it helps to make the work a lot easier for the teacher and school, and secondly, parents need to see for themselves what is going on in the classrooms. He chaperones the children during field trips:

> Like when a teacher … like when some kind of message is sent around, let parents come to school to help their kids or to help participate in class, "Go into the class and help …" Go into the classroom and, you know, or pass food in the cafeteria. Yes, do a lot of things they do in a classroom. So parents' participation is very important because that … makes the work a whole lot easier for the teacher. Because the parent will also be part of the discipline the kid needs to pay attention to what the teacher is saying. And the parents get to see for themselves what their kids are like in their classrooms. So they don't have to be so, maybe, mad at the teacher … anytime the parent gets a note from the teacher, the parent automatically knows what that note is all about. So he doesn't have to go to the school rushing and sweating or doing anything like this because it's just … As a matter of fact … at the beginning of school or during the school year … they normally ask parents to come in and assign parents to different things they'd be interested in, like a field trip. Parents I know have been part of it. A lot of times when I had my days off, we chaperoned my kids. We go with them during bus trips to the museum or to places of interest … So the school allows that kind of input from parents.

Igbo parents volunteer at the schools their children attend. In few cases, it is mandatory for parents to volunteer a certain number of hours in a year. For them, volunteering is one of the practical ways they can be involved in the education of their children. It affords them the opportunity to know what goes on in the school and helps to make the teachers' work a lot easier.

Extracurricular Activities

Other activities that parents are involved in that promote the education of Igbo children include going to the library, zoo, or museum; going on vacations or day trips; attending sports practices and competitions; and taking dancing and swimming lessons.

For some of these activities, Nneka has a network of other mothers she works with. The essence of the network is to help her daughter connect with other people at an early age.

I network with mothers of her age group or a year older. And then she gets to meet them, and she learns from these kids, and they learn from her. And so she's not thinking it's just me and my mommy, but she knows there are other people existing in the world, and there are other things outside her environment. I've been able to take her to museums. I take her to the zoo. We've been able to go to … a beautiful place called Morton Arboretum. It's in a western suburb; Morton is … you have a lot of beautiful flowers. It's a vast ground where … people can take walk for an hour or two and you see nature at its peak. So we've been able to visit Morton Arboretum two or three times now. And she had learned to see nature not just on TV but the way it is. And see the birds and play with other kids. I think that's a plus. And I have also tried to enroll her in swimming because it's not just the fun part of it but in terms of safety. If the child learns how to swim, probably there's a crash somewhere on an aircraft or whatever; that's a plus for the child. So she's presently in swimming class … and also ballet, getting exercise, because these days we talk about obesity and what the child eats and all that. I … for me I think that a child can eat whatever he or she wants, but the thing is how much physical exercise is going in. How much are you breaking down? So that's another … part of education … people make excuses with the weather. "When the weather gets better, I can go out and exercise." But that should not be an excuse. You can do it even while the weather is bad. And so the learning environment she has is good. Again my parish school has a gym inside the school where the kids can play and get physical exercise … and besides the activities, I noticed that she picks up Spanish. Because her age group … her friends that are from Spanish culture or a Spanish background, and their parents … and they are taught Spanish at school, but then she has friends that speak Spanish to their parents or speak it in class. She picked up some of that and brings it home. I don't speak Spanish myself, but I thought it was a plus.

Providing for exercise takes more time and planning for a parent with three kids, because each one of them may be doing something different and sometimes in different places. That is the experience of Njideka. She makes the effort to provide enough space and equipment at home.

We try not to overdo it because of the number of hours in a day, but I mean they have done soccer. They're not doing soccer now. They're gonna start soccer in the summer again. Right now they swim every week. They're taking swimming lessons, swimming lessons. Niini does dance every week. She does tap dance and ballet. Chijioke Jr. does tumbling every week. He's in a gymnastics tumbling class. And I think that's all for outside structured activities. And then … of course they have bicycles and they ride around and whatever they do at school. But those are the structured ones. I think Chijioke Jr. has expressed an interest in karate … they say that's good for boys to focus, so I might try that one too. You know … little Noono my three-year-old was like, "Mommy, I wanna play table tennis with you," and so she was practicing how she could get the paddle and try to hit it on the little miniature one [board]. Yeah … it's small. It's smaller size, so it's for little people. And they have their smaller basketball.

Nnamdi emphasizes that traveling and visiting museums are very good ways for parents to effectively educate their children. He remembers an Igbo adage that says traveling is a very important source of education.

The primary thing for us is traveling. Yeah … you know, I think the best education … is traveling … the Igbo people have a saying that reflects what I am saying—*Onye nje-nje ka onye isi-awo* [gray-hair person] *ama ihe*. A traveler is more knowledgeable or educated than a person with white hair [sign of old age] who seldom travels[19]. Yeah. Traveling is the best form of education … I mean, the things I learned from going to London or to Poland or going to Wisconsin, etc. You know, so when you put a child through that experience, you know, it stays with them for life. I'm getting to meet people of other cultures; I'm getting to meet people of other circumstances. Traveling is a big part of it. Another big aspect of it is going to museums. You know … put a child in the museum of natural art and you take them to 245 BC. I mean go to the Museum of Science and Industry and discover how the airplane came about. So that's all part of it [education] …

Nwakaego wants her children to get the most out of these kinds of activities. So in addition to the suggestions she gets from friends and neighbors, she carefully researches the places she wants to take her children:

You know, this time and age with the Internet, you know, you can get most of your resources, information, online. Sometimes we will ask around. You may not even know anybody that has been there, but you can go to the Internet and get all the information,

---

19   This Igbo wisdom saying takes it for granted that knowledge comes from traveling experience and that gray hair comes with aging.

you know. And somebody else's experience might not be yours, you know … Yeah, so if it's … a place that I think, you know, is really interesting and is age appropriate for them, I will take them and let them experience it. Most of it is not my experience. It's their experience, so let them experience it. If they like it, you know, let them enjoy it … because some places I will take them to, I might not like it, but they are having a blast.

Also, several of Nwakaego's children are members of their parish's children's choir. Extracurricular activities like singing in a chorus provides excellent teaching and learning moments that might not be found in school or in the home.

In addition to other extracurricular activities, Nonye takes her daughter to the movies or the theater, especially those films or shows that are educational:

> We go to see shows, educational shows mostly. We go to see *Cirque de Soleil*, or we go to the theater. Or we go to movies that are popular. Like she didn't want to go to see *Avatar*, and I said, "Well, everybody is talking about it, so we have to go see it." And so we went to IMAX to make sure we saw it in 3D. And she appreciates that …

The children of Nnaemeka are involved in several extracurricular activities, including participating in their parish life:

> And another activity outside the family is that they enjoy going to church, of which they do Mass serving on Sunday, which they have never missed, even one day. They are always there for the 8:00 AM Mass.

Igbo parents in Chicago believe that extracurricular activities, such as team sports, dance, swimming, museums, parks, traveling, movies, choir, and so on, are important educational opportunities for their children. That's the reason they commit so much of their time and energy to make sure that their children experience these activities.

Igbo Language and Culture

Language and culture lessons are also considered extracurricular activities by most people, but in the case of the Igbo language and culture, I am presenting them separately because of the significance they have to the Igbo parents in this study and to the Igbo people in general with regard to the education of their children. Except for one, all of the children in families

I interviewed were born in Chicago or in the USA. In the narratives that follow, you will hear how and why Igbo parents carry out these significant educational activities in addition to all of the others. Apart from giving these American-born Igbo children Igbo names, some parents even send some of their children back to Igboland, Nigeria, to learn more about their roots.

Just like most Igbo parents, Nneka gives her daughter opportunities to learn the Igbo language and culture. She feels that doing this will broaden her daughter's view of the world, help her be a more tolerant individual, and ultimately make her a better American.

> Ogechi is a Nigerian name! So we had the intention of keeping our culture. We embrace some aspects of their [American] culture that are positive and, you know, let go of those that we think are not. Ogechi was born here, so she's a US citizen ... but we are raising her so that she will know both cultures and know where her parents came from, as well as embracing American culture too ... I've taken her to Nigeria twice now so that she will know where Mommy and Daddy came from, who her grandparents are, and what the culture is like. But she's still very young ... I'm sure she's absorbing as much as she can at this point.

> Igbo is our language, so she will learn that. I also liaise with mothers that take their kids for Igbo lessons over the weekend. And I was lucky to have a mother that called me up and sent me e-mails and asked me if I would be interested in enrolling her in ... the Igbo class program, and I said yes, I would definitely. And so that is a big plus, I suppose.

> And then I also speak Igbo language to her at home so that she can learn it. But I think that overall she has an edge because she's multicultural in the sense that she can fit in anywhere she goes. She's not like in a straightjacket like, "Oh, I'm an American, blah, blah, blah." She knows about other cultures. She knows that it's not just America that is in the world. There are other parts of the world and that it's okay to be black, and ... because she lives in a white community, it's not just about being white, that everybody is the same. So she has an edge in terms of that, and she learned to speak English. Her accent is different from mine, believe it or not.

> But ... she has an edge in that she can learn my language, she can learn English, and she can pick up Spanish. And not everybody is willing to ... expose their kids to that. And so that's ... but

it's also a struggle in terms of that's why I try to expose her to different activities and work with other mothers so she will not feel intimidated or anything. She's comfortable in her skin, or wherever she goes, she's comfortable and bold enough to say, "I am who I am," you know.

So coming home, I also try to feed her not just American food. I feed her Nigerian food. So she knows other food, and when people talk outside, she'll say, "My mommy feeds me *fufu*,[20] and I eat *fufu*." And so she has the opportunity of explaining to the other kids … [because] the other kids would like to know what *fufu* is, and she explains it to them as much as she can at this point. And she tells them it's good and all that, and now… from her, other people learn about our culture … you know, but she doesn't think about it that way. She tells people, "I am from [Evanston], Illinois," you know, but she eats *fufu*, you know? This person from [Evanston] eats *fufu*. It's funny. So it's a learning and growing process.

Since she was also born here in the United States, Njideka thinks that teaching American-born Igbo children the Igbo language and culture is an important way of sharing that culture with other people in this country and the rest of the world. She enrolled her children in the Igbo class at a local university and takes them to Igbo functions.

I mean, I guess that's part of their education. That's part of the acculturation. If we're really trying to share this Igbo culture, I think the most important … I think the thing that links me closest to Igbo culture, being that I wasn't born in Nigeria and never lived there, was that I was able to speak the language. Because most people, once they hear … they say, "Oh, you don't talk like you're Nigerian." And so the only thing that kind of buys my, you know, membership is that I can speak Igbo and understand everything they're saying. So I think people … that's like the link, you know? And anytime I can talk to somebody in Igbo, then they feel like, you know, you're one of them. And then if they find out later, "Oh,

---

20 *Fufu* is a common West African food. It has two parts, which consists of a vegetable, meat, or fish soup and semisolid ground grains—flour—of wheat or millet or sorghum or maize or yam or rice, made by boiling water and stirring the mixture of the flour and boiling water until it becomes semisolid, *fufu*. It can also be made by boiling cassava or cocoyam or unripe plantain in water and pounding in a mortar and with a pestle until a desired semisolid nature is achieved. It is eaten by rolling the fufu into a ball, dipping it into the soup, and swallowing or chewing.

you never lived in Nigeria ... really? Oh but you were speaking Igbo. How is that?" Then they know that you must have been in a very Nigerian home for you to be speaking the language. So I take them to Igbo class every two weeks, you know, and then any Igbo functions we go to. Then yeah, it's kind of unstructured after the Igbo class and their academic lesson. It's at the university. They try to stop in the summer, and then in the summertime, they organize the Igbo soccer camp. (Njideka)

Nkolika teaches and gives her daughters the opportunity to learn the Igbo language and culture, because it makes them unique and helps them to know where they come from. She always brings their daughters to Igbo town or state conventions[21], because in addition to socialization, events like this offer a unique opportunity to practice and live the Igbo language and culture. She is impressed that her six-year-old daughter seems willing and able to appreciate and identify with her ancestral culture.

I always go with my kids to our annual convention. Actually, we have a convention coming up in May. Last time it was held in Chicago, and every parent came with their child. Those conventions have things for children to get involved in. They had so many things for them to learn, cultural ... I mean, it was really, really educative [educational]. I really enjoyed it. So we're going to another one in May, and I look forward to taking my kids. Yeah, a lot of things for the child to also know where she comes from, you know ... to try to learn the language. Like we're Nigerians, so I try to make sure that they learn the language. So they had the provision where somebody came and taught them the language, the culture, and all those things. So I really, really enjoyed it.

A child has to know where he/she comes from. Yeah, I think it's very, very important for them to learn the Igbo language because that's what makes them unique, speaking those two languages. That's why I gave them Nigerian names, and I was impressed with my daughter when somebody asked her, "I can't pronounce your name. It's too long." And she said, "Yeah, that's what makes me unique." Yes, that's my first daughter. So I was really impressed, and I was proud of her that she likes her [Igbo] name. She has English name. Her English name is Jennifer, but she wouldn't go with that. She tells you, "No, my name is Onyenye." You know, she hardly calls [herself] Jennifer.

---

21   Igbo people in USA have town or state associations. Once a year, they gather in a convention that represents a social grouping of the town or state.

> She likes that Nigerian name ... that's also part of educating them
> ... that is trying to teach them their roots and then speak a language
> that makes them unique. They speak a little, but ... they do more
> of understanding. (Nkolika)

Nkolika spoke about the time when she and her husband were pleasantly surprised to discover that the "era of speaking Igbo so that the kids don't understand what they are saying" was over in their house. After that time, they could no longer say anything "secret" in Igbo while the kids were there, because the kids had been studying Igbo and would now understand exactly what was being said. Nkolika described an interesting incident with her second daughter.

> We went for a vacation, and they had a wristband, and I wanted to
> take it off of my daughter—the second one. She didn't want it off.
> She wanted to show it to her [classmates and friends] at school. So
> when she came back, I allowed her to go to school with it. When
> she came back, I wanted to take it off. She refused, so I told my
> husband in Igbo that when she goes to sleep I will cut it off. And
> she said, "No!" and started crying. So I was surprised that she heard
> [understood] what I said. So they understand my language, yeah.

Nkolika would even prefer her children to marry another Igbo so that they could carry on the culture. "I would really like them to marry Igbo ... I would like them to marry a Nigerian. You know, the culture and all those things are what I want to carry on."

Besides, there is something Igbo culture brings to the development of American-born Igbo children that will help make them good Americans. Again, it is always an advantage to speak more than one language. These are some of the reasons why Nwakaego exposes her children to opportunities to learn Igbo language and culture.

> We want them to see, you know, the whole ... culture—where
> they are from, what it is like ... as against what is being portrayed
> to them. You know, so we are living examples of our culture, so it
> would be nice for them to see and to try to emulate ... the most
> that they can.

> First and foremost, it always pays to be bilingual. Or quarto-
> lingual, anyhow you look at it. If you want to acquire more than five
> languages, that is always ... an advantage. That is number one. Then
> number two that is their native ... that is their mother tongue. Even
> if they are born in Poland or Czechoslovakia, that is their mother
> tongue, you know? So you don't want them to lose [that] ... you

want them to have at least that mother tongue so that anytime they go back home, if somebody says something in their language, they will be able to understand. You know, so they won't be looking like they don't know what is being said ... and second ... it's not just teaching them about the language. It's the culture too.

And just like every other culture, there are some things, you know, that are people's way of living. So there are some things that we do that can even help mold them, you know, in being good Americans. So teaching them the culture will help them, you know, to ... if they can inculcate that into the American culture, that would be nice. That would be ... because ... I believe we have good culture back home.

In Chicago, it seems apparent that teaching Igbo children their native language and culture is definitely a big part of education for Igbo people. That is the reason why Nneamaka takes her children to Igbo functions in Chicago, like christenings, weddings, wakes, Igbo fests, etc. And beyond that, she explained that one of their sons stayed in Nigeria for a year, solely for the love of Igbo culture and the desire to learn his ancestral language. She noted that the year's stay was very rewarding for him. In this way, her children have established lasting links with their immediate and extended family members:

We have a closely knit Igbo community in Chicago. So you know, activities like Igbo school, Igbo functions ... Igbo fest, you know, marriage ceremonies, wake keepings, you know, parties ... all these activities help to build ... a strong Igbo child. And the role of the parent is to redirect the child, to channel the child in the avenues you want them to progress in. Because I want them to see, you know, what my culture is all about ... you know, I value my culture. I value my background. I love who I am, and I'm proud of my heritage, so I want my children to embrace my heritage. I want them to interact with my people. I want them to see people from the same area where I come from. I want them to have the solid communal association with people of the same character, people of the same upbringing, people from the same culture ... because we have to be united. Otherwise, we can't stay strong. That is a very big part of education that goes on outside of the school, [inside and] outside of the home ...

The world is getting smaller. With the advent of Skype, video cams, and cell phones, they can live here and associate with people in

Nigeria, which is exactly what they're doing now. We call home. We call Nigeria on the phone. They have aunties and uncles. When we visit, they see them, and when they come back, they communicate with them on their cell phones. They will call them themselves. So I wanted the association to be open. So they can live here and still maintain contact with people at home.

One of my children did ... stay one year in Nigeria, so he has more contact with a lot of people in Onitsha[22]. He actually ... stayed one year in a high school in Onitsha ... so he knows a lot—more than the others. He's my third son. So he knows every uncle, every aunt that you can think of. So he still calls home. And the other ones, they visit, and they have friends in Nigeria. So they have linkage with people at home ... so I want the ... communication to continue. So for one year, we purposely sent him home because he loves African culture. He's the one that dances the *Oji-onu*[23] for the community. So we sent him home and say, "Hey, okay, why don't you go home and experience the culture so you have first-hand information about what home is all about." And then he really loved it, so I mean you see him most of the time. He dances with the older folks. Last time he was dancing, you know, the ... what do you call it, the *Igba-Eze*. He danced with them. He danced *Igba-Eze*[24] and *Oji-onu* dance with them. He dances with the elders. He dances masquerades. He loves the culture; my boys love the culture.

Nebeolisa believes that teaching American-born Igbo children their Igbo culture and language and raising them as Igbo American contributes to the essence of being American. It also forms part of their socialization process:

That's all part of socialization. You know, they have to learn, see what we do because that's what my dad did ... so first of all, you learn how to conduct yourself in a public gathering. Secondly, you see what people are doing so that's all part of who you are and ... you are not separate. See, the thing is more or less, they are not separate from me and my wife, because our goal is actually to raise them to be adults and ... not to just keep them as children. So I want them to see everything that ... I experienced; I want them to experience that at their own level because that's where they get their

22   Onitsha is the biggest and commercial city in Anambra State. Anambra State is one of the five states that make up the southeast region—the homeland of the Igbo people—of Nigeria.

23   *Oji-Onu*: one of the Igbo traditional masquerade dances for male

24   *Igba-Eze*: the royal dance, but literally, it means "the royal drum"

education about the cultural things and also community-wise ... wherever we go.

Perhaps they are not going to live ... in the geographic area called Nigeria ... or within *Ana Igbo*, which is the Igbo land. But the truth is that they were created Igbo. Therefore, wherever they are— whether they are in America, in Russia, in Germany, in France, or South America—wherever they are, they ought to see themselves as Igbo because that is who they are. Their cultural identity, ethnic identity, it's who they are. And so that is what they bring to the global table wherever they are within the American space ... because again you know they have Igbo names. And because they have Igbo names and that's the name they will continue to answer [have], that will always raise the question. You are not European; you are not French; you are not Hispanic; you're not ... Brazilian. Who are you? Where is that name from? And ... when he says it's Igbo, he needs to back it up with some cultural content that then says who he is. And people will respect him if he is able to back it up. You know, but if he can't back it up, then everybody is like, "Then why do you answer that name?" Because people want to experience you and your culture. They don't just want to experience you within their own ... you know, within their own culture, especially when they know you are not from around here.

And I have also come to understand that that ought to change within the western thought pattern. Everybody cannot just be the same. There is unity in diversity, and that's really the thing that is American ... one of the key principles out of which America was built ... on which America was built so that the whole idea that people come from all parts of the world to the United States to live and to be part of the American project does not require that they give up who they are, but they can remain who they are while living out the American ideals and values. And those things that we bring as *Ndi Igbo* [Igbo people] now are also what help shape this country.

Due to the importance of teaching the American-born Igbo children their heritage, Igbo parents in Chicago emphasize the learning of Igbo language and culture as part of their education. They also believe that knowledge of Igbo language and culture will help to make their children better Americans.

Dealing with Culture Clash or Conflict
in Igbo Homes in America

Teaching and exposing American-born Igbo children to Igbo culture and language is definitely a big part of their educational process. However, I wanted to know from the parents whether such teaching and learning, in any way, evokes a cultural clash or conflict or identity crisis or related issues among their children. If this is the case, how do they handle it? Do they try to forestall it? I present stories of cultural clashes and efforts to handle them or nip them in the bud.

Nnaemeka accepts that there is conflict but not in the nature of something imploding or exploding because it is the meeting of two cultures in the children they are educating.

> It's conflict, because actually, the child is at two purely different cultures. It is not a conflict that tends to explode or implode. It's a natural conflict that can easily be smoothed out. The thing is that, for instance, they learn from other kids and how [other] kids dress and all that. When they ... for instance, I had one of my kids, he attempted it, and we had to correct that right quick.

There is the subculture, like wearing pants that hangs out from the behind, which drives him crazy. With his voice raised a bit, he talked about how he dealt with it when it reared its ugly head in his family.

> Because you know, the new style of wearing pants, the pants is almost hanging out from the [behind] ... which to me is an irresponsible way of dressing. I never liked it. I don't know the psychology behind it, and it doesn't make sense because it can only delay your movement, and it doesn't help in any way, shape, or form. It does not look decent. It's not safe. It can make you fall. It doesn't look responsible. So when I noticed for one or ... two occasions when he had his pants like that, I was ... yelling. I was mad with him, and he knew I was. I didn't want him to dress that way. I didn't want him to look that way. I thought ... it is not culturally [accepted in] this society, but I think it's a subculture he was trying to imitate, which I didn't think was good, was responsible any way, shape. And of course, he didn't go back to that after that.

> Okay, another aspect of it, of course, is the question of going out to ride his bike with friends and maybe go further away from the limits I've set, that he should stay within the neighborhood. I've got to see him ... other kids, of course, have all the freedom to roam places. But given the way I was growing up and everything, we make

sure that he doesn't go too far away from where we can see him
... from [the] immediate environment here or from the premises
around the house ... so that he doesn't have it in his mind or in
his psyche that he can just be like the other kids. That aspect of it,
I don't want him to belong to that. Another aspect of the culture
is the music thing, which I didn't have to interfere with because in
a way, it complements instead of conflicting with my own culture.
Because they ... sometimes like to dance the Western kind of dance.
In the midst of an African event, where we wanted to have most of
our traditional dances, they would want to [dance Western style]
of course ... what I liked about what they're doing is that they will
seek permission ... before they ... put their own kind of music and
dance their own style instead, you know,... which is okay.

Nsobundu thinks that the issue is not necessarily conflict but what is
morally acceptable to Igbo families here in Chicago and the United States.

Well it's not really much about Igbo. It's about what is morally
acceptable. You know, from where we came from. Like the issue of
discussing about somebody in high school having a boyfriend or
girlfriend and all those things, to hang out, you know. Pretty much
very few, because I know when we are little ... we hang out or we
walk two miles to see a friend. And sometimes your parents won't
know where you are. So I don't think I have much of that problem in
my house. Probably some parents do, but I don't. So we thank God
for that. But the issue of ... you know, boyfriend or girlfriend comes
up. And so even in Nigeria, they do it without ... even discussing
with their parents. So we've been lucky that our kids ... because
that goes to show the kind of parenting we have here, the kind
of relationship that you have with your kids where you guys talk
[with] open-mindedness or open friendship where issues are being
discussed. But in Nigeria, you find kids fourteen, fifteen, sixteen
indulge in all those things undiscussed ... (Nsobundu)

To reduce or avoid conflict or a potential identity crisis, parents like
Nneamaka start to expose their children to Igbo culture early.

That is where the parent comes in. And that's why we expose them
to our culture as early as possible. We bring them along when they
were little. So they ... you know, we brought them with us to all
the functions, meetings ... Igbo parties, Igbo functions. They even
go to Igbo school. So they know from the time they were small that
they are Igbo children. So they don't have a culture shock. They

are comfortable with who they are. They even have organizations in their school that they belong to or they even started … African people organizations … you know, so they [are members]. They know they are Africans in America, and they are proud of who they are … so they … yes, they don't have culture shock. They dress up in cultural dresses. They show up in cultural attires, cultural functions. They love to eat our food because I cook that at home, so they grew up eating, you know, *fufu* for example. They grew up eating farina. They love okra soup, *Onugbu* [bitter-leaf] soup. So … they don't have culture shock.

That's when you start all this—even before they are three. I will tell you what somebody *gwa-lum* [told me] … this was like in the '90s, when my children were like three years, four years, five years old. So the woman said, "Hey, speak Igbo to them in the house. They will learn English when they go to school. That was great advice I received at that early stage in my life. So I spoke Igbo to my children at home. I exposed them to all the Igbo cultures. They go to school; yeah, they know they are Igbos in America so they have to blend in at school. Also when they come home they have different requirements … and they were able to master that effectively … as early as possible, so they didn't have [culture] shock growing up. I started early.

My children were involved in everything that is done in this community. They go to weddings. They clean up. They know they will clean up. They go to functions they know they will participate. It's expected of them that hey, if their parents are here, they will not be over there, and while I'm cleaning up, they will go and clean up. So they knew growing up what they have to do. And when you call upon them to do something, they don't see it as extraordinary. Yes. It's part of their life.

Nwakaego does not believe that what her children experience with regard to learning the Igbo language and culture can be defined as conflict. Rather, she believes that their experiences are normal for children growing up in a home different from the larger culture and society. Exposing them early to Igbo culture has been a great help.

As little as they are now and like most foreigners … they know that they have a [particular] way of doing things. At least they know that there is a norm that they have to follow at home. They know that one. So [it's] the same way when they go to school. They know the difference. Then they will come home, and they will tell me, you know, somebody like this did something like that … somebody said this and that [that] is not good. Or you know the way somebody acted that is not good. So at least I know they know that in our culture we emphasize respecting the elderly more … I mean they follow that … So they know. At the same time, they know when someone is not pronouncing their names correctly, that may be culture clash. So just like me, I know when … Americans get to call my name, like waiting in the clinic and it's time to call my name, I know … there will be a deep breath [laughter] … a deep breath taken before trying to pronounce the name. So with that, I guess they [the kids] will experience the same thing, and it's not fun. But you know, because … they started early … they will grow up not feeling anything. They will adapt to things very well. … they are doing so already because … sometimes they make fun of how they [other people or kids] call [pronounce] their names, how the teachers call [pronounce] their names. They make fun of that … we all laugh at home.

Nneka describes what her daughter experiences and how she accompanies her in the journey of cultural education and adaptation.

I try to expose her to different activities and work with other mothers so she will not feel intimidated or anything. She's comfortable in her skin, or wherever she goes, she's comfortable and bold enough to say, "I am who I am," you know. So coming home, I also try to feed her not just American food. I feed her Nigerian food. But she can tell. She can tell that "Oh okay, I'm black. My friend's hair is curly and all that." She comes home with that, and I say, "Look at yourself in the mirror. Look in the mirror and tell me what you see." And she says, "Oh, I'm beautiful," you know. So it's all part of the world we live in …

When we were at the community college, I remember her coming home and saying something about being black. And I can't remember really the phrase, but the next day, I took it up with the school, and I tried to talk with the teacher and the principal that nobody should make my child feel, you know, she's out of place. And they addressed that issue very well … people have suggested, they say, "Why don't you take her to some other place? Where she won't feel uncomfortable?" But I don't think it's the solution, so I tried as early as possible to put her in the school where she will get a mix. And so … she doesn't think about color or whatever differences. It's not a conscious thing she thinks about. It's natural for her to play with others. She sees them as her friends and age group. She doesn't see any difference between that person and that person. So I think it's a good thing.

The cultural clash or conflicts the American-born Igbo children may experience as they grow is nothing out of the ordinary. In the words of Nnaemeka, it is not in the nature of something imploding or exploding; rather, it is expected in the meeting of two cultures. That notwithstanding, Igbo parents start early to guide their children in cultural education so as to make the best out of their double heritage. They also teach and expose their children to Igbo language and culture so as to prepare them for any eventuality toward that direction.

The Igbo Philosophy of Educating and Raising Children

The Igbo goal of raising and educating children is expressed in the saying *Ekpere nne na nna obula bu onye Igbo bu ka umu ha karia ha*. The prayer/wish of every Igbo parent is that their children will be more successful or better than they are. This is the dream parents have for their children. It also motivates Igbo parents as they participate in the education of their children. The saying takes it for granted that the prayers and wishes of raising more successful children will be backed with hard work. So I wanted to know how Igbo parents in this study understand the saying and what they are doing to achieve the goal of *ka umuha karia ha* (of their children being better than they are). Being better than their parents is not just in terms of money or wealth but in character, values, and morals. After all, according Nnamdi, Igbo people say *Ezi afa ka ego*, which literally means "good name (integrity) is better than money or wealth." It is more worthy to be a person of integrity.

Nnaemeka draws from history to explain how this approach drives development in the world. This saying is not peculiar to the Igbo, as most cultures have a similar attitude. Again, the saying should be backed by action. Nevertheless, it is a saying that motivates him to accomplish something, namely, to see his children become wiser and more responsible citizens of the world.

> I believe it with my whole heart, my full mind, everything that it is saying. And it's true because if all you are doing in life is to make sure that the generation that comes after you makes a step further than you did, I mean you have accomplished something. That's progress. That's development. That's energizing … and if whatever

we do, if we don't pray that our children ... I mean get better, grow, and become wiser and more responsible citizens of the world then we haven't done our job.

So it was because in the history of things, you know, you hope that the generation that comes next will do better. And as a matter of fact, that is how development of things has followed. At the initial stages, when the science of ... influenza and all those other kinds of diseases were present, nobody knew how to tackle it. So many thousands of people died and all that. It was the knowledge of some scientists that came that actually started using some kind of, you know ... and all the rest of them that did their work ... made the discovery of the microscope and all that to see the microbes that are responsible for diseases. It was because the generation that came after the ones before them did something bigger and better. It got better.

So it's a prayer not only from our traditional standpoint. I think for most cultures really, it's the hope that the generations that come after them will do better and get better. Not just praying but also doing. Yeah, the prayer is a prayer with all your being. That means that you're not just praying to God Almighty, but you're also praying with your whole heart that everything you do, all the efforts you put in ... will materialize ... to yield more fruit.

Working to make sure that your children achieve more than you has other benefits. According to Nsobundu, you not only take pride in seeing them excelling but it also brings fulfillment.

I mean it cannot be better said, because you take pride in seeing your kids progress. You die to see your kids do well. You give it all. You starve to ensure that your kids progress. So it's the same thing. And I mean, if you are doing so well, you don't want anything ... that is your blood to do less. Because they do less, it doesn't really measure up to you because you are way up there. You want your kids to be better than you. And if they are better than you ... you are even more fulfilled and happier than even themselves, who are better.

Part of the saying *Ekpere nne na nna obula bu ka nwa ha karia ha* is for your children to complete what you started. Nebeolisa thinks that parents should take two important steps toward achieving that goal while being conscious of the kids' talents.

You know, *Ekpere nne na nna obula bu ka nwa ha karia ha* ... you want your children to be greater than you, to more or less, actually in a way, finish what you couldn't ... do what you couldn't do, get where you couldn't get, you know, and maybe complete what you have started. So the first thing that I think, it's important that I believe in that [saying]. But how you get them there is first to make sure that ... which means that they do not start from ground zero, but they start from a higher platform so that they can leap off to a higher height ... which is why you try to bring them to a higher place of knowledge, understanding, and skills than where you are by downloading your experiences so that they don't need to relearn what you already know. That's one. Two, a lot of it will depend on how you prepare them. You prepare them with an open mind, but being able to know who they are so they can also know what their strengths are. I don't believe in railroading them into things but giving them diverse experiences, and then they begin to make their choices, to make the choice of what they want to do. And you invariably find out that they will choose to do things partly because of what they see you do or because you've exposed them to that experience.

For example, I did not know that my father ... not really my dad, my grandparents had wanted him to be a physician. So ... when they sent him to the United States, my grandmother's hope was that he was gonna come back as a physician. And he started his life early ... in premed, but he didn't like blood. So he went and studied economics and came back very successful as an economist. He built businesses. But my grandmother never "forgave" him for not studying medicine because she had hoped to be known and called *Nne Doc* [mother of a doctor or Mama Doctor]. But think about it this way now. Two of us in the family—my eldest brother and I—are physicians ... but again some of that is not only a dream but a prayer that, in a sense, it's something that God also put in the hearts of the parents to pray about the careers of their children. So sometimes what parents hear and speak could be God speaking to them about the children.

Nneamaka shares her understanding of the above saying. She and her husband are looking beyond what their children will achieve. She also talked about the counseling needed to achieve the goal of *ka umu anyi karia anyi* (of our children being better than us).

I believe in that [the saying], because already the parents have laid down the foundation so the child or children should be able to step up, start from where the parents stopped, and take it to the next level, If they don't … if they are not able to fill the gap and take it to the next level, then they haven't really accomplished a lot. So I tell my children this is where we as parents stopped. You should be able to start on what we have already accomplished and then take it further. The same thing my husband tells them—"Hey, I expect you to train your children in private schools. I expect your children to go to colleges because I went to college. I expect your children …" We are talking about our grandchildren this time. This is a given for them, you see? So theirs is given, okay? All of them must get higher education, not even first degree, okay? So … because the first degree I say it's the minimum, first degree is taken for granted. We are saying take it to the next level with their children. Okay, so for them we know they will accomplish our goals because we are still alive. We are talking of what their children will do. That's what we are worried about right now, because we know that for them, we will make sure that they get to where we want them to be, okay? It is what happens when we are not there. That's really what we're talking about right now. Their father is telling them, "Make sure your children will do this. Make sure you do this for your children because I did that for you."

Igbo parents in Chicago believe in the saying *Ekpere nne na nna obula bu ka nwa ha karia ha.* They work very hard to achieve this ultimate goal in the education of their children. It is fulfilling for parents to see the seed they planted germinate and grow into a big tree bearing abundant fruits.

Future Careers for Igbo Children in Chicago

Igbo parents in this study feel that part of being involved in the education of their children includes discovering and nurturing the potential talents of the children and guiding them to a fulfilling career. As Nsobundu said, parents' role in this regard is like guiding a tree to grow straight. As one would expect, there are different opinions and ways parents perform this function.

Drawing on his personal experience, Nnamdi talks about his role in choosing a career for his first son, Dozie. He does not want to make the same mistake when he was growing up with regard to his choice of career.

What made my son Dozie become a musician? Is it things I'm putting in … it wasn't intentional because, you know, like I put him in a car, and I'm taking him to school. Every day I'm educating myself, and the CD I put in the cassette player while we're going ... so both of them ... actually, what really made him become a musician ... I don't know if you are familiar with the book *The Secret* ... *The Secret* taught people about owning their affairs and becoming what it is they wanna be. I put that book in my son's hand when he was fifteen, sixteen. After he read that book, he was clear as to what it is he wants to become. All this time, we were planning on going to the University of Chicago and studying economics and on going to Harvard Law School. That was the plan. By the time he was seventeen, everything changed.

Yeah, well I take more from my own life, okay? I was gifted as a boy. I was always first in school. Yes, I was very gifted. So my parents did not go to school. My parents were not educated, okay? So my older brother Raymond, who was in school with me—just four years ... My father and Raymond chose that I would be a medical doctor, okay? That doesn't mean I ... that's not me, okay? So up into university level here in the States, I was doing premed before I transferred to business.

So I take a lot from that experience. So ... because everything that will mold us as human beings in this life takes place before we are six or seven. So at that age, I'm constantly watching my children to see where their talent is for them ... My first son, for instance, the one that is a musician—from kindergarten through twelfth grade, he had problems in school, problems, yes. He cannot keep his mouth shut. Talking, talking, and talking. He got suspended twice. Continued ... he's bright. He's bright in school, but he keeps talking. He cannot keep his ... so that's what he's doing right now. The music he's doing, he's talking. Hip hop music, that's what he's doing ... you know, so the issue for me is ... because believe it or not before you were seven years old there were things you knew that were directed toward your mission. The light may have come to you when you were like fifteen, sixteen, seventeen, whatever; but everything that we become is in us before we are six or seven. You know, so I know right now I did not see entertainment in him per se, but I thought that having an argument would not be helpful. You know, so what I do ... is just by observation ... you observe and see where their talent lies and then proceed in that direction. If it's ... a desire that comes from the child's heart then there's no struggle. Music is from Dozie's heart.

Nnamdi wants his sister to learn from his experience when it comes to parents and the future careers of their children.

> But even before I came to the age of choosing what it is I wanna be or do, it was chosen for me. I did not want to make that mistake. My sister made the same mistake. My sister had children. Her first daughter was good in school. She said, "She must be a doctor," and I said to my sister, "That's fine, but what does she wanna do?" And she says it doesn't matter. I said, "Look what happened to me. Learn from that." But anyway, the girl is doing nursing now, and that's not bad because my sister is a nurse as well.
>
> But this is not something I dreamed for my son to be doing, but that's what he wants to do … the other day he wrote on Facebook, "I'm engaged." Yesterday, he said, "I'm engaged." Well I saw it, and I went back to him and said, "Who are you getting married to?" He said he's engaged to his goals. You know so … [chuckles]. As I said, I have never for some reason said, "Dozie, do music" and stuff like that … no, none of that. That's what he wanted to do and … When I found out what he wanted to do … so I gave him things … to strengthen his mind out, because music is about here (pointing to his head). It's not about just show. Music has more vicious people in that business than any other business. Oh God, it's cutthroat. Big time cutthroat, I think, yeah.

Nwakaego says that the key in choosing careers for children is to start directing them early. As a child's career guide, you can make suggestions, but they are to be based on what you observe as the child's education progresses.

> Look at it the way I look at it. You have to have somebody to direct you, okay? … into what they think will be best, you know, into a place where you will be well situated in life, you understand? What I have noticed is that some of these kids … you know, because they are not being directed very well, you see them, they will go and do something … their first degree, they do something that they cannot even get a job with. Then you see them going back to school. They will still be, you know, not doing anything because they are still looking for a job or because they just change their mind. You know … I mean some of them, you see them taking classes, and they don't even know what they want to major in. That's not the kind of thing I want for my children. Of course so you start early, and you say, "You know, you can be this. This is what …" You know, "Hey …

look at this. You can do like this. You can be this." Now when they start growing ... I mean they can change their mind anytime. Just before they enter university, they can change their mind. There is nothing you can do about that. All you can do is to still help them choose ... make a better career choice, you know. That's all the aim in all these things—just to make a better career choice. And you know that's just the way I look at it. I mean of course you have to be there to build their confidence in them that they can be that. My father was like that. You know, you can be this; you can ... he was the one that bought my JAMB[25] form ... whatever for me. He helped me fill out what I'm gonna be.

She adds that even Saturday extracurricular activities can be an opportunity to discover a child's talent or passion.

Like the Saturday activities that we go for that is not academically based. It is activities for them to know the sports they like best or what their hobbies will be ... what they do best. Now ... if they want to be anything in that direction, of course they will still have a good academic ... background for them to be that. I tell them ... if you wanna be a good basketball player or a good actress or whatever, you can still pursue your degree and pursue that one. So ... that is what I am saying. Along the line, even before they enter university, they can change their mind anytime. Now when they change their mind and you see that the person is changing their mind toward a talent that you know they have ... not the one they think they have ... You have to know that they have that talent for them to change then you can support them in that one. If they do not have that talent, no, no, no. You're not getting any support because you don't have the talent. You think you have it, but you don't have it. It's gonna be a waste of time. You have to have the talent so that going to school will now help ... to bring it out. But if you don't have the talent and you are trying to do ... probably it's a little bit late there trying to find out if it was noticed on time ... like somebody is good in music. You start enrolling the person in piano classes or music classes. Now that is something ... you are doing that while still taking the person to school, still encouraging the person to be a doctor or something, whatever, engineer, you know? But along the line, they now decide say, "You know what, Mommy, I don't

---

25   JAMB (Joint Admission Matriculation Board) is an agency under the Federal Ministry of Education that organizes entrance examinations to federal and state universities in Nigeria.

want to go into medical school. I want to go into music." You know, the school in New York for music, okay, because you know that of course you've invested in that part …

Even academically, if you are guiding them toward being a doctor and they find out that they want to be a teacher, that's still good, you know? But just have the basics. What you don't want is a dropout, you know? We don't drop out … I mean, you must have the basics, you know? So I mean they can acquire that and come out and feel like you know what? I am not feeling anything in this medical profession. I want to be an astronaut, you know? They can still go back and be an astronaut.

Guiding children to a career can be a combination of setting expectation and observing where the child is leaning, as Nneamaka explains.

You keep pushing, but somewhere behind their brain, they know "Hey, my mother wants me to be an engineer or wants me to be a lawyer or wants me to be a medical doctor." So these are the things you … tell them, but at the same time, you allow them to … get the general education, get the background, get the foundation. You don't … just want to be myopic and channel them to the medical profession or nothing else because … it can create an imbalance in them. So you allow them to be solid. They have that solid foundation. Even when you want them to be a medical doctor … they will eventually get there, but you kind of channel them. Don't let them fall. Okay, keep working. Keep pushing, yeah. It's a continuous process.

I was concerned that if you have some expectations for your children and somewhere along the line they discover their real talent and disregard their parents' expectations, the children might feel that they somehow failed because they did not meet their parents' expectations even if they become successful." Nneamaka's reaction to my concern is interesting:

No, you don't make the child feel like a failure. That's one thing you don't do as a parent. Even if they didn't measure up to your expectations, you still give them that confidence that you believe in them. You know, what they're doing is, you know, a contributable part of the society. You have to show them that whatever they are, that you are proud of them. Yeah, yeah, that you are proud of who they are as individuals, as your child, your daughter, your son. And then whatever career they have is completely good also. It's acceptable to you, because sometimes they can fight it if they feel you are not appreciative of what they are or who they have become. They can go against your wishes. So it's a trick. You have to support what they are doing for them to know "Hey, Mom or Dad is there." And then they will invariably do your wish even when they don't know they are because they know you are there, you support them. And they will be working toward that.

Nneamaka further shares her experience on how she guides their children; a case in point is her first son, who is gainfully employed. She agrees with Nwakaego that it is very important to start to observe early where a child is leaning and proceed accordingly.

I will say as early as three. Yes. You will see when the child starts preschool. You will see the pattern if the child loves to read, if this child loves sciences, loves math. Actually, once they start talking at … two, three years, they start verbalizing. They start interacting with their peers. You always know where a child is leaning. It's an art, but if you are … for me … who is a teacher. Don't forget I did psychology, so … I am aware of children's psychology, so I am able to know who is going to do what quite early. Because you are able to psychologically analyze them. You know where their inclinations are. You kind of see where they're leaning. You can kind of see how they interact with their peers. Like my son, who wants to be a medical doctor, he's the quiet type … he doesn't argue. He doesn't tell lies, so he cannot defend himself. He can't possibly be a lawyer, so … my first son, he doesn't talk that much, but he is very good with reading. He can read volumes in one … in one … okay. You know that he can read his professional law cases. We know where he is leaning. But we also expose him … you know, because by the time he was in college, the economy was starting to go sour. So we know, hey, lawyers take time … to get a good job. But if you get into science field, you can, you know, make it fast and then you get your law later. So you know he didn't fight it, and he's okay. He's comfortable. He loves that. Now he's working a good job. He gets paid good money. He is now getting into law school. He's currently accepted to … so he will be doing that. There are lots of opportunities. You can take some classes on the Internet and then go to the major ones on campus, and … yeah, so it's there. As early as three years old, you know what a child is capable of doing.

Using the experience of his journey to his current profession, Nebeolisa is applying one or two lessons as he guides his children even at this early age.

His duties as a career guide include making sure that his children get a good education and also to expose them to as many careers as possible.

> For my son, when he gets to be nine, ten, eleven, I can take him to my practice. In the summer, he could help file … you know, just by making him work there does not make him … he will have to make up his mind. My children will go to the workplace with me. I will expose them to other professions … you know, if it's a lawyer, if it's a … you know, my thing with them is to say whatever God … I will support you to do whatever you feel God wants you to do,… and then you hope and pray … I hope and pray that one of them will be an attorney. We don't have an attorney in the family. Yeah, because I keep telling them, "Look, I have people that I really want to make sure that I sue. And I can't pay for it, so I want somebody in the house who will handle it pro bono." But no it's all part of the "see me do" advocacy. So that's part of what may … oh yeah, if I gotta be a good human rights advocate, yeah maybe I'll go get a law degree. But one thing that I hope I could do is to be able to provide for them to be educated … to go … professional training or pursuing a career to the best of their ability and not have to say, "Oh, I can't do this because I don't have the funds for it."

Earlier I wanted to be a physician. Then I changed my mind and wanted to be an astronaut. Then I said no,… I will be an aeronautical engineer. The whole idea of flying … I studied geography. I made sure because everybody said you gotta know geography. So one day we're in the car and … I told my mom … I was in my class five I told my mother I will be … I will do … aeronautical engineering. My mom said, "No, no, no, no, no. I don't want all this … whatever engineering you are doing, you have to do the one on the ground. I don't want all this flying around." So she just put a kabash to it. I took that as a signal that no, maybe this is not cool. So when … I bought my entrance exam JAMB form into the university, my dad … that was the first time he was asking me, "What are you going to apply for?" So I told him I was going to apply for medicine. He said, "Okay, that's fine. We will …," you know. I guess my brother already got into the medical school … you know, I have always had this leaning toward medicine, so yeah.

But for the children, anything they want to be able to do. But you find out that if you leave it open … I've seen that they usually pick up the vocation or the profession of their parents. The things that made their heart throb … that's what the children gravitate toward. If any of my children … but what I will like to press on them is be the best. Get the best training and be the best. My mom was a seamstress. I wish any of them would get into fashion designing … that's a huge career out there. It depends on how you position yourself, you know?

Nonye's daughter is strong willed; nonetheless, Nonye supports whatever she chooses to be. Nonye's duty for now is to constantly remind her daughter of the value of education, "what education can do for her in life." She is also happy that her daughter's focus is not on material things.

So fortunately for me, my daughter is a very strong-willed person, which maybe comes a little bit from my family because we strive for education. So she knows what she wants. I only guide her to know that this is what education can do for you in life. You have to be in a profession that will make you happy. You have to be in a profession where … knowing yourself, this is what you can take; if you can do that profession, be a happy, well-rounded person, you know, where [what profession] you can be yourself. That … you know, that is my dream, but she determines what she wants to do.

What … I am doing to help her dream is that I would like to, before I die, to make sure that I can say, "This is the key to the house. It belongs to you. You don't have to pay rent." So that … she wouldn't have so many worries and can have time and energy … to pursue her own dream. I can … in my case, advise, but … she does what she wants to do, because ultimately she is the one that has to work for it, so I don't think you can … I talk with her every day, and I make sure that at this age, her focus is not to have beautiful hairstyle or to have beautiful dresses or to have nice makeup or material things. I want her to focus on education.

Some parents, in the name of guiding their children, end up imposing a career on them. This is a concern Nsobundu raised. He laments the effects of this on children and points out that parental pressure is a disservice to the child's future career. A child's career should not be the parent's agenda. The parents' roles should be to support and guide the child toward his/her passion.

Those of us who are here now, we've become exposed, enlightened, and we realize that actually … every child has got his own or her own ability. And you know … we also found out that profession doesn't make you who you are. Profession doesn't give you happiness. What gives you happiness is becoming what you want to be. You see?

And what happens in Africa, even when you are a doctor or engineer or a lawyer, you are all those things and you are sad and depressed. You are not fulfilled, but you know you're not going to say it. You just keep it … and you're dying. People die every day in silence at home. But here with our education and exposure, with your child, we know that, you know, being a mechanic … you can make so much money being a mechanic. You can be anything in America or outside America in developed countries, and you can do so well. So being a lawyer or being an engineer or doctor doesn't really take you to the sky. You can get to the sky through other professions. We are so limited in African countries and third-world countries.

For me, we talk to them [my children] and say, "Well this profession we're researching … people are doing so well. This is what it takes. You have options."

You are a guide. And then for you to be a good guide, you have to also watch as he develops and see where his talent is. And I can look at him … you know, I'm from an engineering background … my fourth son, I know he is … when he was maybe five or six years I could see. No matter what he does now, I knew then that he has that ability of manipulating figures. And I see that he's very, very good with language. So I don't know what he's … but I see that closing his eyes, he can speak grammatically very well. I'm talking about him, my last child. So you know … you watch the child and see where he's going … you don't just close your eyes and say, "Well, go this direction. This could be good for you." So that's my experience. But can you make suggestions? I say absolutely.

Like my daughter … you know, we look at different options and my wife, you know she took it from there … And yeah, because … your career doesn't make you; it doesn't make you. I mean somebody could be a doctor and struggling. Someone can be an engineer struggling to make a living because there is no passion. There is no passion. I was discussing with my wife … one of our home girls [our relative], she studied food science, whatever, and had a master's. Eventually left to … try and do something else, couldn't cope. But I know somebody who has a first degree in food science, and she's doing so well. So it's about believing in yourself. It's all about believing in yourself and having passion for whatever profession you like, you know? So I think you cannot force a child to choose a profession which you like. So parents' pressure can be a disservice. Derail you. Yeah it's … I mean, it's a disservice, I'm telling you. So a child has got its own development. You know, like a tree; you can only guide a tree to grow straight by directing, supporting, and propping it up … that is the role of a parent in guiding a child if a child comes home with a problem, you know?

All you have to do is to guide a child. So he's like a tree. And in the end, the child is going to make his own decision because he's going to have a wider scope, you know, to choose from. And the decision that he makes or you made for him may be a disservice to him because you think maybe you see his grades. He does well in math; he will like to become maybe an engineer. But maybe he can also become an economist. Why? Because economists are also very good in mathematics. You need mathematics to become an economist. So if a child chooses any of these two subjects, why should you, as a parent, put pressure on him that because you want him to become an engineer he should by all means become an engineer. So the parental pressure, it doesn't help.

It is important that a child gets into a career or profession that he/she has passion for. Igbo parents agree that it is no easy task. It is delicate because any mistake can ruin the child's future. However, there are certain things parents should not do with regard to helping a child choose a career. First and foremost, a parent should not make the child's future career his/her own agenda. Parents' role, rather, is to discover, sustain, and direct the child where his/her talent is leaning toward. Most Igbo parents start to observe the talents and passion of the child very early and accordingly guide the child to a career.

Relationship between Parents and Children

Parents supervise, monitor, and work with their children in many educational and extracurricular activities. They also make rules and regulations to create a learning-friendly environment for the children. They follow them every step of the way in their education. But how do the kids receive their parents' efforts to assist them in their educational journey? In fact, what kind of relationship do parents have with their children as they participate in their education?

When children are young, they may or may not appreciate the efforts being made for them to have a good educational experience. But as Njideka said, you should keep on pushing, hoping that later they will appreciate all the effort. Children's response to parental involvement might vary.

> They probably wish I would back off. Maybe they will just be like, "Oh, if you weren't …" I know that my son is like, "Ugh!" He doesn't want to do the extra assignments. I mean and that's okay. I think, you know, he's young. He doesn't maybe understand the full, full aspect. Later, he will thank me, but right now the boy just wants to play, and I'm telling him to do assignments besides the one that other classmates are doing. I think my daughter is more into it. She's always begging me, "Can I read some more to you?" She doesn't even want to go to sleep. "Can I read just a little bit longer? Can I read this story to you? Look what I've written for you. Can I write … can I read this story?" You know, so different kids are different and … some of it might be having a girl versus having a boy, but I mean I think they know that education is important. And they know that Mommy and Daddy push it. And … they can write an assignment for school, and I'll look at it and erase the whole thing and say, "I don't like it … the writing was too messy. Start again." And they will be so mad, and later, they'll understand that, you know, it's not just getting the right answer. You also have to have presentable work. So hopefully over time, they will appreciate all my effort.

Nnamdi describes the kind of relationship he has with Dozie, his son. The relationship is quite the opposite of what he has with his father.

> As a father, your job is to get out of the way. That's your job. Up until tomorrow, my father has not gotten out of the way. You follow what I'm saying? If you don't get out of the way, you dissipate the child's life, meaning you corrupt the child's life. You may not agree with me, but food for thought. Yeah. You get out, but you're there. In this land, the age of maturity is eighteen, okay? I'll be fifty this year, but my father still … you know, the way he is. I don't know if it's a tradition or him particularly. [maybe it is Igbo thing.] … by the time Dozie was eighteen, my son, in my eyes, he's a man. In my eyes, okay? So instead of being father … the father that "it has to be my way blah, blah," then I will be a father still, get out of the way, but be your friend because see you still need my advice. You follow what I'm saying? I'm still advising him, but I advise him from the standpoint of "Yeah, this is what you want to do. Do you want me as a mirror?" But not me making the decision for your life.

But I wanted to know, how far do you go?

> "How far do you go?" It has to be something within the confines of the upward mobility of society. That's exactly what I'm saying. Getting out of the way is a huge part of fatherhood. Whatever father understands that rule helps the children more than anything else. Yeah, because you know, you may think you're not six foot ten; but if you have children, in their eyes you're a giant. So at this particular age [eighteen], you have to get out of the way. You *must* get out of the way. You must exit, yeah. So after a while, it has to be the children teaching you because that's a part of the parenting. You learn a lot from them, yes. I can take a look … when I go to pick up my daughter from school, I take one look at the countenance on her face and know how the day was. It's her teaching me from her face, yeah. So education with the children is not just … it's not one way. It's not just me teaching them. They're teaching me a lot. (Nnamdi)

Teenagers will always try to resist efforts to help them, a parent pointed out.

> Teenagers will resist. That's one thing about teenagers. They will try to see how far they can push and how far you are willing to yield. So it's a constant tussle. It's a game they play so well. Sometimes they win. Sometimes you don't let them win. You know? You don't fight everything. The ones you know are destructive to their success, you fight and you don't let them win. The ones you can give, you just pretend as if you don't know they are winning. You know, I let it go. (Nneamaka)

Once in a while, a parent gets mad at a child:

> At times, my daughter gets scared because there are times when she doesn't get it, and I get mad. She gets scared because she doesn't want me to be mad. So … and my husband always tells me not to make her get scared, you know? So when I calm down, she gets whatever I'm trying to teach her (Nkolika).

Igbo parents understand that in being involved in the education of children, it is not guaranteed that parents will have the best of relationships with their children. Part of the reason is that sometimes the children are too young to appreciate the sacrifice of their parents. Sometimes the tendency in teenagers to resist everything comes into play. But all in all, Igbo parents love their children and want the best for them and have good relationship with their children.

Creating a Learning-Friendly Home Environment

The education of children occurs at school, in the community, and at home. Igbo parents see it as one of their duties to create a home environment that promotes the education of their children. Here, parents in this study narrate how they create a home environment conducive to their children's education, including monitoring the use of computers and cell phones, putting limits on seeing and hanging out with friends, establishing curfews and house rules and regulations, cutting down the number of hours spent watching TV, and providing a reading space and materials.

Teaching and learning has to continue when the children come home from school. As Nwakaego makes the effort to create a learning environment for her children, she keeps in mind that "they are not coming back to an empty house."

> You know, that they won't be coming home to an empty home. Creating a good learning environment ... with academics I provide them with as much information as I can get, you know, with the computer and books, good books. Then the library is here, the village library. We go to the library, and we enroll in some summer or winter programs that involve reading. You know, so the more books they read, the more they will be rewarded. And then we still go outside, you know, during the summertime, you know, when the flowers are blossoming, so we use that as a learning experience ... you know, to see how that is ... how that takes place there. We do ... we farm. We plant some food back there in the garden ... so they see that too and they help, you know, in watering that and weeding. So it's still the same educational process ... (Nwakaego)

Besides monitoring TV and computer time and making sure that kids have everything they need for learning at home, Njideka considers a healthy lifestyle (for the kids), including eating, as part of creating good learning environment. Her reason is that an unhealthy lifestyle and eating can trigger health problems that "interfere with things," such as education.

> It's more ... it's an indirect, I would say, connection. If you fight obesity, it indirectly will promote ... education ... like nutritional science would be a subject too. So my kids know about the food groups. They'll say, "Oh, the grain ..." They're like, "How many servings of milk?" because we know that we want to get like three servings. And they say, "Oh okay, well we got ... we get milk at school every day. And we had cereal. There was milk in the cereal. Okay, we need one more ... so they'll say, "Okay, we'll have ...

we'll drink milk for dinner," you know? Or they'll say, "Oh no, we drank juice in the morning." They know ... you need the meat group. You need the fruits and vegetables. They need the grains. They say, "Oh, bread is grain. Farina is grain. Like so they learn that, so that's part of their education. And more importantly, like they know ... like I am an exercise fanatic so, you know, they know that exercise is so important. So then I'll put on my exercise videos, and they will come and join. And say, "Oh Mommy, you didn't do your exercise today. Let's go!" You know and so learning that ... and they said, "Why do you have to exercise?" I said, "Oh because you don't want to get too big." And so they have a concept of ... you have to eat healthy food. They know that we don't have a lot of cookies and potato chips. They don't drink soda unless they're at a special event at a party or something, and they'll ask, "Can we have some of the soda?" you know. So they've learned, you know, very important things about nutritional health. We try ... I don't want to start now talking about obesity per se, although we do have one child that is a little bit overweight. So we know that we have to curtail her portions. And even her siblings will say, "Oh, don't eat too much. Don't eat too much." And then down the road, obviously, obese people are supposedly less healthy. So if you let somebody get so obese then, you know, they could have health problems down the road, which could interfere with things. And there are some, you know, medical problems associated ... like kids with obesity sometimes start having knee problems and this and that. So I guess it's all tied in somehow.

She sometimes watches television with them to help them digest certain programs.

Sometimes I have to sit down with them when they're watching TV so that even with their so-called children's programs, sometimes you'll hear them, you know, yelling at each other, saying bad things. And so you have to use everything as an opportunity to teach and say, "Now would you really want somebody to ... a brother to hit his sister because they came in when they were on the telephone?" And it's like, "No, that's not good." You know, so you have to be able to physically be with them so that you can interpret and help explain some of the stuff that they're, you know, going through. So ... again, it's all about spending time with them. (Njideka)

Television is not completely cut out for Nneka and her daughter. An educational program from PBS is allowed like PBS.org. Sometimes they play puzzles instead of watching educational programs. Another way she creates a learning environment at home is to display Ogechi's schoolwork.

> Making it a learning environment for my child ... I try as much as possible ... well, the classrooms here are well built and things are there. They have books. They have libraries. I let my child use the computer. I try to cut down ... you know, the hours of watching television, because it's a big distraction for the child. I have a billboard for her at home ... where I put all the work that she brings that day and, you know, tells her it's a beautiful work, and I display that for the day. So by the end of the week, she picks out the one that we're going to take down because next week is coming. And so that way she's encouraged to bring more back home. And when she's at school she's doing all this, she knows that mommy appreciates it. You know, she's doing a good job. (Nneka)

Creating a learning-friendly home can be more demanding for families with teenagers. Nneamaka shares her experience, which includes providing educational items, monitoring the use of the computer and cell phones, and establishing a curfew.

> I make things available for my children ... I will say educational items are available to the children, okay? I have ... reference books for all levels of learning. I make available for them a comfortable reading environment devoid of distractions. I have comfortable reading lamps and reading tables and chairs ... where they can learn effectively. I take my children to the library from time to time so that they can also have a reading environment, where they can see other people who are committed to education. I help them with their homework at home, essentially. We study. We read books. I will say we enjoy reading in the house with the children.
>
> And then we have laptops ... computers. We have the Internet, where they can download information with Internet availability. So they have every, I will say ... every opportunity in this house for them to be well educated, because with the Internet they can research and get whatever they need. And we a have wireless connection in the house. I have up to five computers in this house, so everybody ... Everybody has a computer available at any time to do their research work. So I have three laptops and two desktops. Actually, I have three desktops. Two are connected to the Internet, and one is ... for my child in grammar school so that, you know, she is not easily exposed to Internet that much. So ... and then I have laptops

available. So I believe they have most of the things they need to be successful educationally in the home.

I put in some of them parents guard. That's one. I have family computers in the hallway where ... everybody can see what everybody is doing at any time. The laptop is for me and my husband, and then I have two family computers in the foyer—one upstairs and one downstairs, where people can access the Internet, you know, for their schoolwork. And then ... we have to play cop sometimes. You sneak in and sneak out and make sure they don't download materials they shouldn't and make sure you go back and see what's going on. You chastise them. You know, "What you see is wrong," and then you tell them, "Hey, this computer is strictly for education." Don't get me wrong. Once in a while, they go to Facebook and all that stuff. You know e-mails and stuff. But at the same time, they know precisely that the computers in this house are strictly for educational purposes.

There is no television in their rooms. No television in any room. We actually have two televisions. One is downstairs, but it's not cable ready. It's just for ... tapes, you know, if you have videos and DVDs, the Nigerian stuff that we want to shoot for visitors. We only have one working television in the house, and it's in the family room. No television in the rooms because that can be a distraction. No computers in the rooms, okay? It is in the family space, so everybody knows what everybody is doing at any time. I can peak through my door and see what the child is doing. Yeah, you really have to monitor what goes on, especially on the Internet.

Cell phones are another thing ... I don't give them a cell phone until they go to college. Yes, because cell phones can be distracting again. And we have a rule even when they are in college. You come back home, you keep your cell phone in the central charger. We have a central-charger spot. They fight it. Don't get me wrong. They fight the cell phone. They fought it and fought it and fought it. I think they are winning the game on the cell phone, really. The computer, yes, I won. But the cell phones I am still fighting that. Really, I am still fighting cell phone. It's just because I don't want all the texting and all the distractions that go on. So I tell them turn off your cell phone during the day when you are in school. Okay, it's just for emergencies. We even limit the minutes on the cell phone until, I will say, two of them started ... two of them now have unlimited [minutes plan]. But we are still fighting about the cell phones. I don't want to say we are losing the game on the cell phone, but the cell phone one is a little hard because they have to use it for emergencies, especially when they're in college, you know? One of them is out of state, so I have to definitely give her a cell phone. So I'm trying, but I am not winning that game yet. Our children know that … everything we are doing is for their own benefit, okay? We are doing that out of love for them to be successful. You know … you don't fight everything. The ones you know are destructive to their success, you fight and you don't let them win. The ones you can give, you just pretend as if you don't know they are winning. You know, I let it go.

Sometimes establishing a curfew might be necessary in creating a learning-friendly home environment.

Curfew is another thing. It's a big fight. Curfew—what time they can come home—twelve or ten on weekends and so on. So you have to fight, especially when they get in college, because I have two of them that … go [to college] from home, and the reason why they go from home is for me … to monitor, again, what they are doing. So I have cars available for them. They drive to school, and they come home in the night—twelve, one, they are home. (Nneamaka)

Nebeolisa enumerates what it takes to create a learning-friendly home environment, namely, managing time, reducing the distraction of TV, reading to them, and exposing them to learning opportunities.

You know, if the children come home and all they can … there is no quiet environment for them to learn or there is a disinterest or parents are not willing to expose their children to other aspects of learning that they're not receiving in school. The first is the biggest challenge to keep them away from television … you know, help them manage their time. You know, because when we were growing up, you didn't have twenty-four-hour television. So one is to make sure that you keep them away from television so that they have ample time to do more cerebral work. The second is reading to them when they are young. We do that. The third is making them read to you when they start learning how to read. The fourth is bringing them to learning experiences. Just a visit to the museum, to the gallery, to other places where they will see things and learn …

In creating a learning environment, Nonye pays attention to the friends her daughter keeps and limits watching television to specific times.

I made sure that she has, you know, computer access to do her homework, that she has a writing table—a table where she will do her homework. And the TV was limited to specific times. I will make sure that she has finished her homework, and I will monitor how many hours we watch TV and what programs we will watch. So ... and we wouldn't just say, "Oh, let's go to party." No. So we had to make sure that everything is taken care of ... and then I also monitored her friends. Who are your friends? What are their priorities? So it has to be people who value education. And we always talk about education, talk about school every day—how was it today? What can I do to help? (Nonye)

Nnaemeka provides educational television channels and organizes essay competitions and discussions in his family. These are additional ways he creates a learning environment for his children.

As a matter of fact, we have the computer. We have bought all kinds of textbooks for the kids. We provided them with reading materials, and I personally make it interesting for them to do some math, some English, some composition writing, essays. So from time to time, we would pick a topic and start discussing it. Go into competition. We discuss some things about nature and things like that. That provides them an opportunity to grow. They plant seeds and watch it grow in the backyard, and they get to know something about those plants, okay? We can just chase a butterfly in the backyard and then maybe we start describing things. They have books. We go to the library very often to borrow books for them. They have the computer. They are even more computer literate than us, in fact, most of us because they can go there and dig out some information, get themselves educated. The only aspect ... of course, with all this work they also have some leisure time. I allow them a few hours watching the television and, of course, we provide them with like History Channel or those channels that are educational.

Children spend more than half of their daily lives at home, where education also occurs. Besides, Epstein (2001) argues that for any school-aged child, there is no "pure" time out of school or the home since time spent in either affects what happens in the other (p. 33). Igbo parents in Chicago are aware that if children come home and there is no conducive learning environment, their education will be at the risk of being impaired. In order to forestall such risk and create a learning-friendly environment at home, Igbo parents monitor their children's use of the computer, cell phones, and the television and the type of friends they keep. They establish house rules and regulations, provide learning opportunities, and encourage healthy lifestyles for the children. Providing a favorable study space and good reading materials are additional ways they create a learning environment at home. Igbo parents make these efforts because they believe that a learning-friendly home environment ultimately enhances the education of children.

Summary and Analysis

Igbo parents are aware of the important role of schools in the education of their children. They are careful in the type of school they choose for their children. Though there are various factors that influence their decisions, academics is the driving force. In addition to different ways of assisting their children with homework, Igbo parents take time outside the school to teach them important life lessons. They also volunteer in school-related activities, a practical way to be involved in the education of their children, as well as an opportunity to know what goes on in the school. In some schools, however, volunteering is a mandatory contribution (which makes one wonder how the term "volunteer" should apply in that case). Igbo parents consider extracurricular activities as important educational opportunities for their children. Hence, they commit a lot of their time and energy to make sure their children experience these activities. Teaching American-born Igbo children their heritage is an extracurricular activity very dear to Igbo parents in Chicago because they believe that such knowledge will actually help to make their children better Americans.

The cultural clash or conflicts the American-born Igbo children experience as they grow up is nothing out of the ordinary. As Nnaemeka suggested, this kind of conflict is not a surprise, but rather, such an experience of conflict is expected by members of any Igbo family in Chicago, who are educating their children in a new culture. Conflicts in such situations are bound to arise, and Igbo parents consider conflict an important part of the educational process.

Also, it is important that a child gets into a career or profession for which he/she has a passion. There is a tendency in traditional groups, such as the Igbo, for parents to dictate specifically their children's future careers. However, determining the future career of a child is no easy task. It is delicate because any mistake in providing guidance can ruin the child's future. Therefore, rather than dictating, the parents' role in providing guidance is to help discover, sustain, and direct the child to where his/her talent is leading. Most Igbo parents start very early in observing the talents and passions of their children and guide them accordingly to a career.

Igbo parents in Chicago are aware that if children come home and there is no conducive learning environment, their education will be at the risk of being impaired. Igbo parents believe that a learning-friendly environment at home enhances the education of children.

Comparing Igbo Parents and Lopez's Typologies

I noted in chapter 3 that there are many typologies of parental involvement. Lopez (1999), having examined twelve different typologies, suggests seven categories of activities. From the findings of this study, I articulated fourteen different ways Igbo parents in Chicago told me that they practice parental involvement. In comparison, ways in which Igbo parents are involved is both similar and different in respect to other typologies. Here, I will compare it with Lopez's. Table 2 lists and compares Lopez's and Igbo parents' types of activities. (see table 2)

Throughout the interviews, none of the Igbo parents mentioned that they had attended a seminar for parenting skills organized by the school or attended English as a second language class. On the other hand, choosing a school, creating a learning-friendly environment at home, setting expectations and standards, and guiding children to future careers are Igbo parental involvement activities that are missing in Lopez's list.

Igbo Parents In Chicago	Lopez
Laying educational foundation	
Setting educational standards and expectations	
School choice	
Making children ready to learn	Parents as providers of basic students needs
Creating learning-friendly home environment	
Homework	Parents as teacher of their children
Learning and teaching at home	
Igbo language and culture	
Extracurricular activities	Parents as audience and school supporters in school functions
Dealing with culture clash or conflicts	
Future career for Igbo children	
Volunteering	Parents as volunteers or paraprofessionals
School governance and participation in decision making	Parents as decision makers on governance boards
Communication with school	Parents as interlocutors/conduits for school-derived information
	Parents as learners

Table 2: Comparison of Lopez's (1999) and Igbo Parental Involvement Activities

The issue here is not whether one list is better or whether the list is complete or not. Neither does it suggest whether the Igbo findings have to align with institutional practice or not. They are simply different. Igbo parents engage in these activities not because schools prescribed them. Their involvement stems from their understanding of education and schooling. For one, they see themselves as being responsible for the education of their children while working with the school. In other words, these activities for them are duties they owe their children and society. As Nkolika put it, "They are my children; their education will benefit my husband and I, my children, and the society."

Furthermore, Igbo parental activities arise from particular historical, social, political, and cultural circumstances. It is safe to say that Igbo parental involvement typology is shaped by particular circumstances, such as their own education or upbringing in Nigeria, one's particular Igbo heritage, the new American environment, or one's individual profession. I will discuss these factors in chapter 10.

CHAPTER 9

Relationships Between School and Parents

The Igbo parents in this study see themselves as partners with the schools their children attend. The corollary question is what the kind of relationship do these partners in the education of children have? How do they communicate with each other? Nsobundu is of the opinion that if both parents and school keep communication flowing, much will be achieved with regard to the education of the children. In this chapter, I present what schools expect from Igbo parents and the nature and channels of communication between parents and schools.

The questions that provoked their thoughts on this subject—the relationship between Igbo parents and the schools their children attend—are the following:

1. Tell me about your relationship with the school your child attends.
2. What does the school expect from you with regard to the education of your children?
3. How often do you go to the school?
4. What are the reasons you go to the school?
5. What is the nature of communication between parents and the school?
6. What kinds of communication do you have with the school with regard to the education of your child (children)?
7. How do you know how and what your child is doing in school?

What the School Expects from Igbo Parents

Partners in a venture like education have expectations of each other. In the "Role of the School" section of chapter 7, I discussed how Igbo parents understand the role of schools in the education of children. Likewise, schools have expectations of Igbo parents. So when I asked parents what the school expects from them with regard to the education of their children, their responses covered a wide range of expectations, such as getting the children ready for school, creating a learning-friendly environment at home, assisting the children with their homework, participating in school fundraising activities, attending parent-teacher conferences, and volunteering.

Nebeolisa thinks that the fundamental expectation of the school is to have the children show up healthy and ready to learn. He equally believes that if all parents were to diligently perform these duties, schools would function optimally.

> Make them show up. I think that's number one, because people don't think about it. If they don't show up, they're not gonna learn. You know, and I don't think that's a law here that forbids parents not to bring their kids. So at least I have to make them show up healthy, well fed, and well rested. Then I think that's ... and disciplined. I believe that's what is lacking. If every parent did that for the school, the school can function. But what I believe is happening is that a lot of the children come unprepared to learn. Because of different dynamics at home, you know, they were out and, you know, awake all through the night or moving from hand to hand and all that kind of stuff. Secondly, if they ask for a meeting, parents should show up. And then be available to support the teachers and encourage them. And then help sign the homework. If the kid is not doing his/her homework, it's not the child's problem. I think there's a failure at the parental level.

On a general level, Nnaemeka feels that they (he and his wife) have a good relationship with the school, noting that they have access to their children's teachers and usually have open discussions about their children's academic progress and educational needs. The school is always ready to attend to their concerns too.

> We relate very well with them [their children's teachers], and we have no problem getting any answers as to why maybe a child was given any kind of assignment or not. We don't want to give excuses for our children, so we ... they have our permission to make sure our kids get the nature of discipline [that is necessary for them to get a good education].

Using the middle school her daughter attends as an example, Nneamaka gives a long list of what the school expects from her.

> The school expects me to help her with her homework. Help her read at home, study at home, definitely, attend teacher-parent

conferences. Attend some of the functions they have in school, like on the weekends they have some functions. Probably they have a parents-daughter dance, a father-daughter dance. They have some fundraising activities going on. They have some games that you have to bring the child to. They have some functions. You have to fit all these things in on Saturdays. So some Saturday afternoons, we are going to some school functions for her and also some evenings. So if there are like evening functions in the school, they don't usually give them too much homework that evening because they know they will be coming back at, like, six thirty for the school function. So that's how we juggle it. So the days we have functions, of course, we have a schedule. You must have a functional, working schedule to, you know, get all these things in. I have a calendar right on top of my reading desk, okay, where I mark everything that I have for the ... you know for the month. So you have to have your working calendar to be effective.

Schools have high expectations for parents according to Nnamdi. Schools expect parents to pay particular attention to the home environment because television can be a big distraction to the children's educational progress.

Well first and foremost, they expect ... I'll give you an example with my daughter. They have very high expectations. For one thing, they expect the home environment to be conducive for the type of education they are doling out. For instance, they don't want your child watching TV, you know, because they are saying that whatever they teach them in the school, TV takes it away ... yeah, and the video games or even cell phones. Yeah, those are ... or playing on the computer. They are saying avoid all of those things. Yeah, the expectation they have is that you should be hands-on with your child's education, and I like that.

In addition to assisting the child with homework, parents are also expected to volunteer. But Njideka's notion of what the school expects from parents differs from that of Nnamdi. While Nnamdi says that expectations are very high, Njideka says that schools are not really expecting much from her.

Not that much. I mean, they send home ... like they want you to see the children's homework and sign that, you know, you've reviewed the work that was done. They want you to come for these parent-teacher conferences maybe once or twice a year, more if your kid is having problems. They do e-mail just to give you updates so you know what's happening, but it's ... you know, they can ask you to volunteer, to come into the school and either read a book or help them in some special projects. I mean, there's not a lot that the school requires.

For Igbo parents, whether the expectations from school are high or minimal, they, as responsible partners in the education of their children, make efforts to meet these expectations for the benefit of their children's educational progress. School expectations of parents vary. It depends on the school system or whether it is private or special or public school.

Communication with the School

Igbo parents in Chicago have varying means of communication with the schools their children attend. The channels of communication include phone calls, the Internet (e-mail), the school website, visits, parent-teacher conferences, letters, newsletters, report cards, and PTA meetings. Reasons for communication include exchanging information that will boost the child's education, feedback on the child's progress, the welfare of the child, school policy meetings, or invitations to school functions or social gatherings.

While noting the various ways and reasons the school communicates with her, Nneka points out that the essence of communication through whatever channel is to work together for the interest of the child's education. However, she prefers face-to-face communication with the teacher or principal.

> Well, I have to go into the school once in a while, or I call over the phone. But it's always good to go face-to-face. Well they called me at some point and reported that Ogechi ... there was some concern they had, and I had to go in and talk with the teacher. She had to tell me in detail what is going on and we ... myself and her had to sit down to find a solution. Probably ... at some point, she was very upbeat, too playful, and gets tired when others are not. So we worked on her ... giving her more milk so that she can wind down because milk helps you to wind down ... during nap times. So this is one of two examples of things. Or when they need something ... because it's a private school, we jointly fund what they need in terms of paper, tissue, all that. So when they're running out, you know. And so we contribute to that so that the school will have enough. So that way, you are not just ... and paying school fees, you are also participating.

> You are also called when your child forgets maybe her sweater or something. They keep it safe for you, and you pick it up the next day, or if you want to, you can pick it up right away. Again if you're not

there, if you can't make it, they leave you a voice mail and you can … reach them at any point. Like I said, everything is on the Internet. You can also e-mail them and discuss issues that you have.

The good communication between Nneka and the school was evident on one occasion, when her daughter wetted her clothes during nap time at school.

Or sometime, Ogechi … she had come home; she had an accident at school that was … you know she did wet her clothes during her nap time. She had a bed wetting, and we didn't have enough changing clothes, but they had extra at school, so she wore another and came home, and I was curious about that. And they told me what happened, so I sent in more. I thought I had more spare clothes for her. I sent in more, and that's a good way of communicating. They didn't just send her away because … send her back with the wet clothes. They changed … you know, gave her a new one, but then I had to wash and return it and then give them more. So that it's part of the communication with them, and there is also PTA meetings.

I have attended one [PTA meeting], but it was interesting to hear from other parents … where they're coming from. But we also had one thing or the other to contribute. We had ideas that we sold to the school, and they also had … you know, it was a good thing because then you get to meet other parents. And that you form a relationship. And so it makes the world go around … when you know yourselves, and you see the principal and other people who are taking care of your kids. You are meeting them one on one. It's a good thing.

As for parent-teacher conferences … well yeah, it's always good to do that, especially when they have concerns they will let you know. So you go in. Some parents will write letters. I don't think that's good enough. It's good to go and sit with that teacher or make out time to observe the kids in class.

Though Njideka does not communicate excessively, she does not underestimate the importance of communication between the school and parents in the education of children. Her communication with the school depends on the issues at hand. Her preferred means of communication is e-mail, although she will take a call from her son's teacher anytime, even during work. Like Nneka, Njideka underscores the importance of meeting one on one with the teacher to discuss issues in relation to children's education.

I mean, if I need ... I don't have to communicate excessively. But if I did I know they would ... So [I communicate] mostly by e-mail. They send letters home through the children. I mean, I know one ... last year Chijioke Jr. was having some problems where he was feeling sad and sometimes crying in school, and ... I remember the teacher used to call me every day to tell me, "Okay, today was a good day. Oh today he cried a little bit. Oh today," you know, "he was fine. Today he had a rough day." You know she would ... literally call me every day. So I would be at work with a patient, and I would see that it was her, and I would have to stop what I was doing. To say, "Oh, I really need to take this. This is my son's teacher." So when they need to step up the communication and be very involved with me, they do. But this year, you know, there's been nothing. The teacher hasn't needed any special time with me for him.

Yeah. I mean the lessons and the plans for the week are online. I think they said when you get to the higher classes, they'll specifically tell you like, "Oh this project is coming up ..." and they'll have all of these things on the Internet. But the work is not so complicated. It's not so detailed.

I have all their e-mail addresses. I have their voice mail phone number. So if I have to, I can e-mail. Or you can call and leave a message. You can usually ... or you can set up a meeting if you want one.

Yeah, you can set up a meeting. Yeah, it's only ... if there was a ... it's more like if there's a problem. If there was some concerns I had ... I think there was one time, like when Chijioke first started school in kindergarten. I wanted to make sure that the teacher knew how advanced he was and so that they could accommodate that. And by the time I set the meeting and met, the teacher was like, "Oh, I already know. He's the only kid that can read. I'm working on him. I'm gonna have a special teacher come and pull him aside." So the teacher was already ahead of me in terms of addressing my concerns. But yeah, so I haven't really had to do much in terms of looking for them [teachers].

[Regarding parent-teacher conferences], like we had one like maybe September, October, and then there should have been another one in January, but the teacher said, "I really don't need to see you." They said [that] for both of the kids ... both teachers said, "We don't really need to see you. Everything is fine. But if you want to come, you can come," but I knew that everything was okay so ...

Nnamdi once served on the board of trustees of the school his son Dozie attended. That opportunity elevated his relationship with the school. He remembers how he worked with the school to help two of his children, when they had problems at school.

> I take them to school and back ... when they have events ... you know, I was ... my son's school, I was member of the local student council, and I served on their board of trustees, stuff like that. So I served in that. And you know, I won't tell you that I'm the most active parent. I'm not. But I am active. My daughter ... my daughter's school has a lot of activities, and we go to most of them.

> With regard to the parent-teacher conferences, I have attended all of them or most of them. They didn't have any recently. School just started ... The last one my wife went to, but I would say I went to six, eight months ago ... the issues we talked about ... Well, Uju [my daughter], the teacher told me that Uju is her best student, all around in everything. But where she's lacking is social skills. You know, maybe because of how brilliant she is or whatever, you know, she doesn't mix very well with other kids. It's either her way or the highway, and that's what they said we have to work on. We worked on that with Uju a lot ... Dozie, my son, because Dozie ... as I told you Dozie had issues from day one until the last day [in school]. You know, he just cannot sit still like I'm sitting ... like I am right now ... So we worked on that and worked on it, but it was just in Dozie's making. You follow what I'm saying?

Nkolika shares her experience of the first parent-teacher conference she attended. The insight gained from the conference made her work harder with her daughter; that effort yielded good results. In general, she thinks that her communication with the school is good.

> They have a teacher's conference, where the parents come to school and ... I mean teachers and parents' conferences, sorry, where the parents come to school, and they go through your child's report card and ... how your child is doing. And to tell you ... which level your child is on and all those things. Well ... the day they do the report cards, it takes time because they see ... each parent individually. So it takes a long time for you to wait until your turn comes. But you know, they do it in a very good way. You have to sign up for the hour that you want to come in. If it's six, you get there by six, they call you

220

in by six. Usually it takes like fifteen to twenty minutes, even though some people want to ask so many questions. So it depends on how long ... each parent takes will determine how long you will spend. The one that I went to, actually that was my first one. I actually went earlier than my time, so I had to wait for like one hour before they called me in. And when they called me in, I spent like twenty minutes because I just wanted to ask some questions about my girl to know how she's doing. And we went through her paperwork and all that, and I had to sign the papers before coming back. I was asking them what she's doing, because ... they wrote like once she had "passes," and they want her to have "good or ..." So I had to ask them why she had "p." Also I wanted to know if she's the only one ... you know ... to know if she's the only one who's not doing well. And they told me that she wasn't the only one, that by the end of that term, she will get [learn] whatever was hard for her. So ... that's when I took time and started working with her more than I used to do. Yeah, because we had another term, I mean I was really impressed with her work. She had all "excellent" and "good."

Apart from scheduled visits, Nkolika also communicates via telephone and sometimes uses the time for dropping or picking up her children as an opportunity to seek out a few things. But she confesses that she has yet to visit the school website.

Well they have my phone number. Once there's anything wrong, they call me right away, so the communication is really good. And when they can't reach me, they will call whoever is listed as a family friend or something. So I mean, it's very, very good. The communication is perfect ... but they don't use e-mails. But they do more like paperwork. Like if they have activities coming up, they give it to you when you come to pick them [up]. Actually I haven't gone to the website before, but I think they have a website. Yeah. I have their phone numbers ... or if I get to school and I feel something is not right or I have a question, I call them right away ... I think they are really good in communication.

In working with the school for the children's education, Nwakaego combines various channels of communication—visits, e-mails, writing notes, and phone calls—to keep abreast with her children's education.

I visit as much as I can. But since I ... since I went back to school, I only go when ... like I don't volunteer anymore; before I used to volunteer. We can write notes. I write notes sometimes when there is something I need, you know. If there is something I don't understand, I write notes. Then I go to see them. They can be seen before school or after school, you know. And via e-mail too; I have their e-mail addresses so ... I can communicate through e-mail. The school ... they do call. They call when there is ... when there is probably an announcement that we did not get or just a reminder. They have the system set up automatically that will call you. Also, I do visit the website, to see how ... performance-wise, to see how they are performing, you know, compared to other schools. And just update on what's happening on the improvements they are adding, you know.

Like some of the subjects that they had, you know ... there was a time ... we actually went for the meeting where they needed to improve on the amount of time they spent in teaching them sciences, because they concentrate more on English and math. So you know we sort of made it known to them that they need to improve on sciences because I see them coming back with, you know, not too great grades in science and social studies. So they have done that. So they increased the number of hours and, you know ...

I call them, I go to the school, I see the principal. I can talk to the teachers, you know. They are easily accessible. And because almost all my kids went through them, I know them; they know me ... overall communication is good, but there is always room for some improvement in everything you are doing.

On the importance of parent-teacher conferences, she points out that these conferences are not only meant for dealing with negative issues but also to discuss ways to improve performance. After all, there is always room for improvement. Even if the teacher says there is no need for a conference—that is, the child has no problems—Nwakaego believes that there are positive issues to discuss with the teacher regarding the child's education.

Parent-teacher conference ... it's like once every semester, you know, like every ... every session that they have ... it's a good opportunity too, you know? It was good. Of course when you go, they tell you everything is okay, okay, and you don't want to be hearing, "Okay, okay, okay, okay." You want to ... I mean because they are not having any problem. Actually they are impressed with the way the kids are acting in school and their academic performance. But you know, you always want to know... what can the person do better? I'm always like what can he or she do more, or where can they improve more? So it's good. It's good. I mean most of the time they want to dismiss … not that they want to dismiss you. They feel like there is not a problem. You are not the problem here. But you know we are looking … for me that is where I like honesty, you know, like openness to say, "He is very, very good academically, but look at where, you know, he can improve …" or that "He plays a lot or something. He's still a good boy, but he plays a lot." You know, stuff like that. So it's like a forum where the teacher will sort of get to say everything, you know? And you, the parent, can also say what you did the other day or that my child came back with this, I didn't like that.

Nneamaka has an open communication with the schools her children attend. She is available twenty-four hours a day in case of an emergency. She sees communication as an opportunity for teachers to "expose" what they are doing and the kind of help the parent can give to the child's schooling. She is in direct contact with the school and visits at least once a month.

At least every month there must be a function that I will have to go to at the school. It can be a parent conference. It can be an after-school activity. It can be … because my child in grammar school … I mean for the other ones, it was almost every day, because they have either basketball going on, volleyball or baseball. But for … my child currently in grammar school, she's not involved as such in all those extracurricular activities. So basically, I have limited functions to attend in the school, just the basic things. And she doesn't get in trouble, so we don't have to go there to answer to the teacher, you know, so that's a plus. So I don't visit as often as I used to.

The parent-teacher conference [was] I will say in March of this year, yeah, a month ago. It's a good opportunity for the parent to interact with the teacher. I also have their phone number on my speed dial, cell phone, so they can call me or as well I can call them. So you know, we are kind of in direct contact with the teacher. So usually it's the teacher, who kind of exposes what they are doing and where the parent can come in to reinforce what is going on in the classroom, the concepts they are doing at each particular time … from the marking period and that unit they are working on. For example if they are in … their history class, what they are trying to impart for that unit. Or they can tell you the chapter they are on. And then also when they are having tests, which is a big thing. You know, you have to study for the test anyway. So the grade counts, so maybe they have tests on Thursdays or Fridays—this kind of stuff. So you have to drill the child and make sure the child studies, knows the concept you practice, what is being done at school. And then you practice at home to make sure the child is successful on the test because they all count. So basically you visit the teacher. You know what is being done in school so that you can reinforce it at home to make sure the child is passing the classes.

We have open communication with every school my child attends. I mean, direct contact with them. They have my cell phone numbers. They can call me twenty-four hours of the day, anytime. The school can call me … for example, my last child, maybe they are playing in the gym and she falls down and hurts herself. They can reach me. Okay? Also they have … medical insurance information the school requires you to fill out … it's mandatory; they call it an emergency form for all the children. So they know how to reach you anytime there is an emergency, the child can be sick… remember that. If the child is sick, okay, you have to go and pick the child up. There is nobody who is going to pick up the child for you. So the school will be able to reach you anytime if anything happens. Probably the child started being sick at school. The child falls down and was hurt and the school cannot handle it, they have to call you. So in an emergency situation, they must know how to reach you no matter where you are … let's say you have school closing in the morning. They call you early in the morning. There's twelve inches of snow. There is no school. The school is cancelled. They will know how to reach you. So these are the things the school can call you for at any minute, at any time, and you should be there. For example, at times this year, there were schools closing because of the big snow we had this year. So they called like five in the morning that there will be no school today for the children. You know, the school that my daughter goes to. So they should be able to reach you at any time. They reach you in emergency school closing. The other ones they send notes home, yeah, with the child. We also have e-mails.

There are also school websites that we visit to know what's going on. We have parent log-in rights … to view sensitive information, view the child's grades. You can now access the children's grades on the Internet … for example, my child, who is out of state, I can log in and see how she's progressing in all classes every day. Okay, I can log in and see her grades.

I call them too … and I leave a message if nobody is there to pick up my call. And then they usually return my message in about twenty-four hours. I also voice my opinion. I'm an outspoken parent, yes. I voice my opinion if there is something that I don't like that is going on. You really have to. Otherwise, they will intimidate your child. That's one thing as an Igbo parent I learned the hard way. You really have to be involved in your child's education. You have to be visible parents. But … you know, some schools are still discriminatory. So some schools might still … You have to voice your opinion strongly if there is something that is going on you don't like. Tell them, you know, "Hey, I need this to be fixed. I need this to be changed …" And they will listen because they want your money, especially for the private schools, yes. Otherwise, you will pull your child out.

Nebeolisa's reasons and channels for communicating with the school include face-to-face meetings, parent-teacher conferences, visits, responding to notes from the school/teacher, showing up for events, visiting the school website, and requesting for the curriculum.

On some days they have special events like a king and queen dance or this or that. You know, they have social events at the school. As much as possible, I try to go. Or they have … Christmas events, you know … last time … I was in school with my daughter for … They were building a … what was it that they were building? They were … I have forgotten what they called it … something with biscuits. You make a house, you know, decorate that. You know, and I must say actually it is my wife that puts that pressure on because … sometimes you know, men, we can just say, "Oh, let their mother go." She will say, "No, you need to go because I want them to see you in their school." Because if I don't show up, the children begin to read it like, "Daddy doesn't think this is important," [in comparism to how many times mom, my wife shows up] much as mom shows up. So you know how kids kind of like read things. So I try to … she insists sometimes. I will take time and do that.

There was a teacher-parent conference … that was this last school session. It was good. I knew the teacher because she actually was my son's teacher, and now she is my daughter's teacher, so we know her. But it went well. You know, it went well. And usually we try to ask them what can we do … how can we … what do we need to do to help with what she's doing in the classroom, you know. And what are her plans for the class for the next stage, and how can we prepare the child … to be able …

Picking up children can also be an opportunity to communicate with the teacher.

> Whenever my wife goes to the school to pick up the children and she sees any of the teachers, she talks to them. That's one. If she sends … if they send a note home … we will write a response, and we will send it back. We hardly call them unless there is any emergency or e-mail … But it's either face-to-face or written form, notes, yeah. They have our phone numbers. [The school] has a website, where we can check their results. Yeah, you have to sign up for that.

> From the school, basically what one wants to know from the school is what they are teaching the children and then how we can maybe coach them so that they either be in step or ahead. That's really one of the things—what curriculum are you gonna use for this year. I'm interested in the curriculum because I don't want anybody teaching my children any kind of stuff.

Communication between parents and school has to flow, according to Nsobundu, because both have a common mission in the education of children. The information a parent gives to the teacher might assist him/her to help the child at school, and likewise, the information the teacher gives to parents can be useful for working with the child at home. Nsobundu asserts that, generally, schools in America are good at communicating with parents.

> If there is something that is going on, we can write a note. You know, the schools … the American schools are very good at that [communication] … if a child is sick, okay, or if there is something that is going on with the child and if a child has a problem that you think the school can help to control or contribute to, then we will let them know. Like I said, we are partners, not supporters. We are partners, you know? Because if we have communication flowing, you know, at both ends, you can always get something achieved. You can always be aware what is underground. But if one is not informing the other, then one will be at the receiving end all the time.

Nnaemeka believes that the exchange of information between the school and parents promotes a child's educational process. Parents know their children better than their teachers and, as such, are in a better position to provide the teacher with information that will help to create a better learning experience for the child. He shares his experiences of many parent-teacher conferences he and his wife have attended.

> So at the [parent-teacher] conference, we told the teacher about one of our sons, that the class seems to be boring to him, so we need you to give him more homework so that he will get busy when he comes home. If you don't give him enough ... to work on, then he's not using his brain. Then he will just channel it to the TV ...

> So we actually ... especially during the time they received their term report cards, we go, you know, and relay to the teachers what the kids are doing that's very positive, things that they need to prop them up in and those kinds of things, what their dos and don'ts are so ... that helps the teacher know what to do ... how to deal with the child. So as parents ... because we know our kids far better than the teacher does, the teacher ... can only deal with so many kids at a time. And because there is such a short duration of time within the school, and we are ... the ones that spend most of the time with the kids ... from the time they wake up to the time they go to bed and all that. So we know how to relate to the teacher what they ought to look out for when, you know, our kids behave in any way they are not supposed to. So we get feedback from the teachers. That makes life a whole lot easier, and the kids get to learn better under those conditions.

In addition, Nnaemeka is of the opinion that communication has to be frequent to help parents know "what their kids are like in their classrooms."

> So anytime the parent gets a note from the teacher, the parent automatically knows what that note is all about. So he doesn't have to go to the school rushing and sweating or doing anything just because of teacher's remark, which might be negative [which the parent might not like] ... we visit them like monthly. I have called them. We follow up with them to see is there any problem I need to know.

Other channels of communication for Nnaemeka include the telephone, Internet, visits, and newsletters. In general, he and his wife communicate well with the schools their children attend.

> One of the channels of communication, of course, is the telephone. We have ... the school number, and the school has our number both the office and the home number, so if ... for any reason, any problem develops ... like for instance when Chigozie had ... when they were

running school late. He had some kind of … dental check?. Then the school calls, and I go and see … I see the kid. So apart from that … the school is not too far from here. It's only about … I would say about six or seven minutes from here, so I could easily go there or stop by the school and pick them up. Or for any reason when the bus is … you know, is late or delayed for any reason we can easily … They will call us. Or we can call them … we call them.

And they send newsletters for any information that we need to know, any future activity or anything that is coming up in school they will let us know. We always put our signature … for consent to go, let's say … on a field trip. What happens is that we may not be … physically available, and so we can give our signature, permitting them to go with other kids.

And sometimes they give them a card, which we have to sign at the end of the week. The card will tell you that these kids caused no trouble the whole week, and they have to bring it [the card] to the parents. And they [the kids] dare not sign it themselves because they know the dad's signature. So they bring the card back. Then we sign it and give it back to them.

As a matter of fact, I think we have no problem communicating with the school. I know with the new tech and everything that's coming … the avenues of communication are just wide open for us. We use the Internet. They post things through the Internet sometimes. And we can drive down there. So far, we haven't had any problems as a matter of fact. We have no problems with the way the communication takes place.

Summary and Analysis

This chapter started out by presenting what the school expects from Igbo parents as partners in their children's education. Igbo parents understand their role as central in the education of children. But also they are aware that schools have a wide range of school-related expectations of parents, such as getting the children ready for school, creating a learning-friendly environment at home, assisting the children with their homework, participating in school fundraising activities, attending parent-teacher conferences, and volunteering. While such a difference in expectations might cause conflict, as partners with a common educational mission, Igbo parents in Chicago still have very cordial relationships with the schools their children attend. They note that communications between parents and teachers are generally very good, flowing through various channels, such as the telephone, e-mails, the school website, visits, parent-teacher conferences, notes, newsletters, report cards, and PTA meetings.

Communication is More Than the Exchange of Information

The Igbo parents in my study truly believe that they have good communication with the school their children attend. This is reflected in statements like "we have communication flowing at both ends" or "I think they [school] are really good in communication" or "we have open communication with every school my children attend." However, it is important to note that Igbo parents in this study see communication more than as an exchange of verbal or written information. It can also include loving care or acts of charity from the school. During the interview, Nneka shared an example of nonverbal communication with the school her daughter attends.

When Ogechi came home one day in a different dress, Nneka was curious to know what happened, why Ogechi has a different dress, and who changed it. She said that what happened was that Ogechi wet her clothes during her nap time at school and did not have enough spare clothes. But the school had an extra set and changed her dress. Nneka thought she had more spare clothes at school for her daughter. She was delighted that the school did not first request for another dress or sent her home in a wet dress. Nevertheless, she was glad to send more dresses to the school. Nneka believes that she has good relationship with the school and, in conclusion, says, "That's a good way of communicating." One of the reasons why Igbo parents in my study believe American schools are good at communicating with them is because they share a common mission concerning the education of their children, consequently enjoy a good relationship with them. This belief ultimately promotes their children's educational experience.

The next chapter is about what Igbo parents in this study said about the role of their environment as they work with local schools in the education of their children. In other words, they talked about the nature of their environment and how it influences their decisions and activities of parental involvement.

CHAPTER 10

Parental Context of Involvement

During the interview, I asked the participants to recall how their parents were involved in their education in order to get a sense of how the participants' educational lives as children was embedded in relations between their parents and their schools and to see how things change in light of their move to another national context. I also wanted to know whether any of them are using any strategy or knowledge they learned from their parents in their involvement in the education of their own children in Chicago. As we shall hear from their stories, there were frequent references to the way they were brought up or what they learned from their mom or dad or how the system is quite different or how because of the nature of the environment—American society—they made this or that decision with regard to their children's education.

In this chapter, I will consider three main aspects of the Igbo parents' environment that influenced their perception, decisions, and actions with regard to their involvement in the education of their children in Chicago. Two of the aspects are "because of the way [they] were brought up" and the American environment, as these came up frequently during the interviews. The third aspect of their environment is the comparison they made between the Nigerian and American educational landscapes in relation to parental involvement.

"Because of the Way We Were Brought Up"

Igbo parents in Chicago, who work with the schools as they participate in the education of their children, find themselves falling back on what they learned from their parents when they were growing up. Some of those ideas and practices, they try to adapt to their new environment; some, they drop entirely because of the generation gap, the new world order, and the difference in time and place. In short, their present circumstances are different from that of their parents. The way they were brought up influences how they value education, how they choose schools for their children, their notion of discipline for children, and how they participate in the life of the community. On the other hand, it is important to bear in mind that their parents (parents of the participants in this study) were influenced by a different time and society and, to some extent, a different philosophy of life.

As Nneka was growing up in Nigeria, her mom believed that regardless of gender, every child should have the opportunity to get an education, which is the key to a responsible, fruitful, and fulfilling adult life. Nneka absorbed this lesson and has embraced it as she raises her daughter. Among other lessons she learned from both her mom and dad were the importance of breakfast and punctuality.

> Like I mentioned earlier, I grew up in a society … in a culture … that said it's not a priority to put girls into school. And it's not that girls don't go to school. But it depends on the individual parents. But most of them are like because of the culture that the woman will be married at some point and she takes the wealth to another place, so the education is mainly okay for males [boys] because they keep the father's name. So I remember very well my mother said, "No, that's not gonna happen in my house." She had … eight of us. She had five boys and three girls, and we go to school like … I don't know. *The Sound of Music*, I'm trying to remember their family name, the Vaughn family … von Trapp family? My parents were very strict that you'd come home … especially my mother. She had a private business. She didn't work for the government.
>
> She had a grocery store. You may use that word, but she had liquors in it too, you know … she used that as a source of education for us too, in terms of when we'd come back from school … she'd close up her shop and … then she comes home and she asks, "Where is your homework? What did you do today?" And she will expect you after eating to read out to her whatever you did at school. My mom was very, very … she was very strict. And if you missed any word … my mom didn't have as much education as I have now, but I was wondering how she could find what was missing in a sentence … it was interesting to find out that if you were writing a note in class and not paying attention, my mother can easily detect that. Because she will ask you to read your note, and whenever you make a pause, she knows there's a word missing. And she would say, "What is that missing?" because then when you're reading out your note to her

and all of a sudden you stop, she's like, "What is happening? Did you miss anything there?" And then you yourself will tell her, "Oh, I missed something." And she said, "What happened? Were you playing?" And I thought that was a good way of following up from school and educating us. The other thing was that next time when you go back to school, you don't miss anything.

Nneka's mom's shop was also an environment for education.

The other thing she did that was interesting was that when she allows us to come into her business—to her grocery store—she's not just putting us there to be the salesperson. She will ask you questions. She will ask you to multiply. She will ask you questions regarding numbers. She would pull out ... the register and she'd count the money there, and her [she] and you would take inventory. And she would leave you for an hour. She comes back and says, "What happened?" And then she gives you a separate sheet, where you register whatever happens, and then she will expect you to do that addition for what you've had so far and subtract it [from the inventory]. Because then when you are doing selling or whatever it is that you have done within that hour, you have added that money to whatever she had initially. And she would say, "Oh, you have this. So if you subtract this from this, what do you have?" And then you are looking at her and she says, "Write it down. And tell me." And that was a plus because then you learn addition. You learn subtraction. You're learning multiplication. And then she would say if you cannot write it down, then pick those items one by one and put it on the table and add it up. She gives you a lot of time.

Even as a teen, Nneka and her siblings were taught the essentials of customer service.

Besides that, there was also the idea of how you interact with people—that is, being a salesperson and [relating to] customer ... and the exposure ... not being shy, that boldness was in us and how to speak to people. And she said, "You don't have to ... the customer is always right." I remember I learned that from my mom. She said, "You don't have to be rude, but you get your word out and you make your statement." She said this is it. And so my mother educated us in a very unique way. And she kept a schedule for us too. We'd come back from school and ... she would make sure we eat, like I said. We had a nap in between. She gives us time. And then you'd come back to the store, and you'd come with your books, and everybody is busy. And she also made sure we had breakfast ... and this is how I learned when I had my own child ... that breakfast is very important. You don't miss breakfast in my house.

Among other things, she learned punctuality from her father.

My father was a civil engineer. He's retired now. He had to visit so many sites in the morning, so we'd wake up very early. We were very time conscious in my house ... My father had to drop us off at school. We had to be ready ... at five, we're all awake and sometimes four, depending on the sites that he's visiting. And so we are ready and we had to eat. So my mom is up early, and she also says you don't have to choose ... "There's no picky eater in my house. Whatever I put on the table, that's what you eat." And I thought that was a brilliant way of raising a child, even though ... you know, we would always grumble about it, but in the long run, it paid off.

Another thing I wanted to mention that is important about my growing up and education in Nigeria is that even though my parents strived for us all to get an education, we were not on the same level in terms of brilliance. We had amongst us people who were on the extreme, but at some point, I did not pass what they call the GCE[26] exam, and my father didn't find it funny, and he said well ... since I didn't make it once, there was no way ... he's not gonna pay for the second time. And my mom threatened to sell her *abada* [wrappers—her clothing] to register me back so that I can take that exam the second time. That's the effect of culture ... I remember where it kicked in at some point and my father said, "Well anyway, she's going to marry someday, so if this is serious, she has to pass it once." And my mom said, "But you have to give her the second chance." So my mom really believed that education is the key, and that is a culture that I embrace ... I've come to embrace raising my child.

My dad was brilliant, too, in terms of what he does. He was also active, like I said. But because he was an engineer ... he was very good with keeping with the time [he was always punctual]. Besides what we learned, he was very brilliant in terms of what you are doing; what do you want to do with yourself? He always tells us the story of how he was raised by his father amongst his other brothers

---

26 GCE (General Certificate of Education) is a secondary school exit exam organized by the West African Examination Council (WAEC). It is one of the requirements for university admission.

and sisters. How he came to be. That you don't just wait for your parents, you also have to do your own part. He always believed that it's a two-way thing. And so he says, "Even though I pay you guys' school fees ..." My father is always looking forward to ... report cards that we bring back. And but he's always on time ... he said if you're on time, then you're organized. So he likes us to be on time, even at church. Going to church, I remember we were always the first people. Wherever we were going, we were always early. And so my father was also part of us going to school. He paid the school fees ...

Njideka's education has gone well because her dad set high expectations for her. Now she is involved in the education of her children, and she sets high standards because that was the way she was brought up.

People have different ways of going about it [parent involvement] ... You know, some people think too much pressure regarding schooling and education is bad, and they don't want to force their kid to say "Oh, you must get all A's, and you must get everything right." I find myself a little bit on a different ... I didn't grow up that way, and because I feel that my educational background and everything with my schooling has gone well, I want to do things the way it was done to me. So I've set the standard very, very high and ... my daddy used to say if you want to reach for the tree, you aim for the sky. So if you miss the sky, at least you'll get the tree. So I don' tell him that "Oh, just do what you can, and any score you get is good." I'm saying you should get every one right. And I know some people say, "Oh, that puts too much pressure [on the child]." I've met a lot of people who thought that that was too much pressure for kids, and you should just let them be who they will be. So there are different styles, and I think all work.

Back in Nigeria, education was important for Nnamdi's father, and as a result, he pushed his children very hard. However, he thinks that his dad's approach to parental involvement was excessive.

My parents didn't have any formal education. They were just traders. My father had a business in Aba, selling textile ... *akwa umu nwanyi n'ama* [wrapper/clothing for women]. So education was very important for him. Actually my father was very ... maybe the very first person that sent a girl to secondary school in my town. Yeah, my oldest sister ... and then my younger brother went to the university and stuff like that, so education ... You know, meant a lot. And so ... but he built it up ... education to us, so much that it became repulsive. Yeah, and that's why I said there was good and bad about that. You know, so my father was front and center, very principled. He pushed adversely. I mean, it was just like ... you know, like he goes to school and says to the teacher or headmaster, *"omee isike gbuo ya bute lum ozu ya"*[27]. You know, that destroys your self-esteem, and my father was a triple-A disciplinarian, you know, just too much. It's good to discipline children but not ... yeah, not ... that way, that's not the way out.

My dad ... I made him proud. In school cert [school certificate exam], I had grade one. You know so it was something ... it was something he bragged about and stuff like that, you know. So from that standpoint, I made my parents very, very proud. And you know ... but my dad is a taskmaster. It's difficult to satisfy him completely, so there's always an angle ... even if you make an A, and he will say, "Well, A is A, but there is physical work to be done." You know, stuff like that. So he was a tough man. He's a very tough man.

He definitely did learn from the mistakes of his father with regard to parental involvement in the education of children.

Getting out of the way is a huge part of fatherhood. Your question was very, very important. How far away do you go? But that's open to question, but getting out of the way is a huge part of fatherhood. Any father that understands that rule helps the children more than anything else. Yeah, because you know, you may think you're not six foot ten, but if you have children, in their eyes you're a giant. So at this particular age, you have to get out of the way. You *must* get out of the way.

My mom was the person that really got us ready to go to school before you got to that age of readying yourself. You know, her take on education was to do your best. Well in terms of the education, the mold of the person, I get all of that from my mother. Grace, you know. Yeah, it's very important ... you know, in terms of *ndi banyi n'akpo ya asala* [grace in our language is *asala,*] all of that I learned from my mother. Morals ... she gave all of that to me. And then the way you carry yourself, the way you are as a human being, you know. I remember when I was in boarding school when you come

---

27   Literally, it means "if he disobeys you in any way, kill him and send me his corpse—body." This is an exaggeration that gives the teacher or the headmaster the permission to discipline his children in school.

back, my mother makes sure you went and said hello to everybody. The other thing my mother taught me that is very, very important is not to borrow money from somebody, not to go borrowing money. I mean for some reason, she taught us that *na obu ikpali onwe gi* [it is disrespecting one's self]. You know ... learn how to be self-content with whatever it is you have as opposed to ...

Rewarding children's performance is one way to motivate them. Nkolika adapts this lesson she learned from her parents in ways that suit her circumstances in motivating her children.

Like my parents ... my dad ... if you didn't pass very well, you won't get a Christmas dress. So ... everybody in Nigeria looks forward to getting a Christmas dress. So in order for us to get that Christmas dress, you must make sure your grades are really high ... So he played a very important role just like I'm doing now with my kids. ... like you won't get a dress or something like that, I do it the other way. My kids ... when their grades have really improved, when their grades are good, I try to buy things for them. And you know kids love it when you buy things for them. So instead of telling them, "I'm not gonna buy it for you" to get improved, I try to buy things for them to get improvement in their work.

It is interesting that Nwakaego's parents did not have a formal education, yet they made sure that she and her siblings went to private schools. Private schools are good although that they are expensive. Nwakaego brings the same zeal to the education of her children.

Okay first and foremost, my parents did not get formal education ... the level of formal education they got was elementary. They just stopped at elementary. But ... then both of them, they have the zeal for education. I think probably because they did not get it, so they have this great zeal for education ... I mean, my father was a businessman. Not that he was ... exceedingly well-to-do. We all went to private ... primary schools. Then from secondary schools, we all applied, you know ... for the federal government colleges ... some of us went to federal government college. Some went to private secondary schools. Then all of us went to universities ... then even when we came back from school, we still have private tutors ... that come at home and teach us. And when they cannot come, we go for the extra tutorials. I mean you pay them to come to your home and teach you ... and then enrolling you in any ongoing tutorials anywhere. You know ... the fact is that we were given the opportunity to attend the best school available at that time and was expensive … I mean, it can't be better than that. But … it's like everybody must be first. That was always the target—to be first. That is always the target, so you know, to be first every year …

She [mom] was the one that gets most of the textbooks most of the time. You know, that gets the list of textbooks to buy, goes to the store to buy the textbooks, and stay with us, you know, to make sure that … we are being taught well. Yeah. Oh they were very good. Then you know, getting to listen to current affairs … I mean it's like you cannot miss the network news. You must know the things that are happening all around, you know. So stuff like that. So they still got us involved.

Even though Nwakaego learned a lot from her parents she cannot apply some of it because of her present circumstances.

From the time they [my kids] were not talking to the time they started walking and running. Like how to take care of each other, you know. Look after each other. Help clean the house, you know, maintain cleanliness, you know. And just taking an interest in what is happening around them, you know? Then teaching them … you know there are a lot of things they can learn … how to be responsible at home, like you know, folding laundry, just the little things that they can do by themselves … And anything … Education … you know I mean it's expensive. It's more expensive … I mean like the resources are not here. They are not as available as they were back home. So I cannot get the private tutorials to come. So I do the tutoring.

Nneamaka's parents were both educators, and they played an important role in her education. She loved her Catholic school education and is grateful that her parents gave her the opportunity to go to a Catholic school. The fact that she is giving her children the same opportunity here can be traced to her positive experience of Catholic education in Nigeria.

I went to school in Nigeria. And my family played a heavy role in making sure that I was fully educated, you know? My parents sent me to a Catholic girls school … you can see why I love Catholic schools. Because I know I was a product of a Catholic education. So they made sure I had the best that they could afford at that time. They encouraged me to be successful. They exposed me to every opportunity to be sure that I was successful, and I was proud of the opportunities they gave me despite the fact that I am a girl …

you know, when I grew up, girls were not allowed to go to school so to say. But they gave me the opportunity to go to school, and I'm, you know … I am glad that I made them proud because in my community, the girls coming after me are … they are emulating me. I led a very good example for all the girls in my community coming after me … and I'm happy that I made my parents proud. I am the … all the girls in my community kind of emulated my footsteps. And they all went to college … and most of them are successful in their different careers. So I am also happy my parents gave me that opportunity to be educated, a college graduate despite the fact that we are told, "Hey, that's a girl. She's gonna get married and leave your family." But my father always says, "Hey, I wish she was a boy. That I will train her because I know she's going to take care of what boys do in my house." And my father never regretted that.

My father … was actually the headmaster of his school. My mother also was a headmistress, so education runs in my family. And my uncle was the first person that went to high school in my community. So … my uncle Chris … he passed down that knowledge … down to his brothers. So my father went to school, went to college. Oh, he didn't go to college. He went to teachers' training college … to become the headmaster … and my mother went also to teachers' training college, as I said, to become a headmistress also. So I kind of followed in the footsteps of my parents to be a teacher.

But as Nneamaka participates in the education of her children here in Chicago, she tries to adapt some of the things she learned from her parents and the community in which she grew up.

Everything I am doing right now is what I learned from my parents and the community where I grew up. So they are the ones who shaped me. So basically what I'm imparting to my children is learned behavior from my parents, my community, and my culture. So I kind of blend them to suit me at this age and this environment that I'm in. So I will say I'm a product of my parents and my environment. And at the same time, I'm trying to impart to my children to be a product of what I am.

Nebeolisa's approach to school choice is influenced by his dad's.

What I have always said is that I would rather have them go to a public school—have that experience of meeting real people and not just people maybe at a certain social class. But then I can always get them arranged for private tutoring to make up for what is deficient.

That was the way my dad raised us. We went to the public schools in Nigeria, but he had private lessons for us. I think that helped shape who I am and what ... you know, in terms of ... the way I look at life.

I mean, I will say clearly ... first of all, they made sure they chose the school that we went to. And they made those choices based on ... what they knew about the schools. Not so much as where the schools were but who was at the school. You know, the principal is so and so. You have to go to that school because of the principal there is so and so, so I know I went to a place where this kind of person will mentor you or be able to oversee what you're doing ... and even at the primary school level, at the secondary school, they made sure we got to school early. You know they made sure we were not late. He hired private tutors for us and then set the pace. You knew this was what to do. You had no choice. You had to do well. And my mom, like I told you, she was a seamstress, so most of those teachers would come to our house to measure clothes for her, to make those dresses for those women. So you knew she knew your teacher, so you're not going to be goofy now. So all of a sudden you see your teacher come to your house, and you run because you don't want her to see you and tell a story about how you were making noise in school. So ... they were involved, and they provided the funding.

He also learned the importance of extracurricular activities as part of education. Nebeolisa is very active in the Igbo community in Chicago and raises his children with such goal in mind. That, too, is a lesson from his dad.

More importantly, my dad emphasized that education is not just going to school, that you have to also pay attention to other things [extracurricular activities]. I remember one experience in university ... I mean at that point, he had no clue what we were studying. I mean he's not a physician ... but I will come home on vacation, and he will see me reading. Most of it because I'm trying to catch up with work ... because I've not used my time well in school. So he always will prod me and say, "Is that all you do? Read, read, read? What else ... how else do you spend your extra time? What other extracurricular activity do you do?" So he did not know that, yes, I am quite active ... I do things other than books, but he helped me to understand that, yes, there is more to education than just book work. Because ... now he saw me like I'm always reading. But really

I'm trying to catch up. But then he says, "No, no, no, no, no, no
... if you're in school, read. When you come home, relax, do other
things, get involved with the people [community] ..." And like
during ... we get home during the Christmas break, he will make
sure we go to the age-grade meeting. He will make sure we will
go to the village meeting. That morning, he woke everybody up;
"Go and find out where your mates are and go there." This coming
back from school *ana eme oyibo* [conducting yourself with a flair of
superiority] ... You see, and that's why people see us today and they
say, "You're a doctor, but you show up in all these Igbo things." My
dad was American trained, but most people didn't know that he had
a degree ... he relates to everybody from every strata of the society
and at any level. If you see him with a man who is farmer or palm-
wine tapper, you think he's one of them. He had that knack, and
that's the way he raised us. We have no concept of class ... and that's
been useful because there's nothing about the Igbo community,
Igbo land, or Igbo culture ... we experienced them all. *Jee mmalu
ife ... baa n'ogbo* (go and participate in your age grade's meeting;
go and identify or associate with your age mates). The day our age
group started meeting, I was there at the first day; I am a founding
member. So you knew those things. You learned those as you were
coming up. Yet at the time I was doing this, most of those boys were
maybe traders. Even when I come back from medical school, I am
there. It doesn't matter where you are. These are your people ... and
you learn from them ...

Nebeolisa confesses that he is using the "script" of what his dad did as
he raises his children.

First of all ... my concept of education, I think I picked up from
them. The role I am playing now is basically what I saw them do.
You know, he will ask you about school. He will make sure you have
everything that you need. He will press on you to apply yourself.
So a lot of what I do is really what I saw them do, and that is the
power of parenting, that example is what I learned from them [my
parents] ... sometimes you don't even know that's what's happening,
but like I shared with you, the way they raised us, that helped
shape my view of the schools because some people will ask me ...
you know, if these kids are going to Harvard you need to put them
in private schools. And I tell them some of the schools we went to
are far ... this Redwood school is like university compared to the
infrastructure and the layout ... If I bring pictures of the schools

we went to, many of them will not believe that I went to those schools. But we are where we are not because of the structure ... we could as well have gone to school under a tree, but the content and the value of the education that we were given prepared us to be able to perform and achieve in any other society, and that to me is education. It's not the fanciful environment, you know?

Nebeolisa learned a communal approach to educating children from his community in Nigeria. But he is yet to apply that here.

Because that was how our fathers were sent to school. The majority of our fathers went to school not because their parents had money but because the community identified them as smart, sharp, and the community contributed money and sent them to school. Or they rewarded them for going to school. Or they helped them or they assisted them. But there was the communal vision for education. So No Child Left Behind was not just a slogan, but everybody worked toward that ... every child that was seen not going to school when it is school time was dragged by any parent of the community ... you know, that adult drives the child to school and says, "This is where you are supposed to be. Why are you here? Why are you not in school?" You can't drop out ... because the principal will send ... the headmaster will send the big boys to come and pick you up from the house, you know? That's right. It takes a village. You know, and it's not a socialist concept. You know, because once you say, you know, "community," some people start thinking, "Oh, this is socialism." No. ... it's the community. The community must rise up and educate her children. That's one of the things I am quite appreciative about what the president is doing.

Because he [President Obama] realizes that the only way that there has been a lot of social divide, cultural divide, economic divide is because some children are not being educated up to their potential. And so long as we want some people to be at the lower rank—you know, like giving a poor quality education—then you continue to have problems in the inner city and the community. Some of those children, if they ... have the opportunity to go to a good school or be taught well, be educated to their potential, they will rise up and there won't be crime. There will not be stealing. They won't need welfare. They will not need social support. They will be the ones contributing taxes to the community. They will be bringing their resources back to the community.

The love for education by Nonye's parents, even though they did not go far in school themselves, is manifested in the kind of sacrifices they made to put Nonye, her other nine siblings, and some members of their extended family through the best schools. Nonye feels blessed to have had such devoted parents, and she makes similar efforts to be involved in the education of her daughter.

> My situation is very different because my parents ... my mom never went to school. My father went only to primary six [sixth grade]. But their love for education ... my parents used to tell us how they worked seven days a week just to make sure that my eldest brother could go to Germany and study—he is a retired medical doctor now—and how they will be sending all their money to Germany so that he can study. It was only after the war [Nigerian civil war] that we lost a lot, and my parents couldn't do that anymore. But ... my parents achieved so much more than what we could ever achieve.

> What I recall from my parents is that they always sent us to the best schools. You know Government College Umuahia for the boys, Holy Rosary Secondary School ... for the girls, St. Michaels, always the best schools. And then paying for school fees was never a problem. Whenever we said, "We need this for school," my parents always brought out the money. And now looking back as a grown-up person, I wonder how they managed. But they never ... complained. And they always ... it was ... I knew that if there was one day that I missed school, my father would definitely beat us ... one thing I remember ... my first term at Holy Rosary Secondary School, we were like seventy-something girls ... in that class, and I was the third person in the class ... when our report card came out. And I told my father, "Yeah, I am the third out of seventy-something." And he said, "Oh my God, where were you when the other two ... took the first two positions ..." *Ebe ka ino mgbe mmadu gbara* first or second [where were you when some people took the first and second positions]. So I can never forget that. So now ... we strive to have, you know, all A's and do our best. Yeah. I am the seventh of ten children, and I knew that most of my siblings ... the older ones all had mostly A's, you know? So they did very well, everybody.

> I remember ... when I was in Europe ... my mom couldn't read English very well, so I would write her letters in Igbo. But I remember that when my mom was in her fifties and sixties, she went back to night school, and she would lament, "Oh, I wish I went to school.

I know where I would be today if I went to school." So I always appreciated that comment for her, saying that I have the opportunity ... I am blessed to have the opportunity to go to school, and she didn't. And also, I appreciate my parents very much because many of my uncles did not want to send their female children to school. But my parents always paid for everybody, even my cousins. If you wanted to go, female or not, he paid for everybody. So we appreciated that from my father ... who paid for everybody, male or female. So that was exceptional. And ... I make sure that what my parents gave me, I give that to her [my daughter]. I am blessed. I am lucky.

In being involved in the education of his four children, Nsobundu applies some of the things he learned from his dad, an educator with many years of experience as both a teacher and administrator.

My dad was a teacher, you know. He was a headmaster and ... he taught at St. Charles Teachers Training College. He was a senior tutor. He was headmaster in different elementary schools, so my dad taught me just like any other teacher. But when I come home, he teaches me a short way of doing math and all those things. And that's about it. My mom was pretty much about business; she was a businesswoman. She also would help as much as she could. She was not as educated as my dad ... you know, like my first child sometimes, you know, plays music while... doing homework, and my dad always want you to sit quietly, hold your pencil in a particular way, have a different posture when you're studying, you know? And I try and instill that into my kids also, you know, the way of holding your pencil and all those things. You can't be playing music and doing your homework, you know, your attention becomes impaired no matter how smart you are. It's like you're trying to eat your cake and have it at the same time. It doesn't work, you know?

Nnaemeka is proud to indicate that he and his wife are bringing up their children the way they were brought up. Discipline is essential in their approach to raising and educating children. He says that he is a good parent because of his parents and what they instilled in him.

We have one daughter and four boys. We are doing fine, and we've been trying to ... bring them up through the same Catholic faith and tradition we were brought up in. So far we've been doing a good job of it, at least that's what we learn from people around us. Talking about a good education ... our parents trained us and raised us to this level not only through schooling but with good education. Our kids, they were all born here. And we trained them under the roof and the umbrella of what we learned from our own parents. The memory of my dad and parents who have just passed on, I would say that, of course, played a very significant role. As a matter of fact, I wouldn't be the kind of parent I am. I am not being too proud that I'm a good parent, but I know that I wouldn't feel satisfied with the way I'm handling my children if it weren't for my parents that instilled that in me. Of course, it's a whole lot different from my experiences in Nigeria at that time.

So whether it is learning from the mistakes of their parents or using or adapting what they learned from their parents, the way Igbo parents were brought up in relation to their education in Nigeria or elsewhere has become part of the Ecological systems that shapes their perception and practice of parental involvement here in Chicago.

"Because of the Nature of How Things Are in America"

In comparison to Nigeria, America is a high-tech capitalistic society characterized by individualism and a fast-paced life. The quest for freedom and equality, even if not totally realized, are at the heart of the American way of life. Freedom of speech is a value Americans treasure. The country, as a whole, derives its power and authority from the Constitution. The pursuit of education is a big part of American culture and the acculturation process. Immigrants and their children pursue education in order to become part of the larger society. This, in sum, is the nature of how things are in America, the new environment Igbo parents live and function in, including their involvement in the education of their children. The influence of the American environment on Igbo parents as they participate in the education of their children extends to the sociological, economic, and psychological spheres of life.

From the experience of growing up under strict Nigerian parents (in particular, her dad) in the USA, Njideka tries to balance the influence of American freedom and liberty with the need to instill discipline in her children as they grow up. The nature of American society makes her cautious of the kind of activities she wants her children to participate in. She believes that the nature of American society has pressured some Nigerian husbands to jettison some Nigerian approaches to domestic duties brought from Nigeria. Unfortunately, some are yet to change.

Whether they want it or not, Nigerian fathers are doing a lot more and are being more involved just because of the nature of how things are in America. And I think it's good for the children to have real ... more active relationships with their father, you know, on a day-to-day basis and not just, you know, because they made noise or did something to get in trouble. And the more the husband is willing to help, the better it is for the wife, too, to help relieve some of ... the stress. Because I talk to some Nigerian mothers, and their husbands are still doing like *Naija*²⁸ style, and ... and the woman maybe works, you know, the night shift, but her husband still says, "You do everything with the kids. You have to cook everything ..." And it's very stressful for them.

But as for me growing up ... because I'm like the bridge where I know both sides ... I'm one of the oldest ... American-born Nigerians in the country. I'm one of the oldest. You know, because people were coming in during the '60s and early '70s. That's when some of the first immigrants were coming over. And so my dad is one of the pioneers ... who moved to America. So ... I'm one of the oldest kids ... there's only a handful of kids in America that are, you know, older than me. So you know, it was like ... now you have parents and they'll say, "Oh, ask so and so ... because he did it this way." But he didn't have anybody to ask ...

When we go to school and then they'll say, "Oh, there's a school dance." And he'll say, "Why do you need school dance?" You know, "Stay home. Why would you ... go out at night? What is all this?" You know, he didn't even like the idea of sports. He said, "Why don't you just concentrate on your books? Why would you be on the basketball and the softball and the track team? You need to focus on your books. You're trying to be everywhere. You're not concentrating." Or you know, people will have parties. He says, "Why should young people be going to parties ..." you know ... and so all the kids at school would be like, "I'm not inviting you. I know you can't go. Your daddy is too strict. You don't get to do anything." They couldn't call on the phone. They were like, "I can throw away your phone number because your daddy won't even ... let me call you." He will say, "Oh, I called you last night." I said, "You did?" [And the other child says] "Oh yeah, your dad said you're busy with your schoolwork. You can't talk," you know. So it was always like, you know, people would have functions or do things and it was like, yeah. You'd hear about it. "Oh, you missed it. Everybody had a good

---

28   *Naija* is the nickname for Nigeria

time, but your parents are so strict you never do anything. You can't do anything." So over time, you know, they started loosening up a little bit and allowed you to do some things, but never ... you know, like they would have camping trips overnight for like a weekend or five days. "How are you gonna sleep somewhere else?" So I never got to do any of those things, but that's how it is for first-generation Americans.

As she raises her children, Njideka tries to balance her strict upbringing with yielding to every demand her children make. After all, virtue, they say, stands in the middle.

I mean, but you don't want to say, "Oh yeah, go do everything!" you know? Because I don't think it is good to do everything, you know. Like a lot of other people's kids are crazy, and ... you know like everything is, "Oh, let's have a playdate." People will call and say, "Oh ... Chijioke and my son are friends. Let's have a playdate. Come over to my house." I don't want him to come over to your house if I don't know you and I don't know the kind of person you are, you know? So Chijioke is always like, "Oh, all these people got together, and I didn't get to go." It's like well, I don't know his mom. He's like, "Oh, but here's a phone number ..." I can't just talk to somebody on the phone and then leave you to be there for three hours. The first couple of playdates that Chijioke had, like I sat there with the mom while Chijioke was playing with the kid. So you know, after speaking to the mom for a few hours, then I know next time, okay, I have an idea of this woman. You know, I think I understand where she's coming from, that she doesn't seem so crazy. That maybe next time I can, you know, let you stay there. Or maybe tell the boy he can come to this side. But you have to be careful. This country, I think, has more crazy people than maybe other places, and you just don't know. You don't know what you're getting into if you just say, "Yes, yes, yes." Even the birthday parties, they'll say, "Okay, birthday party is from two to five," and then you get there and people have just dropped off their kids and left. But you don't know this person, you know? So I would say, "Oh, can I stay?" They're like, "Oh, you want to ... you want to stay?" You know, so it's just getting used to things. But you have to ... you have to get to know people. Then you can relax. But I think it's good to be cautious.

Nnamdi has more flexible time than his wife, so he takes charge of most of the domestic duties, especially during the busy morning hours of getting ready for school.

I wake up before my wife, and then my wife comes to the kitchen. By that time, I've prepared the food they're gonna eat. And the next step is dressing them up for school. That is the busiest hour in the morning. And then I have to take my daughter first, and I come back to take my son. They are at opposite ends of the city. You know, so he's off at two fifteen, and I pick him up, I put him in the car, and I go get her. And then we get home and eat lunch and play. And then my wife comes … You know, she's in school. And she comes home in the evening. And when she comes home, I retire.

Nnamdi understands the nature of American society, namely, that domestic duties or chores are not meant for wives or female members of the family alone.

American society encourages parents to voice their opinions on matters relating to the welfare and education of their children.

I also voice my opinion. I'm an outspoken parent, yes. I voice my opinion if there is something that I don't like that is going on. You really have to. Otherwise, they will intimidate your child. That's one thing as an Igbo parent I learned the hard way. You really have to be involved in your child's education. You have to be visible parents. (Nneamaka)

The school Nebeolisa's children attend requires that parents take care of some the extracurricular activities, like sports, dancing, etc. This not only requires the parents' time and physical presence, but it can also be cumbersome, especially for larger families. He also offers some suggestions on how to make it less burdensome for parents.

I will say that the only thing … that I can say is the difference is that the parental involvement here is more tasking. Because there were a lot of things that the schools did back home that the schools are not doing here. For example, you have to arrange extracurricular activities for your kid. You know baseball is on the parents, swimming, gymnastics. You know, when we went to school that's all part of the school curriculum. So that the kid went to school, stayed in school, finished with their homework, or did their extra curriculum activities, did sports and games, and then when they came home, they are home. So the parents weren't involved in trying to arrange for them to do this or do that. But a lot of that is on the parents here, and it becomes challenging when you have two, three kids doing different things. So you hear some parents … the husband is three miles away with somebody who has football.

> The mother is ten miles away with somebody who has, you know, athletics. And then you have to run from that to pick or ... to drop off the other one at gymnastics.

Based on his experience, he is willing to offer advice to the school district on how to reduce the burden of parents with regard to this issue.

> So ... if I could suggest to the school district, it would be easier on parents if the children went to school in the morning, stayed 'til six. Release them to us at six. When they finish school, let them go have a snack, do their homework, go and play. Have games, have sports—baseball, athletics, football, tennis, badminton, whatever— and then come home instead of the parents trying to run around town. You know like fortunately for us, the community center is just behind us, so I will sign them up for swimming lessons. So I have to be there from five to five forty-five. And then my son will start by six to six forty-five, so you are there for two hours. Thank God it's in one place. But at some point, you want them to get into basketball. You want them to get into baseball. You want them to do soccer. You have to do that. You see that's the only thing. The music is not so much part of the school. That you have to find ... if your child is musically inclined or something, then you want them to be exposed to music school. But that's the only thing that I find that is different. And then the other part of it is I would like them to have a broader education beyond the American space. Learn about other people, other countries. And that's one advantage maybe I'll say our children have because we will take them home, and they know about home. And they know about people other than just America. Because that's the way ... I mean that's partly maybe our colonial heritage. We studied Europe, and we studied America.

There are certain things in American society that are attractive and sometimes children are pressured to imitate them because they think they are trendy. Parents really have to step in to help the children evaluate and educate them about these influences

> My son came home one day ... he had one of these temporary tattoos. He said, "Daddy, I would like to get a tattoo." I said, "Okay, where did you see that?" He said ... somebody came to school with a tattoo. So I said, "Does your daddy have a tattoo?" He says no. I said, "*Ndi ba anyi adighi* eme tattoo." (Our people don't do tattoos.) It's the same answer I gave him when he says he saw somebody with an earring. Like, "Dad, what about earrings ..." I said no, our

people don't do that. *Umu nwoke ndi Igbo adighi agba ihe nti* (Igbo males don't wear earrings). So it's good because now I'm framing for him a different kind of social and cultural heritage that says there is a way we behave. We are not just Americans. We are Igbos living in America. And so, *na ndi n'eme eto a na ndi Igbo adighi eme eto a* (There are certain things Igbo do, and there are certain things Igbo don't do, even if other ethnic groups or people do them). It's something that they have come to understand. (Nebeolisa)

America is a tough and competitive society. Besides that, things like TV and Hollywood influence the children's upbringing. These help to define the kind of relationship Nonye has with her daughter. She helps her deal with these influences in a positive way.

> I make sure that she studies, and I cook. I cook, she washes up; whenever I tell her to do something, she does it, but I try to do as much as I can because I know she has very tough … competition. It's a very competitive environment.
>
> And of course, the TV and Hollywood does affect her upbringing here. There are so many things that she will talk back about or discuss with me that if we were in Nigeria she wouldn't. She would be silent. She's much more assertive or much more … in Nigeria when you are a woman, you are much more laid back … yeah, you can't talk as much. She's much more open than I would be … it's a good thing because in this society you have to be. Otherwise, you will never be where you want to be because people kind of take you for granted. They will say you are shy. Being aggressive is a good thing here.
>
> But America … has so many chances that you don't have in Nigeria … they don't … go on strike. So you finish your education hopefully when you are supposed to finish it if you study. And you get things like financial aid and scholarships which, in Nigeria, are almost nonexistent. So if you don't have money, you can go to school here. In Nigeria if you don't have money … it's more difficult to go to school.

When it comes to discovering and nurturing a child's career, due to their exposure to American ways of doing things, a parent like Nsobundu knows what not to do—that is, impose a career on a child.

> Those of us who are here now, we've become exposed and enlightened; we realize that actually every child has his own or her own ability.

Being a lawyer or being an engineer or doctor doesn't really take you to the sky. You can get to the sky through other professions. We are so limited in African countries and third-world countries. So we don't do that here. For me, we talk to them and say, "Well, this profession we're researching is ... people are doing so well." This is what it takes. You have options ...

America is a land of liberty. However, that freedom can be taxing for some parents from Nigeria, who are raising American-born Igbo children here in Chicago.

You know, when I came things weren't as ... I mean, not that things have gotten any better now. As a matter of fact, they have gotten worse. But being new in a foreign land, things were very tough and hard; I had to go through the process, first of all, in making the transition from a foreign student to getting my resident card and, from there, to further making myself a permanent citizen of the United States. Yes, so it's been quite a length of time—thirty years.

As a matter of fact, in this day and age, it takes a whole lot more to educate a child not only in terms of discipline, but it requires ... especially here in Western culture ... I'm only referring ... to how kids sometimes have this level of liberty which most of us never had back home. And it takes a whole lot more to get a child educated. Firstly, you have to have their attention to get them interested in the process. And to do that you have to discipline them. And as a matter of fact, that's one of the reasons why we decided ... not that the system is not good here. It's very good. It's just that the culture itself does not permit the level of discipline maybe we want ... Two of our children are back in Nigeria [for secondary-school education].

The memory of my dad and parents who have just passed on, I would say ... they played very significant role. Of course, it's a whole lot different from my experiences in Nigeria at that time. We had to do a lot of things and still go to school. It's not like here, where kids just spend the time mostly in school, and then they come home and do [homework] ... we did a lot of manual labor—go fetch firewood, go to the stream and get some drinking water, do a lot of things and yet come home, read, try to study for school the following day; it takes a lot ... but that level of discipline has made me ... made my family and most people from that area that are now here ... I would say most of them are good parents because they know what it takes to do that.

"Compared with Nigeria"

In this section of parents' environment, Igbo parents in this study compare the Nigerian environment to America in relation to their involvement in the education of their children.

Njideka is fortunate to have a husband who has adapted to American style of life, doing things which ordinarily he would not do if they were to live in Nigeria.

> I mean, it's hectic so you do need help. And so you know sometimes Chijioke, [my husband] might have a schedule maybe where he will … come home a little early. And luckily like in America, it's a little bit different from Nigeria, where the father is more participatory, you know, is participating more than I think they do [in Nigeria] … I don't know if things have changed in Nigeria, but I know that all the things that Chijioke does, I know that his father didn't do, you know? And the more the husband is willing to help, the better it is for the wife, to help relieve some of … stress, but I am very fortunate that I have a great partner, who can help me and has adapted to the American style, you know?

Having a boyfriend /girlfriend is one of the issues that has not really been influenced so much by American culture. Igbo parents are very reluctant to discuss such issues.

> My parents, they didn't allow us to have a boyfriend until we went into college. But over here, some people have a boyfriend at the age of fourteen, fifteen, you know … so some parents don't like it when you ask question about having a boy/girl friend, especially when they are Africans or they're from another tribe.

It is unlikely to find a child in elementary school engage in petty trading or hawking while attending school. American society would not allow such a thing.

> Or like something that happened in Nigeria, I can remember one of my friends … she didn't come from a very well-to-do family. So … her mom used to bake like some groundnuts and things like that … cook and bring some things to school. And during break time … she will be selling those things, you know? So I mean … I remember

how that girl really sold those things to make some money for the parents. She didn't sell it to take the money. She takes it back to her mom. So that's something I really always remember. I can't think of children doing that here in America.

Nwakaego compares the challenges of parental involvement that arise because of the environment.

If you compare [parental involvement] back home, I will say that you have a lot of help, you know, assistance, because most of the things you don't have to do by yourself. Because you cannot split yourself into five parts, you know. So sometimes you have assistance ... I think it's easier though when you put them in a nice school. (Nwakaego)

I then reminded her that not many Nigerians can afford the so-called nice schools for their children.

I am trying to say that the challenge is small back home [Nigeria] ... I mean, if you put them in a nice school, you will see [notice that] it's less challenging, you know. I think the challenge back home is more of the things you have to sort out by yourself, not like you have something helping you here, you know—maybe the Internet or the computer. Here, you have to make use of the library to find the information you need, you know. So you'll be more resourceful in going through textbooks. In fact, you appreciate whatever textbook you have. Back home, because of lack of resources, you appreciate the education more, you know, it's challenging ... for lack of resources, I believe. That is what makes it more challenging. Over here, it's easy ... it's convenient, you know? So that makes it easy for the students, and they do not need to work so hard [to find information], because whatever information they need, they get it, you know?

In Nigeria some parents may not be physically involved, but they are financially involved. Like with making resources available, I know they put them in good schools, the best of schools [for those who can afford it]. They don't mind paying whatever they will pay, if it will get them in the best of schools. Most of them ... even if they [some parents in Nigeria] are not involved ... will get a tutor that will come to the house ... make sure that the tutor comes to the house. Then they will go through what the child went through for that day. They will ask questions. I mean even the ones [some parents in Nigeria] that are illiterate, you know, they will still want to know what the child is learning. (Nwakaego)

Nneamaka briefly compares Nigerian schools with those in America in relation to parental involvement.

[They are] completely different things. At home … you know, the school is like an entity at home. They [schools] are the alpha, the omega. They make rules. The parents really don't have too much contribution to schooling, you know. Again we have boarding schools at home … when they are in high school, but in grammar school, they go from home. And the teacher is an all in all, you know? The teachers can enforce even "capital punishment" on the child, and the parent has no say … I don't know whether it's good or bad, but it kind of makes the child, you know, adhere to the norms of the school and the teacher. So they [Nigerian and American schools] are completely different … they are like night and day, really. Here, the parent is more involved, unlike at home. At home, the job of the parent is to make sure that the child goes to school every day. That's … okay. The children know they have to do their homework. You don't have to, you know, tell the parent, "Come on, did you help them do their homework."

So they don't really help the child, you know, in their homework like here. The schooling is completely done at school, unlike here, where the schooling also takes part at home because the parents have to help the child do the homework. Here, there is too much overlap because if you don't do it, your child is not gonna pass, and you don't want the child to be failing. So the parent definitely has to help with the homework, the projects, the tests, the whatever. You know, you have to take the child to the library to do the research work, download things on the Internet, make copies, print, and make sure they are well bounded … they call it portfolios … to make sure that the child is successful.

At home, hey, you don't even drive the child; the child walks to school. If they are in boarding school … they can take the bus or the cab to the school, and that's it. You stay in the boarding school. You know, you must be successful. It's a given. There is no two ways about it, because the grades are posted. You don't want to have your name—oh, you failed. You failed in your high school. You get grade three or grade four. You must work hard to … get grade one. And for you to get grade one, you have to work hard to make aggregate six or ten[29].

---

29   This is the system of grading secondary school exit exams. The grading

They are quite different ... the system is quite different. At home the system is that, hey, you must pass. You are expected to pass. Here, the system doesn't really require you to pass. That's the difference, okay? Wherever you are at any stage in your life you must ... you can find some job. But at home they whip you. If you don't pass one level, you cannot go to the next level, so you must make sure that you pass that level before you are expected to ... go to the next class. But here, whether you pass or not, you know, you can still go to the next level, but you will be at the bottom of the class. So you don't want your child to be at the bottom of the class.

Back home, most parents will fall back on the extended family as their support system. Nebeolisa bemoans the lack of it here. However, in his community, there is a network of families that support each other, although that is merely an imitation of what they have at home.

You don't have the support system. You are by yourself. Most families are, apart from the network of families that we have developed to serve as a support. But imagine if we are by ourselves. You have to be everything to the children. You have to do everything for yourself. Unlike when we were back home, you had a huge support system that made it a lot easier. If you felt the child was not doing well, you sent them to an uncle who is a teacher. Then he leaves there and comes home for vacation ... if that child is not really paying attention, then the parent says, "Look, I don't know how to handle it. Let me send him to somebody who is in education who can handle him or her."

When it comes to a child's discipline, Nsobundu prefers the Nigerian system because the teachers and school do not have to worry about litigation from parents as they perform their duties in educating children. Secondly, other adult members of the society are involved in the disciplining of children. After all, it takes a village to raise a child.

I think it's better at home because the society is more ... involved in children's education. Because if you see my child misbehaving over there, you're gonna whoop his butt right there at the spot. So the society is also more involved. The teachers also know you. They communicate with you without holding anything back. You know, there are no legal worries about disciplining a child when a child is getting out of hand. So I think the Nigerian system is pretty good. However, the only thing I don't like ... is labeling a child too early,

---

system combines the use of numbers and letters.

whom I know is going to be great, because now you're dealing with someone in school. And then ignoring the fact that some people it takes ... it takes some people a little time to develop.

Nnaemeka has two of his children in Nigeria for secondary-school education. He compares the two educational systems, noting their advantages and disadvantages.

> Educating children here is ... challenging; and equally challenging but on a different scale is educating children back in Nigeria. I feel that the children back in Nigeria are going for the experience; they are going for the knowledge, and I think that will be very beneficial for them in the future. The challenge, of course, is that they will have to deal with all the inconveniences, which we feel maybe is not quite suitable for them. But they [my kids] have not experienced that in a way that would discourage us because they seem to go along with living without the conveniences ... of course, their tuition and the boarding ... is something we really try to make sure we provide for them so that they will continue without any hesitation or without any fear of not having their tuition and everything paid for them. They are more relaxed. I mean, they feel more relaxed over there, maybe because of the nature of the social support group. They have friends, relations, extended family members that are always around them. But I would think that they'd rather finish their high school there ... finish everything about their college here and continue with their education at university level. The ones [my other children] here, while they itch to go over there, not knowing what they will face over there ... they don't know that there is a lot of work involved if they go over there. So I feel for the ones here now, who haven't had that experience yet but are trying to go over there, that they will really need to be as disciplined as the ones over there, be able to live over there. I'm thinking eventually, you know, they get to learn that ... But education for them over there would be a solid foundation for them to continue at a higher level here. Because I feel their education there will ground them, make them better persons, more mature, more responsible than if they just stayed with the system over here. Not that I am belittling how their education process goes here. It's just that the nature of liberty, the nature of a carefree way of life is not going to ... is not the same as they would face when they go home ...

Educating children in Nigeria has its peculiar challenges because of the fact that the Nigerian educational system has its roots in the British system of education, which is different from the American system. Another point of comparison is that democracy, which has permeated the American way of life, including its education system, is not the same in Nigeria. Besides, the Nigerian educational system lacks amenities, and the teachers are poorly motivated.

Summary and Analysis

During the interview, the participants to referred to the way they were brought up or what they learned from their mom or dad or the nature of how things are in America as the underlying influences of parental involvement decisions and activities. The value of education, which these Igbo parents in my study have, can be traced to their parents back in Nigeria, who left no stone unturned in educating them. It is interesting to note that some of their parents in the homeland had little or no formal schooling, yet they were still able to set high educational standards and expectations, and they worked very hard to meet them. Their love for education was simply infectious, compelling their children (now parents in Chicago) to follow the same path, when it came to the education of their own children. So whether it is learning from the mistakes of their parents or using or adapting what they had learned from them, the way the participants were educated by their Nigerian parents has become part of the Ecological systems that shapes their perception and practice of parental involvement here in Chicago.

The nature of American society is another major part of Igbo parents' context as they work with local schools in their children's education. The main characteristics of their new environment include capitalism, individualism, a litigious society, and a fast-paced, technology-driven life. Freedom of speech is a value that Americans treasure, and democracy permeates all aspects of American life, including education. The quest for freedom and equality, even if not totally realized for all people in the USA, is at the heart of the American dream. The ability to communicate well in English is an important part of their context too. One of the obvious influences of American society on Igbo parents is the sharing of housework and other domestic duties. Apart from the common influences they share, each participant has his/her specific context due to family size, profession, and time of arrival in the USA.

Liberty and Freedom in the American Society

A common theme often heard is that America is "the land of liberty and freedom"—that is, that a person, even an immigrant, can be anything and do almost anything, individually directing his/her own success in America. But most of the Igbo parents were brought up in a society where the expression of freedom is quite different: families, as a unit, act to control their destiny, and children must follow the lead of their parents and not put themselves beyond family definitions of freedom and other rules. Regarding this discrepancy, one of the parents said that the level of freedom and liberty that American children enjoy can also be a problem, leading to a lack of discipline. "I'm only referring to how kids [here] sometimes have this level of liberty, which most of us never had back home ... the nature of a carefree way of life" (Nnaemeka). While acknowledging that the American education system is very good compared to Nigeria, Nnaemeka and his wife chose to send two of their children to Nigeria for secondary-school education because "the culture itself [the system here] does not permit the level of discipline we want ..."

For Igbo parents in Chicago, the issue becomes how much freedom you allow your children. Can parents redefine freedom outside of how the larger society within which they now reside defines it? As part of their parental involvement, Igbo parents aspire to balance American-style freedoms with a more rigid idea of "freedom" that many of them experienced while being raised by their own Nigerian parents. Igbo parents do not claim to have a clear-cut solution to this. Some of their strategies are based on trial and error, and others are arrived at by consultation with other parents. Some experiment with sending their children to Nigeria for some part of their schooling or by sending their children to faith-based schools that emphasize discipline, while others try to incorporate Igbo standards of behavior in their teaching and learning at home.

Educating Igbo American Children in an Individualistic Society

A major characteristic feature of American society is its individualism. This generation of Igbo parents in Chicago is coming from a communitarian society, where the extended family system is still operational (Oke, 1986; Ohuche, 1991; Ogbaa, 2003). For immigrants like the Igbo in Chicago, it's almost impossible to change the features of their new environment. They will either have to abandon their own traditional attitudes or they will have to accommodate both American individualism and their own communitarian attitudes toward life. For most in this study, they still value their communitarian approach to life, wanting their children to learn the same. To achieve this aim, they engage their American-born

Igbo children in various Igbo gatherings and activities, like graduations, wedding parties, wake keepings, or home-town or state networks and associations.

The next chapter will address two main issues regarding Chicago's Igbo parents' involvement in their children's education. They are the challenges they face and the support they have or their coping mechanism.

CHAPTER 11

Challenges and Support

Having heard the stories of how Igbo parents in Chicago understand and exercise their involvement in the education of children, I next inquired about the types of challenges they face and the sources of their support or how they simply cope with the challenges. The questions I posed for this purpose are the following:

1. What types of challenges do you experience in your involvement in the education of your child (children)?
2. What are your sources of support?

Challenges

The challenges they face can be time, the nature of American society, being a single parent, finances, or the need to support family back home in Nigeria. As a single mother, Nneka faces a lot of challenges:

> One of the challenges I face at this point, besides finance, is just the idea that she can go out there and get something and bring something home in terms of getting sick, because not every parent believes in vaccinating their child or immunizing their child. Every parent has a different view on what immunization they're giving their child. But I give my child all the vaccinations or immunizations that she needs. And so she comes home, maybe she's sick or something, so I'm really like worried where she got this because kids need to play together.
>
> The other one is the idea of coordinating all this and balancing it out, being a mother, a student, and just doing the whole thing. It's really not easy ... to create a balance as a mother ... a single mother and a student at the same time. It's quite demanding. And to be

able to raise your child the way you want to see your child, so that's a big challenge, and so I try not to keep it in, not to just do it all by myself.

The other thing I don't like is the weather when it gets too cold because I'm from a warm climate. I would like to share that because … I tried to get used to the cold, but sometimes you cannot get used to it. It's sometimes unbelievably cold. Weather that is too warm is not good either. But that's it.

The authority parents enjoy here can pose a challenge to working with the teachers, especially in situations where you have overzealous parents, who are not prepared to dialogue with teachers on what is best for the child.

Especially with the extra activities … some parents have their kids in five activities, and that is really crazy, because you can't do it all. And some parents have this expectation that their child … must be a lawyer. And the teacher is saying, "You know, I think this child is good in math. Let's work with this child's talent and see where …" and the parent is insisting that … well, the teacher can only do so much. The authority is the parent, and so it brings more conflict when the parent is expecting the child to be what his or her parents want … you know, how their dream is not the child's own dream. And so the teacher can only do his or her best and leave it to them to handle it. And so it doesn't … always go well when you push the child to the extreme. So you have such parents going, "My child must be a doctor. My child must be … this and that. My child must be a Hollywood star." It doesn't always turn out that way, so it's just a balance; creating the balance. (Nneka)

Time is a challenge for Njideka. She finds herself not meeting daily or weekly goals due to lack of time and energy. Other challenges she faces include being a working mom.

Just mostly having enough time to do all the things you wanna do. Sometimes I'll make notebook lists of things that I'm hoping to accomplish with the kids. But the problem then becomes the time to do them. Another thing is … I think kids today are so … like they want to question everything you do, so if you're trying to suggest something, they will say, "I don't think I want to do that," you know? "I don't think that's a good idea." Spending so much time trying to convince them sometimes … I know what I need to do, and it's just trying to have enough time and energy to do it. It's the energy. Sometimes you come back, and they say, "You said you were gonna do our spelling bee. We were gonna practice spelling today." And you're like, "Oh, let me just have a minute. Let me have a minute ..." You know, just trying to have enough energy to do everything is sometimes hard ... maybe that would be solved if I didn't work as much, but you know, it's give and take ...

Sometimes the inability to do all one plans to do in relation to parental involvement makes Njideka consider whether she should stop working so as to devote more time to the education of her children.

So you really start second-guessing yourself so much, so much. And I would say, "Chijoke, maybe I should stay home." And he's like, "Mmm." [no] He's like, "Mmm. Are the other kids doing better than yours?" And the truth is that they weren't, you know, both in behavior and academics. And you know, again I try to follow the model that I know has worked, and that was my parents'. And my mom worked. You know so although my dad was kind of at home ... he lived between Nigeria and the States because he had a business in Nigeria. So he was back and forth. So my mom was kind of a single mom at times, whereas it could be three, four months that daddy would be in Nigeria, and she was handling it by herself ... but then when he was here then he was just home, and so he was on top of us and knew everything. So it was kind of ... so that kind of tells me that it's possible to do it with a working mother, although it's helpful to have somebody who is around. So I think that's what kind of convinced me ... like it's always been my goal to work but maybe not work so much. So I've been negotiating with my employers. I know after having the fourth baby, I said, "Look, I'm not gonna come back and work five days a week." And I said ... you know, so the best I could negotiate ... they said for a short time, "We'll let you go for three days a week." And so I know I was about three days a week for sixth months, and then the plan that they agreed to was that I had to go to four days for another like two or three months. And so when that ended, I said ... I called another meeting and said, "I know that my time is supposed to be up, but I can't ... I can't go back to five days. I need that extra day to be able to do other things for my family." And they agreed. So I'm kind of permanently on four days, but they wouldn't allow me to go to three.

It is interesting what Njideka thinks of some parents who have two jobs and, in some cases, might be a single parent with regard to parental involvement.

You can't ... I mean I don't want to say "you can't" because some mothers who don't work at all will say you can't work and do this. And I do that. But if those people think that I can't do it, I don't know how the person who works two jobs and is by themselves can do it. I think even in those cases, you would have different supports. Maybe you're a young mother, and so you have a mother that's around or other relatives. The problem is that we're here in Chicago with no relations. And so like if I lived in New York, even if I did work two jobs ... I mean that wouldn't be ideal but at least I have my father there, my mother, my sisters, my brothers there, like everybody else will be chipping in too. And so I assume that people who have to work so hard, they have to rely on some supports. Maybe it's family. Maybe they have a neighbor that they're very close to that helps. Like nobody can do anything alone. Even though we don't have family here, so we have to pay people to help us, you know? So you might have, you know, a babysitter, a driver. You hope you have some relatives from Nigeria that can come and stay and help, you know?

Nnamdi has a different perspective on the challenges parents face in relation to parental involvement.

I define it [the challenge] differently. I don't see it as a challenge. I see it as being a father. Whatever I have to do, it's an end game, okay? The "end game" meaning the final product, okay? Because believe it or not, success to me means that they are happy and they can think for themselves. You know *aku na uba* (wealth) is fine. That has not been my motive. It was my father's motive for me, but we come from different worlds ... so are there challenges? Of course there are challenges, but that's ... you know, there are challenges being a priest, there are challenges being a man, and there are challenges being a son. But that's what God and nature chose you to be. So do I like it all the time? No. But you know, one has to do what one has to do. Yeah. I don't ... and that's my approach to being a parent.

He has his own business and determines his schedule. Therefore, it is a lesser challenge to him compared to other parents who "are under somebody else's clock."

The time factor, I think a big part of it is being in your own business. Yeah, that's a big part of it. Being in your own business you make the time. But parents that are working for somebody are going to and fro from that job, so that's a big ... they are under somebody else's clock … It's just circumstances. Circumstances! Time is a big thing. Time is the biggest factor in the United States because of … right now business is very slow for us. Business is very, very slow because … real estate is hit hard in the economy. You know, so money is not as readily available as it used to be. Yeah. You know, but we are managing. So I think that time constraint is not a huge issue for us in my family. The reason is I control my own time.

Parental involvement is already tough for Nkolika and her husband. Both work, and in addition, her husband is in school. She wonders how single parents cope with the demands of parental involvement.

The difficulty was when I had to change my shift, you know? It was really hard, and it's still hard, but I have to do it because of my kids. The second one is the financial part of it. At times, it's hard, but you just know this is something we have to do for our children. I don't know how the single parents do it. It's tough for them [the single parents]. I mean, it's very hard. It's really hard, especially for the single parents because me and my husband, we take turns to drop them off. But with single parents, you have to do everything by yourself. You're on your own, so I don't think I ever want to be a single parent because I know it's really hard. With small kids that you have to take out, drop them off, pick them up … it's really hard.

Nwakaego has other challenges, but as she expressed, time is the biggest one, especially now that she has gone back to school to upgrade herself. Like Nkolika, she too wonders how single parents are able to cope with the demands of parental involvement in an American environment that is tough, competitive, and stressful.

Resources! Time! Resources! Time! Time! Time! Time! Time! Yeah, the time, you know, to be able to do everything you want to do with your children. Then sometimes getting your hands on good, you know, resources, materials that you want to use. You know, because sometimes we want to do something, but you don't know where to … but with the Internet you can get all the information you want. Then sometimes the cost, that's a big challenge too, the cost. Some programs that you want to enroll them in, they are very expensive, and you know, the programs are very good, but you can't do that, and then you have to do it on your own. It's hard. It's challenging, though … It's challenging, no doubt. I mean … with two parents doing it, it's challenging. How much more challenging do you think it is with one person doing it? But sometimes that's the only option they [single parents] got, you know?

Parental involvement is hard work and challenges parents' strength. Nneamaka says parents have to maintain a healthy lifestyle so as to be able to face the demands of involvement in the education of their children. She imagines the struggles of a single parent who works long hours.

> The challenges? The challenge is having the strength to get up every morning and do what you do best. That is the challenge—being strong enough because you can't be sick. So one thing you have to be sure of is that you are not sick. You do whatever it takes. You eat good food, exercise, be strong to get up every morning, and do it over and over and over and over. Because if you are sick, nobody does it for you. So the number one key is being healthy, eating good, okay?

> Being able to ask for strength, too, divine intervention. I am sorry, but I believe in that too. I know [for some people] it has no place in education, but I also believe in divine intervention. Okay, you ask for strength every day. You ask for wisdom, okay? Because one small deviation will mess everything up. And when you fall, you get up the following morning, and you ask for strength, and you move on. It's a lot of challenge.

> It's hard work, yes. It's hard work, and yes, I understand what they are struggling with, single parents, because when you come home at six, it's a lot different from when you come home at three, three thirty. Because at least if the child comes in two thirty and you are there by three, three thirty, at least you get up to ... four good hours of studying time with the child before the child goes to bed. But when you pick up the child at six ... six in the evening, you get home at like seven. The child will eat dinner, and it's time to go to sleep by nine. So you will be struggling to get in homework if you are lucky to get some homework in. But anyway, most of those people they stay in day care after school, so they do their homework in day care. That's one of the requirements of those day cares, yes. The children have to do the homework in day care.

Among others, time—quality time—is the biggest challenge for Nebeolisa. There is also the challenge of being a new immigrant. He is hopeful that the next generation of Igbo immigrants will not face similar challenges because there will be a system in place to fall back to. The fact that education is very expensive in America is equally challenging.

> It's time. Time is the biggest challenge, time with the children. And not just time but the quality of the time because there are so many things that demands one's time ... work, extracurricular activity; that's why most times, you know, I kind of like make them tag along because that's the only time ... If I keep them away, you know, I don't really have blocks of time with them. So I think one of the keys is time. Two, the sacrifice is enormous. You know, to really, really get the children to where you want them, there are certain things you don't do.

> I ask some of my friends ... what were you doing for your children at the stage where my children are? I ask them that. Then you know, you hear that "Oh, so and so is taking this exam to go into this special school." I say, "Oh by the way, when do you take that exam? Okay, why is your child in this school?" "Oh, this is what happened ..." Unfortunately, there is no central place where people acquire information about what to do because we didn't grow up here. There is no place where we are told ... those are the things you need to do for your child. Or if you want to get your child into magnet programs, special schools, academies, you know, there are programs that universities run in the summer, or there is summer school just to kind of give your child an extra edge, those things you kind of like find out in bits and pieces, you know? I think those are the challenges.

> Education is expensive here, very expensive. We went to school where it was heavily subsidized by the government. Heavily! Also, understanding the system, because yes, you know, it's not just, you know, send them to school; but you have to understand the way the system works and helping them navigate through that educational system, you know? So those are the challenges to me, and that's what I always discuss with a friend of mine.

> But the other thing that is part of it is the challenge of being a new immigrant; you are trying to first settle down. You are trying to gain ground, you know, get a footing. And then you are grappling with ... and then more importantly you have not found your own operational ... what I call operational principles. You are just kind of like living day to day, trying whatever works, you know, and

then hopefully it works well. But then the next generation of Igbo, for example, that will come to Chicago will not experience what we have experienced because … they will have people who can share with them their information. And hopefully actually create a system that will make it easier for them.

Nonye sees the challenges differently. For her, parental involvement is a pleasure, the demands notwithstanding. However, she accepts that financing her daughter's education is a big challenge, as she intends to go to medical school.

I pay for her education wherever she wants to go. So it takes everything to educate a child. Yes, and that's my priority. But it's something you want to do. It's a pleasure. It's not work. It's not a chore. It's a pleasure, not a challenge. No, it's not at all because it's part of you. It's a pleasure, because education is what you live for, so … as a parent I am grateful that she is studying. I am grateful that she is reading. I am grateful that she wants to do it. What would I do if she said no? So I am lucky. It's a pleasure … I mean … there is a challenge. The challenge is I wish that I don't have to worry about paying for the school fees; that $55,000 a year is something I can't just write a check and say, "Here is your $55,000." Okay, "Here is $60,000 every year for med school 'til you're done." That's really the only challenge, I would say.

Sometimes doing homework with the kids can be frustrating. Because of the nature of the homework that the kids bring home, you need a certain level of education to be able to assist them. These are some of the challenges Nsobundu faces with regard to parental involvement in his children's education.

Well here in America you face a bigger challenge than you face at home. Because I will say in Nigeria the kids are scared of their parents. But here Americans have more … American kids are so much exposed that when they see something that does not marry well with their thought or whatever they are taught in school, they are taught to ask questions—why? But you do not ask why to your parents at home. You don't dare ask why. You do what you are asked to do. So here ,it's more challenging because they bring out their good and their bad, so you're gonna have … a challenge. You've got to be ready all the time. Like here in school, they bombard them with homework. They bombard them with advanced things so that if you are not educationally well exposed, you can't help the child. You can't.

But what happens is that sometimes my kids, when they bring their homework, you know, especially my first one and my second one, you try and tell them a way to do it better and all those things ... for some reason, they think their teachers know better than you. Know better than you. Like you are trying to teach your son or daughter how to do math and all those things ... this is the easy way to do it. It's like they're closing their ears. They listen to their teacher. I said, you know, these teachers, some of them probably have ... just one degree. I have two degrees, you know. It's like they are closing their ears. I am telling you. I mean sometimes I feel frustrated, but you know, that's the age. That's the kind of respect they have for their teacher. [They perhaps think] "All you are is my dad. You can't be anything else but my dad," you know ... but for me ... I remember when I was in elementary five or four or six, where my dad taught me how to do long division.

Life is a challenge for everybody. Thus, an immigrant parent is not immune to the social and financial challenges of parental involvement, according to Nnaemeka. Like most Igbo families here in the United States, he has to support his extended family at home. He started doing this several years ago, when he came as a student, and continues to do so even though now he has his own family.

I had to make the transition after the job I had, which was basically to support my family here and at home. For those of us that came ... we spent time actually earning to support those at home. So we didn't really try to just to educate only ourselves. We were trying to help those back home, so that was kind of detraction from the main goal of ... getting ourselves educated. So that slowed finishing up in time, to graduate in time, and all that. So that was, you know, what happened with me. Over the years I've been able to get back into the mainstream of life.

The challenge I think most parents face is trying to provide the necessary tools they need to further their education—financially, socially, whatever it takes to help them do this. And it's never been easy, especially now that the economy is so bad and unemployment is double digit. With all the kinds of things that are happening now, it's really very difficult. And ... of course, not only do we have to take care of those back in Nigeria. We have to also keep an eye on the ones here with us, make sure we provide for them, provide all the necessary things they need to progress. It's quite some challenge, no doubt about it. It's not easy. Life itself is a challenge, and we have to live with it because we know that when all is said and done, some good will come out of this.

Parental involvement is a lot of work. It poses lots of challenges that are physical, social, financial, and psychological. The Igbo parents face these challenges with the hope that some good will come out of it. However, considering the enormous challenges Igbo parents face, how do they cope? What kind of support do they have?

Support and Coping Mechanisms

To help Igbo parents face these challenges, there are certain support systems and coping mechanisms built into the society or created to compensate for the lack of the extended family support system that most Igbo families are used to. Other supports are ideas being put forward that will, in the long run, help reduce the challenges. Sources of support include family, friends, community, government programs, etc.

As a single mother, Nneka relies a lot on her community for support. She also has a network of mothers in her community, whose children are similar in age to her daughter, and a group of Igbo mothers she liaises with.

I went back to school in 2005, so I had her with me at the Willmar College, which is a good community college. They have day care there, which has been attended by kids of the staff ... and some students too ... they have a good program, where they use ... one of the psychology models for their program. I also told Ogechi [my daughter] we're not going to day care. She's going to school. So she has never used the word "day care." All she knows is that she is going to school.

I also liaise with mothers that take their kids to Igbo lessons over the weekend. And I was lucky to have a mother that called me up and sent me e-mails and asked me if I would be interested in enrolling her in ... Igbo class program, and I said yes, I definitely would. And so that is a big plus, I suppose. So that way, I network with mothers of her age group or a year older. And then she gets to meet them, and she learns from these kids, and they learn from her. And so she's not thinking about it's just me and my mommy, but she knows there are other people existing in the world, and there are other things outside her environment. Because it's not just me … raising a child is not just about the parents and the teachers. We also have to work with … other mothers. We trade babies at some point. Some days she gets to go to these mothers, and they take her with their kids out there and expose her to whatever they feel like, you know … they will let me know, and I will approve … where they're going. And some days, I take the kids myself, and … she's not learning in an environment like she's in class all day, doing all these things, so it's interchanged with play depending on her age because she's five now. So they learn through playing. I try to get activities … like … puzzles that keep the brain working. It's not about adding and subtracting, but putting those puzzles together takes the brain to figure out what this is going to be.

When Nneka is unable to, some members of her faith community volunteer to pick up her daughter or take care of her.

> Some weekends I'm not there, we have a nun that comes in to help us and sit with her. Sometimes they take a shuttle bus and go around Evanston, or they go to the Evanston Library, depending on what they are doing. Or they take a walk to the park if … the weather is good.

> Well, I have a good relationship with the teachers. I know their names. I know Ms. Brookmoor, and then I know the principal … I have a good relationship with them. They give me feedback. And I also, in terms of paying school fees … sometimes we get behind … if I'm not meeting up … I call and let them know, you know, I might be late. And they also help me get organized in case of emergency. I have an emergency personnel record, but they also try to help me organize it well in terms of who and who picks her up at what time, and … you know, how to work with these people so we don't have any problems. So they have the names of people that are picking up Ogechi because I don't pick her up all the time. I might pick her up twice in the week, but I have a very good … I will say, friends of my community. I have good support, so I have parents that volunteer to pick her up at different times. So that way the school … know when to call these people if they are running late or have not seen them. And if anything happens, they will let me know. They have my cell phone number. They can reach me anytime, so it works out well.

The case manager and public health nurse are also very supportive. Nneka considers the public health nurse as her "biggest resource."

> As a single mother and a student at the same time, it's quite demanding. I'm thankful that we're in a community and that it's a

blessing. They are very supportive and have ... most of the resources that we need to live here. So each time I try to see what is out there, what are the resources. Sometimes I tend to work with a case manager. Or a public health nurse at Evanston, so I try to find out what the community has for us. So I tend to meet the public health nurse at the public health office and talk to her about my concerns. So she is ... my biggest resource, you know, person. So she gives me probably booklets ... you know, where I can call ... urgent care numbers, relevant numbers. If it's getting shots, what I can do each time. If there are a group of mothers organizing something, she lets me know and asks me if I'm interested. She gives me the number. She also lets me know ... when to get the shots. Even though I get it in the mail, she gives me a second call and says, "Don't forget to get this done."

To cope with the challenges, Njideka sometimes hires drivers to transport her children to different activities.

There are only so many hours in the day. And because I work at least four days a week, I have to get help transporting people to the different activities. I mean ... sometimes I have to employ drivers to help, to get some things, yeah. We definitely get help. So either we have drivers, or you know, you pay babysitters to help. I talk to other moms, both moms ... like I try to connect with people who are in my similar situation, so I have maybe my friends from the university ... and I have a group of other young Nigerian women, who are trying to balance work, mothering, and "wifing." And those are the [support network] ... just because we're all so close. We have the same background and everything so that's helpful. I talk to ... even though some of those mothers don't work, like there are still things, you know, that I can learn from them in terms of things that they're doing. I remember when I went to Igbo class this Saturday, there's one lady ... we just connected, and I didn't know who she was; she didn't know who I was. And we introduced ourselves and, you know, I had four kids, but she had five kids, but they're much older ... so she was just telling me all the things that she was doing, you know, to make sure these kids were productive, good citizens. And she was trying to like counsel me and tell me how much she had to make them work and make them do dishes and make them clean and make them you know ... so it was just ... good to hear that, just to say that, you know, you have to be serious with it now so that you don't wait 'til it's too late to try to correct such bad habits that have developed. So you want to find the right mentors and peers … who have the same ideology and same goals.

She equally appreciates the support from her husband.

I know that all the things that Chijioke, my husband, does … his father didn't do, you know? When we didn't have like a babysitter helper when it was just me and Chijioke, we had to find a school that allowed you to drop early and pick up late. And so I mean the one we have nearest here, the hours are six to six. Or six fifteen to six fifteen. And even to get there by six fifteen, I was struggling because coming from the city to here, sometimes that can take forty-five minutes to an hour. And I can't always get out at five, five fifteen, so I would be struggling to get to them at six fifteen. And it was crazy … if you're trying to be at work at eight or nine, that means dropping them at seven or seven thirty to get down to work … so they're there ten, eleven hours a day. And then by the time you pick them up at six fifteen they're starving, so you're rushing home just to cook food, food, food. What are you gonna eat?

Even now that her mom does not live with her, she still takes care of her grandchildren once in a while whenever Nkolika needs help.

When my mom was living with me, she was really a source of support because … she was taking care of the little one because she wasn't going to school. And even though right now she's not living with me, when I have some place to go and I don't have anybody to watch them, I take them to my mom's place … and at times, my friends do too. They try to watch my kid if I have someplace I have to go, just for a couple of hours, and that's it.

In addition, Nkolika feels that the ability of Igbo parents to speak English is a big advantage.

Like some parents who have language barriers, you can see their children are not doing well because of the language barrier. So for us, we don't really have a language barrier in this society.

Again, she learns from parents and colleagues at work, who have children of the same age as hers. Knowledge from such sources helps her to develop some coping mechanisms.

Especially at my job, people who have children the same ages as my kids, I try to ask them what their kids are doing to see if my kids are really improving or doing what is right or doing what their ages do. So at times … we communicate, you know. We find out what other kids are doing, and we see at least you are happy that your child is on the same path.

Nwakaego refers to her husband as the powerhouse of the family because of the kind of support he provides. But first and foremost, she believes that God sustains her and keeps her going.

> What can I do? Where will I get the money to train them? That is the powerhouse (*pointing toward her husband who sat on the floor during the second half of the interview*). That is the powerhouse there. Yeah. So it's, you know, first and foremost, God, just so you persevere more, you know, just to give you the endurance sometimes or the patience that you need.

She also sources for relevant information from the Internet.

> I share experiences, even online. I get experiences from people I don't know, you know? Like for me, what I like to do is get the curriculum from other schools, you know? Other districts that I think are better than my own district, you know? So I get the curriculum and I compare, you know, what they do, and I try to get my child to that level, if they have not gotten to that level. Then some learning experiences that other parents encounter, you know, maybe the one that my child hasn't had yet. Some learning experiences are a lesson to them and … I listen and wait for that to happen or something or work toward that. So yeah, it is always to get information. Just like I was saying with … this time and age with the Internet, you know, you can get most of your resources, information, online. Sometimes we will ask around. You won't even know anybody that has been there, but you can go there and get all the information, you know. And somebody else's experience might not be yours, you know … but you adapt it …

Praying to God for wisdom, guidance, strength, and good health sustains Nneamaka in the demanding job of parental involvement.

> Divine intervention, like I said. I get tired. Don't get me wrong. At the end of the day, some days I get tired. I'm out. I take a nap … to have some strength to continue. But you always ask for strength, you know? "God help you today. God bless you today. God direct your thoughts, your children." You pray. Prayers also help us in this house. There is really nothing we can do without prayers. I mean you pray for guidance. You pray for direction because we don't know it all. We really don't know it all. You pray for wisdom above all so that you make the right decisions for everybody … at any time. You

pray for guidance at your job place too. You pray for strength and good health. And you pray for God's blessing, and so far he hasn't failed us. He hasn't failed me. And when I fall short, I get up with the confidence that I know it's gonna be good.

Her son, who is gainfully employed and doing well, energizes her too.

My first son, who graduated last year, has a good job … He travels all over the world. You know, he recruits people. He visits colleges, recruiting minority students. He comes to Chicago almost every two months to recruit potential candidates. They go abroad. So he is the minority face of their company as young as he is. He wears a lot of hats in his company … and I'm proud of him, and I'm happy for him, and I told the other ones "Hey, come on, let's go, guys. Push it, push it, push it." The second and the third boys, I ask him [my first son], "Hey, can you talk to them?" Because I knew when he was growing up, he was like, "Mommy is too hard on me." Can you tell them now? Now you have a good job. Aren't you having fun? Aren't you enjoying it? So you guys better listen to Mommy. I'm like, "Oh okay, good. I rest my case. Guys, come on. Let's push it." It's not easy, but at the end of the day, you will smile like your brother is smiling.

Nneamaka believes that other parents may have helpful information with regard to parent involvement. That is why she shares experiences with them informally.

Whenever I see something that is good in a child, I call the attention of the parent and say, "Oh, I like that. I saw your child there. I loved what the child did. What happened? How did you do this? How did you get that child to do this?" And usually they will share. We share knowledge. We share information that is appropriate for our children … yeah, we share knowledge on how our children … will progress academically, socially, and other ways. And we also cherish the good things we see in our children. We cherish them a lot. Yeah, we cherish that a lot.

In Nebeolisa's community, support is impressive with regard to picking up children from school. According to him, much of the credit for this support they enjoy goes to the women of the community. They are able to create an extended family support system (kind of) because a good number of Igbo families are living in the same neighborhood or community.

But the interesting thing that happens here … because my wife is available, let's say Mondays and Fridays, to pick them up in the evening … the days that she cannot pick them up, the women from our community here, any of them that goes to the school will pick them up. You see that's the beauty of community. You know, I was really impressed … one of my off days, I had to go to the school to pick them up. By the time I got to the school, I didn't see my children. But one of the ladies from my community, one of the Igbo women, had already picked up all the kids. Because what they do is if one of them arrives by three, all the kids will follow them. They know everybody goes with whoever comes … like if it's winter, they will go to their car and wait. So as other parents pull up, you pick up your own children. So by, say,… fifteen minutes after three … none of us is coming, the woman will take the children to her house or call on the cell phone and say, "What's holding you up?" And I say, "Okay … somebody is at the house. Drop them off for me while you go to your house." So that has really been quite helpful. In fact, we had said maybe we need to move. But I say no. Because when we go to other communities … everybody is on their own. You have to start building up … but to me the benefit of this community … there are about twenty, twenty-four of them [children] that are growing up together. I think that's good. That's good because I want them to know each other, create now those relationships … They will all … scatter with time, but they will know that they all went to the same school. The women in the community, the other families, I will say … that is the key. You know, the major thing that you want is who is gonna help me drop off my child, pick up my child? You know, sometimes we are at work and they call. "Oh, so-and-so is not feeling well." So you may call around and find somebody who is available … who can pick up the child. And that is important because the children want to play … you let them, you know, just decompress by just playing. So you bring their friends over, and they all play … running around. They are happy, you know, because if they are just there with you, they don't get to play.

Nebeolisa has an idea about how to reduce the challenges Igbo parents experience in relation to parental involvement in the education of their children.

I said we really need to start our own school because then we can have control over what happens and actually train our children well. Like every other community has them. [As an] immigrant community, at some point you try to take control of how your children are educated so that you marry the cultural education together with the secular training and all that … we were just laughing, you know … talking about if we had our own school then … I mean if you want to be there, you come in a uniform, you know it's not … you got your pants trying to drop off of your knees. Everybody will be properly dressed with the kind of discipline that we were raised with, you know, so everybody is well dressed and the school is disciplined. You know, because discipline is the key to learning. The environment has to be permissive for learning. That way every child isn't in charge, and the teacher is begging the children to sit down to learn, you know? And I think given the kind of education we had, if we bring that style here, our children will benefit. The larger community that we are living in will also benefit because it will be properly structured.

Apart from friends, the Igbo association, and Catholic nuns who provide emotional support, Nonye's wonderful family in Nigeria is a great source of support. According to her, they are a very close family and always work together to solve each other's problem, even though her brothers and sisters have their own families to take care of.

My support is my family at home and, of course, the Catholic nuns. If I need emotional support they [are available to provide that], … my family at home and my friends. I have a wonderful, great, strong family. Yeah, I don't think that … I never think there is a problem in this world I can't solve. Because I know my family would solve it for me and my friends too. I always know there is a solution to any problem I may have … we are very close in my family. We always keep in touch. We have our family e-mails that we send. Any problem is solved together, yeah.

The NCF—the Ndi-Igbo Cultural Foundation—their meetings bring us together once in a while and we put … and also they are the only Igbo group that brings the younger ones, the young adults together. I am happy to have them here. It's good to have your own people that give you that support, immediate emotional support … I'm not extremely happy with them. I don't see humility and grace; grace in the Igbo community … the support could be better.

Nsobundu says that coming to America at a young age and learning one or two things about the system here helps him cope with the demands of parents' involvement in the education of their children. His spouse and family are a tremendous source of support; otherwise, he is virtually on his own.

Well our support is that … we as parents came here as young

adults in our twenties. You're going through the American system individualistically. You've gone through the rough ages. And when the child is born, you summon a different momentum to deal with [to take care of] that child. You don't ... you cannot give up. It's just someone with a bigger energy says you know what? I'm gonna help this child. I'm going to make him get to where he wants to be. But that's not now. You don't get support anywhere. The support is inside you.

Even though all children are different, Nsobundu can pick out a few ideas from discussions with other parents and try them out.

Each child is very different. Each child is completely very different. I can't take what one is doing ... with her child or his child and try and use that on my child. It might not work. But you know, when we have a discussion you listen and you see how some parents deal with their kids' issues ... then you go home, maybe you think you can piece one or two things together to see if it can work with your child. It's a trial and error thing. It's not like one plus one is two ... God created us differently.

Nnaemeka is aware that parental involvement is a challenging task. Besides support from his spouse, family, and friends, the hope that some good will come out of his daily toiling helps to keep him going.

It's not a piece of cake, but we know that it's a kind of investment that will yield some dividends in the future ... with that, we don't mind going through the agony or the pain of sacrificing or doing what it takes to get them educated or trained. Life itself is a challenge, and we have to live with it because we know that when all is said and done, some good will come out of this.

Igbo parents in Chicago face various challenges in parental involvement. Sources of support include family, friends, and community. They get ideas and inspiration from other parents or from websites. Some of these ideas are generic, which they adapt to suit their circumstances and purposes. Each child is different. They miss the extended family support system at home, in Nigeria.

Summary and Analysis

Participants pointed out that time is their biggest challenge. Because most wear multiple hats (for instance, mother, wife, employee, and student), it is difficult for them to find time to meet their goals in their children's education.

Education is expensive, even in the cases of families with no more than two children. In addition to paying tuition (for those at private schools), Igbo families have to bear other financial burdens that come with raising children in an American society. To meet up with these financial demands, both parents have to work, which cuts into the time they devote to their children and their education. There is not a wide repertoire of Igbo American experiences to tap into, so they rely on trial and error as they navigate the American society. One of the participants said he was hopeful that the next generations of Igbo Americans would have a system to fall back on. The extended family system is still a value among Igbo people, even in the diaspora. They not only maintain contact with their home, but they also send money for family expenses, which adds to the financial pressures. In fact, some find themselves taking care of both families here and at home.

Common and Personal Challenges

Igbo parents in this study face parental involvement challenges that are physical, social, financial, and psychological as they work hard with teachers and schools to provide the best teaching and learning experiences for their children. The challenges are on two levels, namely, common and personal. Challenges commonly experienced by all the participants include time, the nature of American society, finances, and the need to support the family back home in Nigeria. Personal challenges stem from marital status, family size, and profession. Igbo people in Chicago are a rather new immigrant community, having mostly arrived within the last forty-five years or so[30]. In addition to common immigrant challenges, they also have to deal with the fact that they are black and foreign, which amounts to being a double minority.

On a personal level, some Igbo immigrants have large families, which means that they have to work extra hard. Few of the participants are single parents. The demand of parental involvement is already tough for two-parent families, and they often are amazed at how one-parent Igbo families are able to meet the demands of parental involvement in an American environment that is already tough, competitive, and stressful. Whether the challenges are common or personal, community networking is one of their support structure.

---

30   The earliest to arrive among the participants came thirty years ago. But there are Igbo who came to Chicago before the Nigerian civil war.

Community Networking

An example of dealing with the challenges of their new American environment is how families pool their efforts to pick up children after school. Not surrendering to the lack of communal support, a group of Igbo families have fashioned a way to support each other in providing after-school transportation. Because a good number of Igbo families live in the same neighborhood, they are able to recreate the extended family support system they were familiar with in Nigeria by creating a carpool system. According to Nebeolisa, much of the credit for this idea goes to the mothers in the Igbo community, who put together the plan themselves. Further, the success of this system has inspired him to want to establish an Igbo community center for weddings, graduation parties, wakes, and other social functions in their neighborhood.

Igbo parents in Chicago have certain support systems and coping mechanisms as they work with schools to provide their children with good education. Some of the support systems are already built into the society, or if necessary, Igbo parents develop their own systems to compensate for the lack of the support system provided by the extended family that most Igbo families would be used to. Other support systems are still mere ideas being put forward that in the long run will help reduce day-to-day challenges.

They are also strengthened in the face of these challenges by the hope that some good will come out of their struggle to give their children the best education possible in this new land. They keep going forward, spurred by the hope that their sacrifice will produce responsible and fulfilled adults, who, in turn, will contribute to the progress of society.

CHAPTER 12

Igbo Parents' Involvement Through the Lenses of Epstein and Bronfenbrenner

In chapter 5, I presented brief biographies of the participants in this study. In chapters 6–11 we hear the participants' voices and perceptions regarding the issues covered in this study. I combined the conversations of the ten interviews into a story that thematically followed each of the different subthemes that were behind the interview questions. For each theme under focus, the voices and opinions of several participants were heard, each contributing his or her own experiences regarding the themes. We also heard how their upbringing and social environment influenced their parental involvement decisions and activities. Their different voices gave color and texture to the story of how Igbo parents in Chicago are involved in the education of their children. At the end of each theme or chapter, I identified issues I considered analytical points and discussed them.

In the present chapter, I will now turn to the two main parts of the theoretical framework, namely, Joyce Epstein's theory of overlapping spheres of influence and Urie Bronfenbrenner's ecological systems theory. The purpose is to reflect on the data through the lenses of these two theories. The two guiding questions in this chapter are the following:

- What is the nature and degree of Igbo parents' overlapping and nonoverlapping influences in working with the local schools to educate their children?
- How do different levels of context play out in Igbo parents' involvement in the education of their children?

I will begin, however, with a brief discussion of how the two theoretical frameworks are related to each other.

Linking the Two Theories

Epstein's theory posits that parents, family, community, and school exert overlapping influences on the education of children. Bronfenbrenner's EST asserts that the development of individuals and life activities do not occur in a vacuum, but rather in a context. In this study, I used the two theories as a dyad: the *overlapping (and nonoverlapping) spheres of influence*, which parents, family, school, and community bring to bear on the education of children occur in *specific context*. Put in another way, the specific contexts within which Igbo parents in Chicago live and function define the nature of overlapping (and nonoverlapping) spheres of influence in the education of their children.

Both theories shed light on the nature and dynamic of the alliance between Igbo families in Chicago and local schools in providing the best learning environment and experience for their children. They also give a conceptual explanation as to why Igbo parental involvement—in overlapping and nonoverlapping spheres of influence—is similar as well as different in some respects to, for example, Lopez's typology as we saw in chapter 8 (see table 2). I will start by summarizing the theory of overlapping spheres of influence and then, in light of the theory, discuss the findings.

The Theory of Overlapping Spheres of Influence

Epstein's (2001) premise that the education of children takes place in the environments of home (family), school, and community is key to understanding her theory of overlapping spheres of influence. The lives of children take place in all three settings. The theory of overlapping spheres of influence posits that none of the environments can adequately educate children alone, because there is no "pure" time out of school or home for any school-aged child; time spent in either affects what happens in the other (p. 33). Thus, these environments tend to influence each other and affect the education of the child.

As they work together, there are some spheres of influence that overlap while others do not overlap. Epstein acknowledges that the degrees of overlapping and nonoverlapping spheres of influence are likely to vary due to particular circumstances. For example, the education of a mentally challenged child is likely to have more overlapping spheres of parents, teachers, and a social worker than that of a child without such a challenge. In the same manner, a high level of overlap of home and school influences in preschool and early elementary school children would be expected. It is hard to determine the degree of overlapping and nonoverlapping spheres without the knowledge of prevailing circumstances.

From the accounts of Igbo families in Chicago in this study, parental involvement involves the exercise of influence in spheres that include the social, cognitive, psychological, moral, physical, and spiritual development and education of children (see chapter 8: "Parental Involvement Practices"). Likewise, there are both overlapping and nonoverlapping areas of influence across these aspects of a child's education and development. But what actually shapes the overlapping and nonoverlapping areas of Igbo parents in this study? Similarly, what kinds of negotiations go on within these overlapping and nonoverlapping spheres of influence? Epstein (2001), in explaining how the theory works, pointed out the importance of perception. It all starts in the mind. So the point of departure for understanding what goes on in the overlapping and nonoverlapping areas of the spheres of influence is to recall some of the Igbo parents' fundamental perceptions with regard to education in general and the role of the agents of their children's education.

Overlapping and Nonoverlapping Spheres

In the accounts of parental involvement of Igbo parents presented in chapters 6–11, one might wonder about the degree of Igbo parents' sphere in relation to the school (and community) spheres in the education of their children. Getting a sense of the nature of overlapping and nonoverlapping spheres of parental involvement of Igbo parents in Chicago begins with asking some pertinent questions concerning their perceptions of education in general, the role of school, and the parents' role in the education of children. There are always links between perception and practice (Dauber and Epstein, 1994; Lopez, 1999; Epstein, 2001). Likewise, certain perceptions underlie the overlapping and nonoverlapping aspects of the involvement of Chicago's Igbo parents in the education of their children. I will outline some of these perceptions.

Nneka, like other parents in this study, believes that parents and teachers have to work together, listening to each other with the aim of finding a happy medium for the benefit of the child's education. They simply share a common mission in the education of children. Using the eyes as a metaphor, Nneka further stresses the role of the school as the second eye of the parents. As the second eye, the school helps to identify the child's strengths or weakness for the parents to develop or follow up on.

Nwakaego is more emphatic in saying that it is impossible for the school or parents alone to adequately educate children. She further noted that supporting what the school does is not enough. Parents must be involved because children live, function, and learn both at school and home. This understanding of the role of the school by Igbo parents is reflected in school and family becoming allies and sharing activities in the education of children.

Participants in this study believe that the primary responsibility of educating their children falls on the parents' shoulders. Some say that in working with the school, they are the "senior partners" of the relationship. Yet another belief is that the school is there to serve their needs in the education of their children. Positioning parents as the senior partners or perceiving that schools serve parents in their more primary responsibility suggests a different relationship that is not evident in much of the parent involvement literature. It implies that more responsibility sits on the shoulders of parents, who are primarily accountable for the education of their children. Much of the parent involvement literature situates parents as the support so schools can do their jobs better, thereby positioning schools' perceptions, needs, and responsibilities as primary.

Igbo parents believe that there are multiple benefits—to the child, family, and society—in educating children. According to Nkolika, these benefits are manifested in the level of sacrifice they are willing to make to educate their children. Parents in the study make lot of sacrifices for the education of their children, with the hope that it will yield dividends. They not only plant seeds, but they also tend, fertilize, prune, and weed, hoping that it will yield abundant fruit. Igbo parents hope that their investments will result in responsible and fulfilled adult Igbo American citizens, who will contribute to the development of society. From the interviews, the amount of time, energy, and resources Igbo parents invest in the education of their children are indicative of the nature of their overlapping and nonoverlapping spheres as they work with the local schools in the education of their children. This flows from their understanding of education and what it takes to educate a child.

The idea of working with the school to educate the whole child is another element that helps to shape the nature of overlapping as well as nonoverlapping spheres of influence. According to Igbo parents, good education is holistic— that is, it tends to the intellectual, social, ethical, spiritual, and emotional development of the child. Education for them must aim far beyond "mastery of the basics, far more than the possession of tools for economic competitiveness" (Scherer, 2007, p.7). This boils down to the notion of educating the whole child. Nneka and Nonye agree that good education is not just about textbooks or grades. It involves everything that makes an individual a well-rounded citizen of the country, a responsible and informed citizen. In addition to good grades, it requires character, values and social aspects—how you relate to other people.

There is another element that determines the overlapping and nonoverlapping spheres. According to Igbo parents, because there are so many children in class, they are not likely to get the teacher's personal attention. Participants agree that it is not the teacher's fault; rather, it is the nature of the system. Due to this situation, parents have to take up where the teacher leaves off. It falls on the parents to take the children to the library, supervise homework, and engage the children in educational extracurricular activities. This directly influences the overlapping nature of the relationship. The implication of this for participants is that education of children is like a circle. It starts from home to school and community and back to the family.

I will now name some these activities that overlap. These includes assisting with the children's homework, volunteering, attending meetings, creating a learning-friendly home environment, extracurricular activities that provide educational opportunities, getting the children ready to go to school every day, following up on schoolwork and complementing it, providing good meals and other nutrition necessary for learning, learning and teaching at home, setting educational standards and expectations, guiding and nurturing Igbo children's future careers, communicating with the school, and participating in school governance and decision making.

Overlapping Spheres

The nature of overlapping spheres of Igbo parents as they work with the school in their children's education can be traced to their beliefs about education, the way they perceive the role of the school. The school as a partner is there to serve their needs in educating their children. Though the education of their children also benefits society, they believe that it is primarily *their* responsibility (see figure 7).

In figure 7, you will notice that the circle representing the Igbo family is bigger than that of the school and community because participants believe that they shoulder more responsibilities regarding the education of their children. In other words, the bigger size of the circle reflects Igbo parents' perceptions about their greater responsibilities in the education of their children while school is there to serve their needs. However, I will subsequently describe some Igbo parental involvement activities while noting that these activities contributed to enlarging the circle that represents Igbo family in figure 7.

Laying a Foundation of Education

Parents start to influence their children's education at birth. This means that before the child begins school, parents have done quite a lot of the basic work in the area of intellectual, social, and psychomotor development (Nwa-Chil, 1984). Igbo parents regard laying the foundation of education as a crucial step in education; hence, they are a major influence in setting the path of their children's education. Nneamaka gave an example about having taught her children to read even before they started their schooling

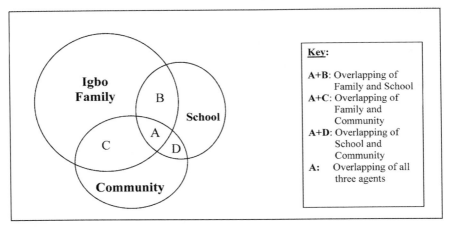

Figure 7. *Overlapping* spheres of influence of Igbo families, the school, and the community.

Adapted from Epstein, J.L. (2001). *School, Family and Community Partnerships.* Boulder, CO: Westview Press (p. 28).

Setting Standards and Expectations

The educational process naturally incorporates goals, standards, or expectations. In addition to school standards and expectations, Igbo parents as partners have their own goals as they join forces with other agents in their children's education. Igbo parents work with the school their children attend to reach these goals. Among others, these goals include being well educated, responsible, successful, happy, and fulfilled citizens and to be able to live a good, decent, and less stressful adult life. They recognize the importance of school in attaining these goals.

Teaching and Learning at Home

Education is a continuous process that includes teaching discipline, social skills, moral values, dealing with failures, hygiene, and integrity. These lessons that Igbo parents undertake at home and outside the school is another way of ultimately enhancing the educational process of their children. They share this function with school.

Homework

According to Nneka, "[w]e have to participate in their homework, whatever it takes to get them ... get it done." Nneka speaks for the rest of Igbo parents, who see homework as an important aspect of their children's schooling and education. That is the reason they make such an effort to assist them, "whatever it takes." Various ways they assist their children include simply being present while the child does his or her homework. The school generates the homework assignments, and parents assist their children with it.

Volunteering

Most Igbo parents see volunteering as an opportunity to participate in the life of the school and the education of their children. Activities to which Igbo parents volunteer include assisting teachers, chaperoning during field trips, preparing for social events, serving food in the cafeteria, reading to children, or supervising and playing with children in the playground.

Extracurricular Activities

Igbo parents in Chicago believe that extracurricular activities, like sports, dancing and swimming lessons, visiting museums and parks, traveling, going to movies, church choir, etc., are important educational opportunities for their children. That's the reason they commit time and energy to make sure that their children experience these activities, which help them to internalize what they learn at school.

Creating a Learning-Friendly Home Environment

Creating learning-friendly home environments is another important activity Igbo parents undertake to enhance the educational performance of their children. They create a home environment conducive to their children's education. They are very strict about the use of computers and cell phones, their children's social networks, and TV watching. They are careful to provide a beneficial reading space and appropriate materials. Nneamaka makes sure that whatever the school is doing, she reinforces at home also. Igbo families, by providing a positive and enabling home environment, contribute significantly to the education of children (Constantino, 2003).

Future Careers for Igbo Children

Igbo parents feel that part of being involved in their children's education includes discovering and nurturing potential talents and guiding them to a fulfilling career. Nsobundu saw the parents' role in this regard as "guiding a tree to grow straight." Nwakaego said that the key to choosing a career for a child is to observe the talents and passions of the child and that, as a child's career guide, you can make suggestions, but they have to be based on what you observe as the child's education progresses. While schools (ideally) contribute to the development of those talents and passions, they are often not explicitly involved in guiding students into particular careers, except through the limited opportunities available in tracked systems.

Ensuring Regular Attendance and Making Children Ready to Learn

Nneamaka, like other Igbo parents, think that the school might not be able to fulfill its role if this basic step of making children ready for school is lacking. So they do their part in the home to make sure that Igbo children go to school daily, well-nourished and ready to receive the knowledge from the school. Nebeolisa states it well: "If they don't show up, they're not going to learn. So at least I have to make them show up healthy, well fed, well rested … and disciplined."

School Governance and Participation in Decision Making

Nnamdi was a member of the board of the school her son Dozie attended. Igbo parents attend PTA meetings, which gives them the opportunity to influence and participate in the decision making of the schools their children attend.

The above activities represent overlapping spheres of Igbo parents and school in their children's education. However, there are other areas where there are little or no overlapping spheres of influence as they work together in the education of children.

Nonoverlapping Spheres

Figure 8 indicates nonoverlapping spheres of Igbo parents and school and overlapping spheres of community and Igbo families. The circles representing Igbo and school do not intersect while it (Igbo family) intersects with the circle representing the community.

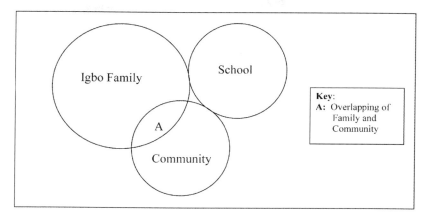

Figure 8. *Nonoverlapping* spheres of Igbo families and school but *overlapping* spheres of family and community.

Adapted from Epstein, J.L. (2001). *School, Family and Community Partnerships*. Boulder, CO: Westview Press (p. 28).

Using the religious formation of children as an example, an intersection occurs because the community provides structures and programs which parents willingly access for the religious formation of their children.

I will now describe some activities indicating the nonoverlapping aspects of the influence of Igbo families and school.

Religious Education

Most Igbo parents in this study come from a strong religious background and consider religion and spirituality as very essential to their children's education. One of the nonoverlapping aspects of working with the school is choosing whether or not to make religion a part of their children's education.

Njideka and her husband are believers and would not like to raise their children without faith. They faced a tough decision-making process when sending their children to public school with a good academic program but without religious education. In this case, they chose the public school and decided to set up a family religious education program to make up for what is lacking in the public school. They also enrolled their children in their parish religious lessons program. In the end, the religious education for their children, which is important to them, does not overlap with the school (see figure 8). However, there is an overlap with the community (see figure 8), namely, their parish that provides faith formation in addition to their family fellowship and religious education.

On the other hand, the religious formation of Igbo children overlaps when they attend faith-based private schools. Nneamaka knows that she does not share the responsibility of her children's faith upbringing with the school; hence, she is free to decide how to go about it. The decision and choice of religious education simply does not overlap with the public school's sphere. She believes that a faith-based private school will be helpful in this regard, hence her choice.

Nneka grew up in a very strong faith-based family and believes that it has helped her. She exposes her six-year-old daughter Ogechi to religion so she's taught about God at an early stage of her development. Other reasons for early exposure to religion include (a) so that it won't be foreign to her when she goes to a public school and (b) so she doesn't hear it for the first time in the media or get lost when people are discussing faith. The goal of these efforts is to help Ogechi form an opinion and decide for herself as an adult based on her experience.

Like other parents in this study, such a choice (religious formation) does not overlap. Of course, this raises a question: since religious formation is so important to Igbo parents for their children's education, why is it that the school's sphere of influence does not extend to this? The ecological systems theory and how different levels of context determine what overlaps and what does not, which I will discuss in the next section, will shed more light on this.

School Choice

The American educational system offers Igbo parents—like all other parents—the option of sending their children to a public, private, or special school. As I found out, it is not only an essential way in which parents are integrally involved in the education of their children, but it is also a big decision-making process. Though they research the opinions, at the end of the day, it is entirely their decision. The decision-making process to send their children to a particular school does not overlap. The overlap begins after the decision is made—that is, when schooling starts. Nebeolisa decided that his children should attend public school because it will afford them the opportunity to meet and interact with people from every strata of society. He does not like the exclusivity of private schools. He also thought of moving to another neighborhood but changed his mind after deciding he would miss the network of Igbo families in the area. Some Igbo parents even go to the extent of sending their children to Nigeria for secondary-school education.

Values

The Igbo parents in this study arrived in the United States with their Igbo heritage, which they treasure and want to pass on to their American-born children. There is no guarantee that the values the schools teach will always be in agreement with those of the Igbo families in Chicago. The question is how much overlap and nonoverlap occurs as school and parents work together with regard to the teaching of values. For instance, Nneamaka made it no secret that her children go through a process of "detoxification" when they come back from school. The aim is to separate what they learned into what is acceptable in the house and what is not. She goes on to add that they build on what is acceptable and discard what is not. Determining what is acceptable in the home is the sole responsibility of parents like Nneamaka and her husband and, as such, is not overlapping with the school's sphere of influence.

Discipline

Nebeolisa pointed out that discipline is key to children's education. Both school and parents teach discipline. But like the issue of values, parents and school sometimes differ about the nature and methods of discipline. According to Nsobundu, American teachers and school are hesitant to discipline children because of litigation from parents. Some Igbo parents, distrusting the discipline here, send their children to Nigeria for secondary-school education, where they, the children, will receive the type of discipline acceptable to them. There are different forms of and approaches to discipline. When those at school and at home don't agree, they are perceived as not working in unison.

Igbo Language and Culture

Due to the importance of teaching the American-born Igbo children their heritage, Igbo parents in Chicago emphasize the learning of the Igbo language and culture as part of their education. They also believe that knowledge of the Igbo language and culture will help to make their children better Americans.

Again Igbo parents teach their American-born children to be rooted in Igbo heritage and cultural identity as a way of preparing them for a multicultural world. For this reason, Nneka provides opportunities for her daughter to learn the Igbo language and culture. She feels that will broaden her daughter's view of the world, make her a more tolerant individual, and, ultimately, a better American. The schools Igbo children attend, whether public or private, have no contribution in these areas, as they don't teach either the language or culture. Rather, it is the prerogative of the Igbo community in Chicago.

Dealing With Identity Crises or Conflicts

American-born Igbo children may experience an identity crisis or culture clash as they grow up at home with Igbo parents and continue to learn from the wider society of Chicago. It "is not in the nature of something imploding or exploding" (Nnaemeka), but rather, this kind of conflict is something that is to be expected in the meeting of two cultures. That notwithstanding, Igbo parents start to guide their children early in cultural education in order to make the best out of their double heritage. They also teach their children the Igbo language and culture to prepare them for any potential crises or conflicts. One would not be surprised to learn that school has no influence on this because of the lack of what might constitute a conflict for American-born Igbo children.

Epstein (2001) points out that there is never a complete overlap because, as we saw, both Igbo families and schools their children attend maintain some beliefs, values, functions, and practices that are independent of each other.

Conclusion

There are areas of both overlapping and nonoverlapping spheres of influence as Igbo parents work with schools and work independently in the education of their children. There are certain decisions parents have to make in relation to their children's education that are outside the sphere of the school. Likewise, decisions, like the hiring of teachers or the development of school curriculum, are outside the sphere of family (see figure 9).

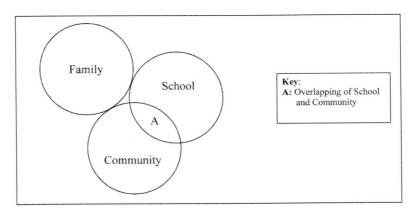

Figure 9. *Overlapping* spheres of school and community but *nonoverlapping* spheres of Igbo families and school.

Adapted from Epstein, J.L. (2001). *School, Family and Community Partnerships*. Boulder, CO: Westview Press, (p. 28).

These are nonoverlapping spheres of influence in the education of their children, despite the fact that children's education takes place both at home and school. However, examining the findings of this study through the lens of Epstein's theory shows that there are several activities where spheres of family and school overlap. This is because they share primarily the same educational mission for Igbo children. The nature of overlapping and nonoverlapping spheres of influence of Igbo parents as they work with school in their children's education can be traced to their beliefs about education, the way they perceive the role of school. The school, as a partner, serves the needs of Igbo parents in educating their children. Again, though the education of their children also benefits the society, they believe that it is primarily their responsibility.

Next I will discuss Bronfenbrenner's ecological systems theory in relation to the role of context in defining the Igbo parents' overlapping and nonoverlapping spheres of influence in the education of their children.

Ecological Systems Theory and Igbo Parental Involvement

In this section, I will examine Igbo parental involvement as narrated by the participants through the guiding theoretical lens of the ecological systems theory. The essence of the discussion is to highlight the influence of context as Igbo parents in Chicago work with local schools in their children's education. I will summarize the propositions and structure of the theory, briefly explore the sources of influence for a community, like the Igbo in Chicago community as they work with the local schools in their children's education, and finally, discuss Igbo parents' ecological systems and their parental involvement activities.

A Recap of the Ecological Systems Theory

The point of departure for Bronfenbrenner's theory is that an individual's development is not "context free" (1989, p. 202). An individual's development does not take place in a vacuum but in a very particular environment. This applies to Igbo parents' involvement in the education of their children—that is, their engagement with the local school in their children's education, which contributes to the children's development, is not context free. Essentially, families, parents and communities are interlaced in social networks, institutions, and traditions (Comer, 1984, p. 325). A context-free discussion of Igbo parental involvement would resemble a corresponding discussion on the climate and culture of a given school community without reference to its environment. Such a discussion would imply that the culture, class, or setting in which people live and function are all the same or not relevant (Bronfenbrenner 1989). As that is not the case, one can understand why participants often referred to the influence of their profession, the American society, Igbo heritage, or the way they were brought up when they described their decisions and activities regarding parental involvement. All these influences constitute a significant part of the context that influences the development of Igbo children in Chicago.

Context includes psychosocial, economic, and historical aspects (Delgado-Gaitan, 1992). Context changes with the movement of time (chronosystem). Context shapes the ways that parents become involved in and understand their relationship with schools.

Structure of Ecological Systems Theory

Bronfenbrenner delineates the Ecological systems into five different layers (see figure 6). The constituents of these layers can include social, economic, geographical, historical, cultural, and political factors. The EST, which is represented visually as a set of concentric circles surrounding the child (in the middle), portrays the complexity of these multiple levels and helps to explain the mechanisms through which children and their families are influenced (Weiss, et al. pp. xiii-xiv). The delineation serves to distinguish the immediate setting and larger context and their corresponding consequences on the developing individual. An important proposition of the theory is that the closer a subsystem is to the developing individual, the more the interaction and, consequently, the more potent the influence.

I will briefly outline these five layers that include microsystem, mesosystem, exosystem, macrosystem, and chronosystem.

The microsystem is the environment closest to the child. It includes family, home, school, and peers. The mesosystem is the interrelationships of the microsystems of the developing child. The exosystem is the third layer, which indirectly influences the developing individual. Its elements include the parents' workplace, the media, agencies of the government (local, state, and federal), the distribution of goods and services, the means of communication, and transportation facilities. The macrosystem has an overarching influence that passes through all layers to influence the developing individual. Elements that make up this layer include cultural values, religious beliefs, attitudes and ideologies, the global economy, scientific discoveries, and national and international politics. The chronosystem is the influence on developmental changes triggered by life events and experiences. It is ever present in all the other layers of the ecological system[31].

EST defines and delineates context and consequently addresses various degrees of influence. Thus, it presents a picture of the level of influence that each subsystem wields in the development and educational process of children. In this regard, EST contributes to a better understanding of Igbo parents' perceptions and practices of parental involvement in the education of children vis-à-vis their context. On the other hand, it has a drawback in that the configuration of EST does not likely fit every community and culture like the Igbo community in Chicago.

Context and Sources of Influence

What are the sources of the influences on Igbo families' involvement in the education of their children? One can appreciate the importance of the above question in light of the Latin adage, *nemo quod non habet*—"no one gives what he/she does not have." In other words, Igbo families can only use the means their circumstances permit to influence the education of their children.

Families tap into what Epstein (2001) describes as "the accumulated knowledge and experiences of parents" (p. 31) or "funds of knowledge," defined as "the historically accumulated bodies of knowledge and skills essential for household functioning and well-being" (Gonzalez, Andrade, Civil, and Moll, 2001, p.116). In essence, the funds of knowledge are the resources, including tacit knowledge and wisdom, that parents have at their disposal as they influence their children's educational path. This means that irrespective of being a newer immigrant group, Igbo parents and families possess resources that enable them to contribute to their children's and develop meaningful relations with schools and the broader community.

Igbo parents' relationships with the schools their children attend aim at providing a better learning environment and educational experience for the children. Like all human behavior, their relationship with the school happens in their unique context here in the Chicago area and through their particular histories. The Igbo parents' environment itself is subject to the vagaries of the larger ecological system. That is what shapes and reshapes the overlapping spheres of influence on their children's education. In other words, the perception and practice of Igbo parents' involvement in the education of their children cannot be divorced from their ecological system. They made that clear during the interviews. The parental involvement activities of Igbo

---

31   For more detailed description of these five subsystems, refer to chapter 3, pp. 66–70.

parents in Chicago, which I presented in chapters 6-11 are results of their interactions with their environment as they work with local schools in the education of their children.

Now focusing on the words of the participants, let us see how each subsystem and their constituents influence Igbo parents' perceptions and activities in relation to the education of their children.

Igbo Parents' Ecological Systems and Parental Involvement

During the interviews, most parents referred to how the ways in which they were brought up influenced what they are doing now with regard to parental involvement. Other influences referred to were being in a new American environment (in the United States, a foreign land) and efforts to maintain a link to their Igbo heritage, language, and culture. Also, some parents said that their professions were an important influence in their practice of parental involvement. These historical, cultural, social, psychological, and economical element form part of the Ecological systems of Igbo families in Chicago, of which I will now discuss to their parental involvement activities.

Historical and Cultural Elements of Igbo Parents' Ecological Systems

Elements that constitute the way they were brought up include culture, community, values, beliefs, family members, parents, and so on. These elements are located in different subsystems of the ecological system. For example, community is located at the mesosystem; beliefs and cultural values are found in the exosystem and macrosystem respectively. Bronfenbrenner, it should be recalled, notes that the chronosystem is ever present in all the systems. This helps to explain why Igbo, who rely on the way they were brought up, blend those learned behaviors because of the different time and place in which they live and function.

Igbo parents in Chicago, who interact with the schools their children attend, found themselves relying on what they had learned in Nigeria from their parents when they were growing up to provide the best possible educational experience for their children. The way they were brought up influences the way they value education, choose a school, discipline their children, and participate in the life of the community. On the other hand, it is important to remember that their Nigerian parents were subject to the influences of a different society and time and, to some extent, a different philosophy of life. So participants were creative by adapting some of these ideas and practices to their new environment. Some they discarded because of the generation gap, the new world order, and being in twenty-first-century USA. Igbo parents in this study narrated how these historical and cultural elements of their ecological systems influence their parental involvement decisions and activities.

Nneamaka made it clear that everything she is doing now in working with the school to educate her children is what she learned from her parents and the community where she grew up. Her parents, community, and culture shaped her as they did the other participants. She is the product of her parents' influences and environment. Nevertheless, having found herself in Chicago—a new environment—she blends those learned behaviors to suit her present age and environment. She hopes that by what she imparts to her children, they, too, will become products of her influences and their present environment.

Education is the key to a responsible, fruitful, and fulfilling adult life. As Nneka was growing up in Nigeria, her mother believed that regardless of one's sex, every child should have the opportunity to get a good education. She demonstrates this attitude consistently through her involvement in the education of her daughter.

One of the reasons Njideka thinks that her education has gone well is because her dad set high expectations for her. Now that she is involved in the education of her children, she sets equally high standards because that is the way she was brought up.

Nneamaka's Nigerian parents were both educators, and they played an important role in her education. She loves Catholic education and is grateful that her parents gave her the opportunity to go to a Catholic school. The fact that she is giving her children the same opportunity in Chicago can be traced to her positive experience of Catholic education in Nigeria.

Similarly, Nebeolisa confessed that he is using his father's "script" for child upbringing and education. He picked up his concept of education from his parents. Besides, his parenting role now is basically what he saw his parents do. Nebeolisa gives an example in his approach to school choice, which is heavily influenced by his father's attitude toward choosing schools for him and his siblings in Nigeria. His children attend a public school in their neighborhood because that is the way they were raised. Public schooling afforded him the opportunity to meet real people and not just those from a particular social class. That helped shape him and his outlook on life in general.

Discipline is essential in their approach to raising and educating children, and these parents have well-defined notions of what discipline should be. Nnaemeka is proud to say that he and his wife are bringing their children up with emphasis on this form of discipline because of the way they were brought up. "I am a good parent. If it weren't for my parents and what they instilled in me …," he added.

Nnamdi learned from the excessive authoritarian upbringing he experienced, especially from his dad in Nigeria. Such a negative experience has rather made him a better parent, one that has a good relationship with his children.

Community networking is another influence brought over from their Nigerian upbringing. For Igbo families, even in the diaspora, it still takes a village to raise a child. A group of Igbo families evolved a communitarian way of picking up their children from school. Two or three parents of the community pick up all the Igbo children from school, and later on, the rest of the parents pick up their children from these two families.

The Igbo community of Chicago, as recent immigrants, is in a new environment, which influences their parental involvement activities.

Geographical, Social, and Political Elements of Igbo Parents' Ecological Systems

American society has a great influence on the choices and behaviors that Igbo parents make with regard to their children's education. Of course, they can accept or reject certain influences, but whichever direction their choice goes in is believed to be in the best interest of their children and society. They have no control over some influences, such as the weather, except to put up with it and make the best of the situation. Elements of American influence on Igbo parents include attitudes and ideologies, community, social institutions and agencies, the parental workplace, and values. These elements are found in the mesosystem, exosystem, and macrosystem of the ecological system.

From the experience of growing up under strict Nigerian parents in the USA, Njideka tries to balance the influence of American freedom and liberty and the need to instill discipline in her children as they grow up. The nature of the society makes her cautious about the kinds of activities she wants her children to participate in. She also believes that the nature of American society has influenced some Nigerian husbands and fathers to jettison some approaches to domestic duties that they brought over from Nigeria. Again for Njideka, the more the husband is willing to help with domestic duties, the better it is for the wife. As a mother, wife, and employee, she knows how hectic it is for most mothers. These mothers, who wear multiple hats in the family, need help in order to relieve some of their stress.

Njideka is fortunate to have a husband who has adapted to the American style of living, doing things he ordinarily would not do if they were living in

Nigeria. Sometimes Chijioke, her husband, arranges his schedules to come home a little early to help, because he knows that America is a bit different from Nigeria in that fathers here tend to participate more in domestic duties.

Nnamdi has more flexible time than his wife does. He understands the nature of American society, namely, that domestic duties or chores are not meant for wives or female members of the family alone. He takes charge of most of the domestic duties, especially during the busy morning hours of getting ready to go to school.

American society encourages parents to voice their opinions in matters relating to the welfare and education of their children. Nneamaka learned this lesson and so is not only involved in her children's education but is also a visible parent at her children's school.

There are some things in American society that are attractive, and sometimes children are pressured to imitate them because they think they are trendy. Parents really have to step in to educate the children about these influences, helping them evaluate them. Nebeolisa shares how he educates his son on what is acceptable to Igbo people living in America. Nebeolisa's son came home from school one day and engaged his dad in a conversation suggestive of his desire to have earrings. He tells his son that they are not just Americans but also *Ndigbo* living in America. Therefore, there are certain things *Ndigbo* do, and there are certain things *Ndigbo* don't do, even if other ethnic groups or people do them.

When it comes to discovering and nurturing a child's career, because of their exposure to the American ways of doing things, a parent like Nsobundu knows what to do, i.e., you do not impose a career on a child. American society has made him appreciate the fact that every child has his or her own ability. So in matters relating to his children's future professions, he talks with them and researches certain professions to let them know about areas where people are doing well. He learned also that parents, as career guides, should focus on identifying the child's passion.

Regarding the disciplining of children, the perception of American as a litigious society makes Nsobundu prefer the Nigerian system, where teachers and schools do not have to worry about litigation from parents as they perform their duties in educating children. In Nigeria, adult members of the society are always involved in the disciplining of children, whether at home or at school. "It takes a village to raise a child."

Economic and Psychosocial Elements of Igbo Parents' Ecological Systems

A parent's profession is part of his or her Ecological systems and can affect the overlapping influences in the education of the children in different ways. Nnamdi is self-employed, hence, is flexible and has more time for involvement in the education of his children. The time factor, according to him, depends on whether you work for somebody or not. Parents who work for somebody else go to work and come home according to their employer's clock. This is unlike having your own business, which affords a more flexible schedule.

Conclusion

In this chapter, I discussed the activities of Igbo parents as they work with schools in the education of their children in light of the theoretical framework of this study. Igbo parents in Chicago live and function in a unique environment and accordingly shape their understanding and practice of parental involvement. What influences the involvement of Igbo parents in Chicago are their professions, their new American environment, the way they were brought up, their Igbo heritage, the ability to speak English, and being new immigrants. We can see these parents holding on to Nigerian perspectives while being challenged by American context to work within the norm. In general, Igbo parental involvement is not school centered nor is it merely following a ritual designed by the schools their children attend. It arose from their ecological system.

The uniqueness of Igbo parental involvement broadens the space and discourse of family-school relationships. Whether the Igbo parental involvement perceptions and practices align with institutional preferences for parental involvement is not the issue. The question is how the behaviors of Igbo parents in Chicago, within the context of their ecological system, promote the education of their children.

The next chapter will present a summary of the study, revisit the research questions, and propose implications of this study for practice. It will also recommend future research.

CHAPTER 13

Conclusion

The Igbo diasporic community in Chicago is part of the larger Ndigbo, who are the third largest ethnic group in Nigeria. Together with the Hausa, the largest ethnic group, and the Yoruba, the second largest, they constitute 66 percent of the total population of Nigeria (Ogbaa, 2003). Nevertheless, here in Chicago, Ndigbo are a double minority—black and foreign—but are part of the growing minority community in the United States that will become tomorrow's majority. Though the quest for education was the primary reason the majority of Ndigbo came to Chicago, there were other reasons, including the desire for better political and economic conditions. Most of the new arrivals are beneficiaries of the American government's diversity-friendly immigration policy that resulted in a sharp rise in Nigerian immigration (Rong and Preissle, 2009).

As the Igbo community in Chicago grows, so does the number of their children. For immigrants, as well as native citizens, education is an essential tool for survival in the United States. Education, which is more than schooling, includes learning that occurs outside the school setting. Simply put, it takes place both in school, in the broader community, and at home. It is a duty parents, family, community, and school jointly undertake for the benefit of the individual child and society. Igbo children attend both private and public schools in Chicagoland. Education is essential for their survival in the United States. But how are Igbo parents involved in the education of their children? Answering that question is the primary goal of this study.

There are sets of beliefs and activities that are widely accepted in both literature and practice as standardized types of parental involvement. These institutionalized forms of parental involvement often reflect the experiences of the middle class and mainstream culture, which themselves are unique contexts. Using examples from research, I was able to argue that there are other parental involvement approaches and practices which, knowingly or unknowingly, are ignored simply because they do not fit the standardized or prescribed forms. An obvious consequence of the conscious or unconscious neglect of these other valid parental involvement beliefs and practices is the tendency to project the phenomenon not only as exclusive but it also narrows the space for its potential discourse and practice. There is a need to broaden the understanding and practice of parental involvement. This research, which seeks to find out how Igbo parents are involved in the education of their children, is an effort in that direction—to broaden the understanding and the space for parental involvement practice.

Epstein's overlapping spheres of influence and Bronfenbrenner's ecological systems theory are the conceptual lenses of this study. For the most part, I used the two theories like a dyad in the study. Combined into a unit, it reads, "the context in which parents, family, and school live and function shapes the nature of the overlapping spheres of influence they exert on the education of children." For me, the combined theory served as a tool to explore the nature of parental involvement among Igbo families in Chicago.

New contexts emerge as civilization marches on. As a result, parents, family, and school are compelled to face the challenges of adapting and responding to the demands of the new environments vis-à-vis the parental involvement in the education of children. Similarly, the phenomenon of parental involvement evolves, adapting and responding to the demands of new educational environments. For Igbo families in Chicago, it includes applying the old but essential concept of parental involvement in their new educational landscape that the ever-evolving society engenders.

Again, because communities exist in different contexts, it is extremely difficult to know how parental involvement plays out in each context without hearing the parents' experiences or getting a fair knowledge about the ecological systems of the school community (parents, family, community, and school). Simply put, different contexts lead to varied understandings and practices of the concept. The nature of parental involvement is not and cannot be the same across the board even though parents have common aspirations.

Research Questions Revisited

This study explored three main issues with regard to Igbo parents' engagement with local schools in the education of their children. They include their perceptions and practice of parental involvement and the challenges they face. The study found that Igbo parents' perception of parental involvement can be traced to their notion of education, which is primarily to educate the whole child—a comprehensive understanding that includes the intellectual, social, spiritual, psychological, and physical education of the child. Given that stance, the study indicates they believe that neither the family nor the school alone can adequately educate children to be responsible and fulfilled citizens. Both must work together. Their notion of the role of the school is that school is there to serve their needs, because the primary responsibility of educating their children falls on their shoulders. Furthermore, their accounts of their practical ways of involvement show that Igbo families and the schools their children attend have many overlapping spheres of influence in the education of children. These include volunteering, supervising homework, creating a learning-friendly home environment, extracurricular activities, two-way communication, getting children ready for school, attending PTA meetings, etc. However, there are certain aspects of their children's education that are nonoverlapping, such as religious formation, certain approaches to discipline, and teaching the Igbo language and culture.

As for the challenges they face, the study shows that it is struggle for the parents to educate and raise their children as Americans rooted in their Igbo heritage. As a newer immigrant group, they haven't planted their own two feet firmly on the ground. Perhaps as of now, they can be likened to the proverbial chicken (in a new environment) that walks around with one leg, trying to familiarize itself with a new environment before putting both legs on the ground. Though not peculiar to them, Igbo families face the challenges of time and finances. As for the challenge of the Igbo approach to domestic activities, some Igbo husbands and fathers are quickly adapting to the fact that house chores must be shared by the male members of the family.

Based on their cultural heritage, the concept of parental involvement in the education of children might not be new to Igbo families. However, the newness of their environment, which the participants frequently referred to, played a role in the way they responded to the demands of parental involvement. The answer to the issue of how Igbo parents face the daunting challenges of parental involvement in their Ecological systems are embedded in the stories they shared with me about their engagement in the education of their children.

Participants made it known to me during the interviews that education is central in raising Igbo children. As a result, they make enormous sacrifices to see that their children get the education they need to be responsible and fulfilled adults. This enormous sacrifice is a kind of investment they strongly hope will yield some dividends in the future—*ka umu anyi wee karia anyi*. It is immaterial whether their particular involvement fits the prescribed or standardized form of parental involvement found in the literature or in practice elsewhere.

Implications for Practice

This study provides knowledge about one of the largest African immigrant groups in Chicago and their children's education. Not all immigrants group are the same. They have both similarities and differences. There is something to learn from them all, hence the need to acknowledge the Igbo parents' spheres of influence in the education of their children. Educators should develop an interest in understanding how Igbo families live and function.

One of the educational goals of Igbo parents is to raise their children as responsible and fulfilled American citizens rooted in the Igbo heritage; thus, they value education that acknowledges this double heritage. According to Igbo parents, it is a goal that will enrich the American society and make their children better citizens. It would be useful if educators working with Igbo parents learned about Igbo families and their culture so that what happens at school would support (or at least not undermine) the goal of developing a dual identity.

Efforts to learn about Igbo people in Chicago and their culture will help to reveal areas of nonoverlapping spheres in the education of children and the struggles of communitarian immigrants as they raise and educate their children in an individualistic society. This effort would support Igbo parents' belief that the school is there to serve their needs in the education of their children.

Recommendations for Future Research

Further work could be done to deepen our understanding of Igbo parental involvement in Chicago and ultimately broaden the scope and discourse of parental involvement in general. First, a study could identify Igbo parents who arrived in the USA fairly recently (in the last five years) to examine their experiences and what they learned from the challenges earlier Igbo immigrants faced. One of the participants of this study hopes that other Igbo immigrants coming after them will not have to start from scratch and will be able to learn from their predecessors' experiences.

Another study could focus on the male parents' involvement in the education of children. Most participants during the interview alluded to the fact that the American environment has influenced the attitude of Igbo males toward the home front, including their involvement in the education and upbringing of children. What does this shifting pattern of involvement look like and what influences it?

As American-born Igbo children are becoming parents, it would be interesting to see how they are involved in the education of their children as a second generation. Almost all the participants of this study received a significant part of their education in Nigeria. As they pointed out, that education influences their approach to parental involvement here in Chicago. So what will parental involvement be like for Igbo parents who were born and educated here?

This study interviewed parents with children at different ages and levels of schooling. Further research into parents' involvement in Igbo children's education focusing on a particular level of schooling would help to illumine the practice of this essential phenomenon in the education of children.

Concluding Remarks

One of the powers of story is that it has the ability to provoke thinking, stretch the mind, raise questions, and suggest answers. This study is a story about the perceptions, practices, and challenges of parental involvement of Igbo people in Chicago as they work with local schools with regard to the education of their children. It is also a story of Igbo parents efforts on the road to *Ka umu wee karia anyi*. A well-told story helps a listener or reader to think and develop a relationship with the characters in the story. I believe that the stories of these ten Igbo parents will have a similar effect on other readers.

References

Adamu, A. U. (2003). Community Participation in Universal Basic Education (UBE) in a Dwindling Economy: Lessons from World Bank Reviews. *UBE FORUM – A Journal of Basic Education in Nigeria,* 3, 47–66.

Adesina, S.A. (1999). A Review of the Fundamental Function of the Family Institution Toward Meeting Challenges of the New Millennium. In Sodipe, N.O; Nwanyanwu, O.J., Salawu, K.A., Akinnusi, O., Ojelade, K., and Asade, B.K (Eds). *Education in Nigeria: A Futuristic Reflection* (pp.52–63). Ibara-Abeokuta, Nigeria: Visual Resources Publishers.

Ake, C. (2003). *Democracy and Development in Africa.* Ibadan – Nigeria: Spectrum Books Limited.

Akyeampong, E. (2000). Africans in the Diaspora: The Diaspora and Africa. *African Affairs*, 99: 183–215.

Aluede, R.O.A. (2006). Universal Basic Education and Cultural Development in Nigeria *Journal of Human Ecology,* 13(1): 53–56.

Aluede, R.O.A. (2006) Universal Basic Education in Nigeria: Matters Arising. *Journal of Human Ecology,* 20(2): 97–101.

Alutu, A. N.G. and Aluede, O. (2006). Secondary Schools Student's perception of Examination Malpractices and Examination Ethics. *Journal of Human Ecology,* 20(4): 295–300.

Anya, O. A. (2004). *When Will Nigeria Take Charge of Nigeria*: A lecture under the auspices of the Gindiri Old Boys Association, Hill Station Hotel Jos, Plateau State Nigeria on November 6, 2004. Retrieved September 6, 2006, from http://www.dawodu.com/anya1.htm

Auerbach, E. R. (1989). Toward a Social-Contextual Approach to Family Literacy. *Harvard Educational Review*, 59(2), 165–181.

Barbour, C. and Barbour, N. H. (1997). *Families, Schools, and Communities: Building Partnership for Educating Children.* Upper Saddle River, New Jersey: Prentice-Hall, Inc.

Barton, P. (2004, November). Why Does the Gap Persist? – The Home-School Connection. *Educational Leadership*, 62(3), 9–13.

Bayor, H. R. (2003). Series Forward. In Ogbaa, K. (2003). *The Nigerian Americans.* Westport, CT: Greenwood Press.

Becher, R.M. (1984). Parental Involvement: A Review of Research and Principles of Successful Practice. *ERIC Clearinghouse on Elementary and Early Childhood Education*—[National Institute of Education, Washington, D.C. ED247032]

Berger, E. H. (2000). *Parents as Partners in Education: Families and Schools Working Together* (5th Edition). New Jersey: Prentice-Hall, Inc.

Brandt, R. and Robelen, E. (1998, May). Listen First. *Educational Leadership*, 55(8), 25–30.

Bronfenbrenner, U. (1977). Toward an Experimental Ecology of Human Development. *American Psychologist*, 32, (July), 513–531.

Bronfenbrenner, U. (1979). Context of Child Rearing-Problems and Prospects. *American Psychologist*, 34(10), 844–850.

Bronfenbrenner, U. (1986). Ecology of the Family as a Context for Human Development: Research Perspectives. *Developmental Psychology*, 22(6), 723–742.

Bronfenbrenner, U. (1989). Ecological systems Theory. *Annals of Child Development* 6, 187–249.

Chavkin, N. F. (1998). Making the Case for School, Family and Community Partnership: Recommendations for Research. *The School Community Journal*, 8, 9–21.

Chavkin, N. F. & Williams Jr., D.L. (1990). Working Parents and Schools: Implications for Practice. *Education*, III, (2), 242–248.

Christenson, S. L., Godber, Y. and Anderson, A. R. (2005). Critical Issues Facing Families and Educators. In Patrikakou, E., Weissberg, R., Redding, S. and Walberg, H. (Eds.), *School-Family Partnerships for Children's Success – The Series on Social Emotional Learning* (pp. 21–39). New York: Teachers College Press.

Clandinin, D. J. and Connelly, F. M. (2000). *Narrative Inquiry: Experience and Story in Qualitative Research.* San Francisco: Jossy-Bass Publishers.

Cogan. C.A. and Ibe, C. (2005). Nigerians. *The Electronic Encyclopedia of Chicago,* Chicago Historical Society. Retrieved November 11, 2008, from http://www.encyclopedia.chicagohistory.org/pages/891.html

Coll, C. G. (2005). Learning in the Shadow of Violence: Community, Culture and Family Involvement. In Weiss, Heather, B., Kreider, Holly, Lopez, M. Elena and Chatman, Celina, M. (Eds.), *Preparing Educators to Involve Families – From Theory to practice* (pp. 158–168). Thousand Oaks, CA: Sage Publications Inc.

Comer, J. P. (1984). Home-School Relationships As They Affect the Academic Success of Children. *Education and Urban Society,* 16(3), 323–337.

Constantino, S. M. (2003). *Engaging All Families – Creating A Positive School Culture By Putting Research Into Practice.* Lanham, Maryland: Scarecrow Education: The Rowman & Littlefield Publishing Group, Inc.

Cooper, T. and Maloof -Miller, V. (1999). Parent Involvement in Teaching Elementary-Level Chinese, Japanese, and Korean. *The Journal of Educational Research (Washington, D.C),* 92(3), 176–183.

Council of Chief State School Officers [CCSSO] (2006, November). Parental Involvement at Selected Ready Schools. Retrieved January 20, 2008, from http://www.ccsso.org/contents/pdfs/Parent_Involvement_at_Ready_Schools.pdf

Creswell, J. W. (2003). *Research Design: Qualitative, Quantitative, and Mixed Method Approaches* (2nd Edition). Thousand Oaks, CA: Sage Publication Inc.

Crotty, M. (2003). *The Foundations of Social Research: Meaning and Perspective in the Research Process.* Thousand Oaks, CA: Sage Publications.

Dambatta, S. N. (2005). A Glance at UBE. *Nigeriaworld.com.* (Nigeriaworld is a website dedicated to Nigerian social, political and economic affairs) Retrieved September 22, 2005, from http://nigeriaworld.com/

Dauber, S. and Epstein, J. (1993). Parent Attitudes and Practices of Involvement in Inner-City Elementary and Middle Schools. In Henderson, A. T. and Berla, N. (Editors) *A New Generation of Evidence: The Family is Critical to Student Achievement* (pp. 55–56). Washington, DC: National Committee for Citizens in Education.

Davis-Kean, P., E and Eccles, J. S. (2005). Influences and Challenges to Better Parent-School Collaborations. In Patrikakou, E., Weissberg, R., Redding, S. and Walberg, H. (Eds.), *School-Family Partnerships for Children's Success: The Series on Social Emotional Learning,* (pp. 57–73). New York: Teachers College Press.

DeCuir-Gunby, J. T. (2007). Negotiating Identity in a Bubble: A Critical Race Analysis of African American High School Student's Experiences in an Elite, Independent school. *Equity and Excellence in Education,* 40, 26–35.

Delgado-Gaitan, C. (1992). School Matters in the Mexican-American Home: Socializing Children to Education. *American Educational Research Journal,* 29(3), 495–513.

Djamba, Y. K. (1999). African Immigrants in the United States: A Socio-Demographic Profile in Comparison to Native Blacks. *Journal of Asian and African Studies,* 34(2): 210–215.

Dodd, A. W. and Konzal, J. L. (2002).*How Communities Build Stronger Schools – Stories, Strategies, and Promising Practices for Educating Every Child.* New York: Palgrave Macmillan.

Ebelebe, C. A. (2007). *The Mission Theology of the Holy Ghost Fathers in Igboland, 1905-1970, in the Light of the Changing Face of Mission Today: Toward a Mission Theology for the Igbo Church.* Unpublished doctoral dissertation, Marquette University.

Ekenachi, I. D. (2001). *Education for Change in a Changing Nigerian Igbo Society: Impacts of Traditional African and Western Education on the Upbringing of Igbo Children.* Unpublished doctoral dissertation, University of Southern California, University Park, CA.

Emenike, T. (2002). Tradition – Breaking of Kola Nut *Isu Oji – Omenala ndi Igbo.* Retrieved July 17, 2010, from http://www.amaigbo.plus.com/ files/orji.html

Epstein, J. L. (2001). *School, Family and Community Partnership: Preparing Educators and Improving Schools.* Boulder, Colorado: Westview Press.

Epstein, J. L and Sanders, M. G. (1998). What We Learn from International Studies of School-Family-Community Partnership. *Childhood Education,* 74(6), 392–394.

Epstein, J. L. and Sanders, M. G., Simon, B.S., Salinas, K.C., Jansorn, N.R., and VanVoorhis, F.L.(2002). *School, Family and Community Partnerships: Your Handbook for Action.* Thousand Oaks, CA: Corwin Press, Inc.

Epstein, J. L and Salinas, K. C. (2004, May). Partnering with Families and Communities. *Educational Leadership,* 61(8), 12–17.

Epstein, J. L. (2005) Forward. In Patrikakou, E., Weissberg, R., Redding, S. and Walberg, H. (Eds.), *School-Family Partnerships for Children's Success: The Series on Social Emotional Learning* (pp. vii-xi). New York: Teachers College Press.

Ezeani, E. (2005). *Education in Nigeria-Problems, Dilemmas and Perspective: A Handbook for Teachers, Students, Researchers, Scholars and Policy-makers.* London: Veritas Lumen Publishers.

Feinberg, W. and Soltis, J. F. (2004). *School and Society* (4th Edition). New York: Teachers College Press.

Finders, M. and Lewis, C. (1994). Why Some Parents Don't Come to School. *Educational Leadership,* 51(8), 50–54.

Ford, M. S., Follmer, R., and Litz, K. (1998). School-Family Partnership: Parents, Children, and Teachers Benefit. *Teaching Children Mathematics,* 4, 10–12.

Fullan, M. (2001). *The New Meaning of Educational Change* (3ʳᵈ Edition). New York: Teachers College Press.

Fuller, M. L. and Marxen, C. (1998). Families and Their Functions—Past and Present. In Fuller, M.L. and Olsen, G. (Eds.), *Home–School Relations: Working Successfully With Parents and Families* (pp.11–39). Needham Heights, MA: Allyn and Bacon.

Fuller, M. L. and Olsen, G. (Eds.) 1998. *Home–School Relations: Working Successfully With Parents and Families.* Needham Heights, MA: Allyn and Bacon.

Fuller, M. L. and Tutwiler, S. W (1998). Poverty: The Enemy of Children and Families. In Fuller, M.L. and Olsen, G. (Eds.), *Home–School Relations: Working Successfully With Parents and Families* (pp.257–272). Needham Heights, MA: Allyn and Bacon.

Fafunwa, B. A. (1967). *New Perspective in African Education.* Lagos: Macmillan & Co.

Fafunwa, B. A. (1991). *History of Education in Nigeria* 9ᵗʰ Edition NPS Educational Publishers LTD Ibadan –Nigeria.

Fafunwa, B. A. and Aisiku, J.U. (eds.) (1982). *Education in Africa: A Comparative Study.* London: George Allen and Unwin Publishers LTD.

Fukuyama, F. (May, 1993). Immigrants and Family Values. Retrieved January 19, 2009, from http://www.cs.ucdavis.edu/~matloff/pub/Immigration/ImmAndTheFamily/Fukuama.html

Gestwicki, C. (2004). *Home, School, and Community Relations: A Guide to Working With Families.* (5ᵗʰ edition). Clifton Park, NY: Thomson Delmar Learning.

Gonzalez, N., Andrade, R., Civil, M. and Moll, L. (2001). Bridging Funds of Distributed Knowledge: Creating Zones of Practices in Mathematics. *Journal of Education for Students Placed at Risk,* 6(1&2), 115–132.

Gore, A. (1997). Partnership for Family Involvement in Education: Vice President Gore Highlights importance of Teacher Preparation for Family Involvement in Education U.S. Department of Education teleconference, Richard W. Riley (host) November 5, 1997. Retrieved May 11, 2007, from http://www.ed.gov/G2k/community/98-01.html

Hanhan, S. F. (1998). Parent–Teacher Communication: Who's Talking? In Fuller, M.L.and Olsen, G (editors) 1998: *Home–School Relations: Working Successfully With Parents and Families* (pp.106-126). Needham Heights, MA: Allyn and Bacon.

Hawaii State Department of Education, (2007). Family Support. Helping Students Learn. Retrieved December 10, 2007, from http://familysupport.k12.hi.us

He, M.F. (2002a). A narrative inquiry of cross-cultural lives: lives in Canada. *Journal of Curriculum Studies,* 34(3), 323–342.

Henderson, A.T., Marburger, C.L. and Ooms, T. (1992). *Beyond The Bake Sale: An Educator's Guide to Working With Parents.* Washington, D.C.: National Committee for Citizens in Education in collaboration with: The institute for Educational Leadership and the Family Impact Seminar.

Henry, M. E (1996). *Parent-School Collaboration: Feminist Organizational Structures and School Leadership.* Albany, NY: State University of New York Press.

Hulsebosch, P. and Logan, L. (1998). Breaking It Up or Breaking It Down: Inner-City Parents as Co-Constructors of School Improvement. *Educational Horizons* 77(1), 30–36.

Jacobi, E. F.; Wittreich, Y.; and Hogue, I. (2003). Parental Involvement For a New Century. *The New England Reading Association (NERA) Journal,* 39(3), 11–16.

Ketefe, K. (June 20, 2006). 47% of Nigerians are Illiterate—Survey. *The Punch Newspaper Online Edition.* Retrieved June 20, 2006, from http://odili.net/news/source/2006/jun/20/414.html

Lana-Khong, Y.(2004). *Family Matters: The Role of Parents in Singapore Education - Teaching and Learning Series.* Singapore: Marshall Cavendish International Private Limited.

Laosa, L. M.(2005). Intercultural Consideration in School-Family Partnership. In Patrikakou, E., Weissberg, R., Redding, S. and Walberg, H. (Eds.), *School-Family Partnerships for Children's Success: The Series on Social Emotional Learning* (pp.77–91). New York: Teachers College Press.

Lareau, A. (1987). Social Class Difference in Family-School Relationship: The Importance of Cultural Capital. *Sociology of Education,* 60(2), 73–85.

Lightfoot, S. (1978). *Worlds Apart: Relationships Between Families and Schools.* New York: Basic Books.

Lightfoot, S. (2003). *The Essential Conversation: What Parents and Teachers Can Learn from Each Other.* New York: Ballantine Books.

Lincoln, Y. S. and Guba, E. G. (1985). *Naturalistic Inquiry.* Newbury Park, CA: Sage.

Lincoln, Y. S. and Guba, E. G. (2003). Ethics: The Failure of Positivist Science. In Lincoln, Y. S. and Denzin, N. K (editors). *Turning Points in Qualitative Research-Tying Knots in a Handkerchief* (pp. 219–237). Walnut Creek, CA: AltaMira Press.

Lofland, J., Snow, D., Anderson, L., and Lofland, L.H. (2006). *Analyzing Social Settings: A Guide to Qualitative Observation and Analysis* (4th Ed.). Belmont, CA: Wadsworth/Thomson Learning.

Lopez, G. R. (1999). *Teaching the Value of Hard Work: A Study of Parental Involvement in Migrant Households.* Unpublished doctoral dissertation, The University of Texas at Austin.

Lopez, G. R. (2001, Fall). The Value of Hard Work: Lessons on Parent Involvement From (Im)migrant Household. *Harvard Educational Review,* 71(3), 416–437.

Lopez, G.R., Scribner, J.D. and Mahitivanichcha, K. (2001, summer). Redefining Parental Involvement: Lessons From High-Performing Migrant-Impacted Schools. *American Educational Research Journal,* 38(2), 253–288.

Mbiti, J. S. (1990). *African Religions and Philosophy* (2nd Revised and Enlarged Ed.) London: Heinemann.

Mattingly, D.J., Prislin, R., McKenzie, T.L., Rodriguez, J. I., and Kayzar, B. (2002). Evaluating Evaluations: The Case of Parent Involvement Programs. *Review of Educational Research,* 72(4), 549–576.

Meisels, S. J. (April 2005). Testing Culture Invades Lives of Young Children. *FairTest: The National Center for Fair and Open Testing.* Retrieved December 2, 2009, from http://www.fairtest.org/testing-culture-invades-lives-young-children

Moles, O. C. Jr.(2005). School-Family Relations and Student Learning: Federal Education Initiatives. In Patrikakou, E., Weissberg, R., Redding, S. and Walberg, H. (Eds.) *School-Family Partnerships for Children's Success: The Series on Social Emotional Learning* (pp.131–147). New York: Teachers College Press.

Molnar, C. (1999). *Parent and Teacher Views of Parental Involvement in Local School Governance: Master's Thesis* University of Regina: SSTA Research Centre Report #99-06. Retrieved October 26, 2009, from http://www.saskschoolboards.ca/research/parent_involvement/99-06.htm

Monke, L. W. (2006). The Overdominance of Computers – Our Students Need Inner Resources and Real Life Experiences to Balance Their High-tech Lives. *Educational Leadership,* 63(4), 20–23.

MyUSGreenCard (2007). United States Green Card lottery Result 2007. Retrieved January 19, 2009, from http://www.myusgreencard.com/lotteryresult.html

National PTA (2000). *Building Successful Partnerships: A Guide For Developing Parent and Family Involvement Programs.* Bloomington, Indiana: National Educational Service.

Nderu, E. N (2005). *Parental Involvement in Education: A Qualitative Study of Somali Immigrants In the Twin Cities Area.* Unpublished Doctoral Dissertation, University of Minnesota.

Ngidi, D. and Qwabe, J. (2006). The Partnership of Parents, Educators and Principals in Creating a Culture of Teaching and Learning in Schools. *South Africa Journal of Education,* 26(4), 529–539.

Nnaike, U. (July 3, 2007). *Oando* Adopts School in Calabar. *ThisDay Newspaper-Online Edition.* Retrieved July 8, 2007, from http://www. thisdayonline.com

Nwabuisi, E. M. (2000).*Values and Education.* Onitsha –Nigeria: Spiritan Publications.

Nwa-Chil, C. (1984). *Family and Education.* Obosi, Onitsha-Nigeria: Pacific College Press Ltd.

Nzekwe, A. A. (2003). *Dropping out of High School in IGBO (Nigeria) Society: A Qualitative Study of Societal Influences and School Experiences of Selected UMU OKOROBIA.* Unpublished Doctoral Dissertation, University of Akron.

Nzekwe, A. A (2007). *Silent Resistance: High School Dropouts Among Igbo-Nigerian Children.* Bloomington, Indiana: AuthorHouse.

Obanya, P. (2002). *Revitalizing Education in Africa.* Ibadan, Nigeria: Stirling-Horden Publishers Ltd.

Obanya, P. (2004). *Educating for the Knowledge Economy.* Bodija – Ibadan, Nigeria: Mosuro Publishers.

Obidi, S. S. (2005). *Culture and Education in Nigeria: An Historical Analysis.* Ibadan-Nigeria: University Press PLC.

Ochu, C. (February 3, 2009). One Million Nigerians live In US-Envoy. *ThisDay Newspaper-Online Edition.* Retrieved February 3, 2009 from http://www.thisdayonline.com

Ogbaa, K. (2003). *The Nigerian Americans.* Westport, CT.: Greenwood Press.

Ohuche, R. O. (1991). *Ibu Anyi Ndanda:*The Centrality of Education in Igbo Culture. *Ahiajoku Lecture Series: The 1991 Ahiajoku Lecture.* Retrieved August 29, 2005, from http://ahiajoku.igbonet.com/1991/

Oke, A. E. (1986). Kinship Interaction in Nigeria in Relation to Societal Modernization: A Pragmatic Approach. *Journal of Comparative Family Studies,* XVII (2), 185–196.

Olivos, E. M. (2006). *The Power of Parents: A Critical Perspective of Bicultural Parent Involvement in Public Schools.* New York: Peter Lang Publishing, Inc.

Ozigbo, I. R.A. (1999). *A History of Igboland in the 20th Century.* University of Nigeria, Nsukka: SNAAP Press LTD.

Patrikakou, E.N, Weissberg, R.P, Redding, S and Walberg, H.J. (2005). School-Family Partnerships: Enhancing the Academic, Social, and Emotional Learning of Children .In Patrikakou, E., Weissberg, R., Redding, S. and Walberg, H. (Eds.), *School-Family Partnerships for Children's Success: The Series on Social Emotional Learning* (pp.1–17). New York: Teachers College Press.

Patton, M.Q. (2002). *Qualitative Research and Evaluation Methods* (3rd Edition). Thousand Oaks, CA: Sage Publication Inc.

Peppler-Barry, U. (Ed.) (2000). World Education Forum Dakar- Senegal 26–28 April, 2000. *Final Report,* Paris, France: UNESCO.

Phillion, J. (2002). *Narrative Inquiry in a Multicultural Landscape: Multicultural Teaching and Learning.* Westport, CT: Ablex Publishing.

Rabusicova, M. and Emmerova, K. (2002). The Role of Parents As Educational and Social Partners of Schools In the Czech Republic: Legislation and Media Analysis. *European Educational Research Journal,* 1(3), 480–496.

Ratha, D.; Mohapatra, S.; and Silwal, A. (July, 2009). Outlook for Remittance Flows 2009–2011: Remittances expected to fall by 7–10 percent in 2009. *Migration and Development Brief 10: Migration and Remittances Team Development Prospects Group, World Bank.* Retrieved November 29, 2009, from http://www.worldbank.org/prospects/migrationandremittances

Reynolds, R. (2002). An African Brain Drain: Igbo Decisions to Immigrate to the US. *Review of African Political Economy*, 92: 273–284.

Reynolds, R. (2004). "Bless this Little Time We Stayed Here": Prayers of Invocation As Mediation of Immigrant Experience Among Nigerians In Chicago. In Farr, M. (Ed.) *Ethnolinguistic Chicago: Language and Literacy in the City's Neighborhoods* (pp. 161–187). Mahwah, New Jersey: Lawrence Erlbaum Associates, Inc.

Rich, D. (1998, May). What Parents Want from Teachers. *Educational Leadership*, 55(8), 37–39.

Riggins-Newby, C. (2003, April). Families as Partners. *Education Digest*, 68(8), pp. 23–24.

Riley, R. W. (1999, March). Partnership for Family Involvement. *Teaching PreK-8*, 29(6), 6.

Rong, X. L. and Preissle, J. (2009). *Educating Immigrant Students in the 21ˢᵗ Century: What Educators Need to Know* (2ⁿᵈ ed.). Thousand Oaks, CA: Corwin Press.

Rubin, H. J. and Rubin, I. S. (2005). *Qualitative Interviewing: The Art of Hearing Data* (2ⁿᵈ Edition). Thousand Oaks, CA: Sage Publication Inc.

Sanders, M. G. (1996). Building Family Partnership That Last. *Educational Leadership*, 54, 61–66.

Sanders, M. G. (1998, Jan/Feb). School-Family-Community Partnership: An Action Approach. *High School Magazine,* 5, 38–49.

Sanders, M. G. (2006). *Building School-Community Partnerships: Collaboration for Student Success.* Thousand Oaks, CA: Corwin Press.

Sarkodie-Mensah, K. (2000). Nigerian Americans. *Gale Encyclopedia of Multicultural America.* Retrieved February 13, 2009, from http://www.encyclopedia.com/doc/1G2-3405800116.html

Scherer, M. (2007, May). Perspectives: Why Focus on the Whole Child? *Educational Leadership*, 64 (8), 7.

Sharlin, S. A. and Moin, V. (2001, Summer). New Immigrants' Perceptions of Family Life in Origin and Host Cultures: In-group and Out-group Favoritism Effect. *Journal of Comparative Family Studies*, 32(3), 405–418.

Schram, T. H. (2006). *Conceptualizing and Proposing Qualitative Research* (2nd Edition). Upper Saddle River, NJ: Pearson Education Inc.

Sergiovanni, T. J. (1999). *Building Community in Schools*. San Francisco: Jossey-Bass Publishers.

Shenton, A.K. (2004). Strategies for Ensuring Trustworthiness in Qualitative Research Projects. *Education for Information*, 22, 63-75.

Smith, D. J. (1997, Spring). Indigenous Peoples' Extended Family Relationships: A Source for Classroom Structure. *McGill Journal of Education*, 32, 125–38.

Smith, D. (2008). *Hope and Perspective: A Qualitative Study of the Relationship Between Parents and Professionals in Special Education*. Unpublished doctoral dissertation, DePaul University.

Strauss, V. (2006, October 10). The Rise of the Testing Culture. *The Washington Post*. Retrieved December 2, 2009, from http://www.washingtonpost.com/wp-dyn/content/article/2006/10/09/AR2006100900925.html

Sullivan, P. (1998, May). The PTA'S National Standards. *Educational Leadership*, 55(8), 43–44.

Swap, S. M. (1993). *Developing Home-School Partnerships: From Concept to Practice*. New York and London: Teachers College Press.

Takougang, J. (2003, December).Contemporary African Immigrants to The United States. *Irinkerindo: A Journal of African Migration*, 2: 1-15 (online edition). Retrieved January 19, 2009, from http://www.africamigration.com/archive_02/j_takougang.htm

Tomlinson, C. A. and McTighe, J. (2006). *Integrating Differentiated Instruction and Understanding by Design: Connecting Content and Kids*. Alexandria, VA: Association for Supervision and Curriculum Development (ASCD).

Ugbala, S. I. (2003). The Position of Kola-Nut in the Cultural Life of the Igbos. *Igbo Net: Kola Nut Series*. Retrieved July 17, 2010, from http://kaleidoscope.igbonet.com/culture/kolanutseries/ezeugbala/

Ukaegbu, J. O. (2003). The Kola Nut: As an Igbo Cultural and Social Symbol. *Igbo Net: Kola Nut Series*. Retrieved July 17, 2010, from http://kaleidoscope.igbonet.com/culture/kolanutseries/jukaegbu/

UNDP Human Development Report (2006). Human Development Indicators: Country Facts Sheets: Nigeria. Retrieved August 21, 2009, from http://hdr.undp.org/hdr2006/statistics/countries/country_fact_sheets/cty_fs_NGA.html

United States Department of State-Bureau of Consular Affairs (2006). Instructions For The 2006 Diversity Immigrant Visa Program (DV-2006) Retrieved January 19, 2009, from http://www.diversity-immigrant-visa-program.com/inst2006.asp

Universal Basic Education Commission (2005a). Some Information on Universal Basic Education UBEC, Abuja-Nigeria. (www.ubec.gov.ng.)

Universal Basic Education Commission (2005b). *The Compulsory, Free, Universal Basic Education Act, 2004 and Other Related Matters* UBEC, Abuja–Nigeria

UNESCO. *At a glance: Nigeria - Statistics*. Retrieved November 30, 2009, from http://www.unicef.org/infobycountry/Nigeria_statistics.html

Walker, D. F. and Soltis, J. F. (1997). *Curriculum and Aims* (3rd Edition). New York: Teachers College Press.

Weisner, Thomas S. (2005). Ecocultural Understanding. In Weiss, H., B., Kreider, H., Lopez, M. E. and Chatman, C. M. (Eds.), *Preparing Educators to Involve Families: From Theory to Practice* (pp.130-135). Thousand Oaks, CA: Sage Publications Inc.

Weiss, H., B., Kreider, H., Lopez, M. E. and Chatman, C. M. [Eds.] (2005). *Preparing Educators to Involve Families: From Theory to Practice*. Thousand Oaks, CA: Sage Publications Inc.

World Education Forum [WEF] (2000): *Final Report*: Dakar, Senegal April 26–28, 2000. Paris, France: UNESCO. Retrieved November 30,2009, from www.unesco.org/education/efa/ed_for_all/dakfram_eng.shtml

Wright, K. and Stegelin, D. A. (2003). *Building School and Community Partnerships Through Parent Involvement*. Upper Saddle River, NJ: Pearson Education, Inc.